Model-Integrating Software Components

Mahdi Derakhshanmanesh

Model-Integrating Software Components

Engineering Flexible Software Systems

With a foreword by Prof. Dr. Jürgen Ebert

 Springer Vieweg

Mahdi Derakhshanmanesh
Koblenz, Germany

Dissertation, University of Koblenz-Landau, 2014

ISBN 978-3-658-09645-8   ISBN 978-3-658-09646-5 (eBook)
DOI 10.1007/978-3-658-09646-5

Library of Congress Control Number: 2015938592

Springer Vieweg
© Springer Fachmedien Wiesbaden 2015

Printed on acid-free paper

Springer Vieweg is a brand of Springer Fachmedien Wiesbaden
Springer Fachmedien Wiesbaden is part of Springer Science+Business Media
(www.springer.com)

To my grandmother.

Foreword

In software engineering, models are used to represent relevant knowledge about software systems. For instance, in the course of collecting requirements for a new system, the concepts of the application domain, the relevant workflows to be supported, and the main use cases may be modeled by diagrams in a precisely defined modeling language. In *model-driven software development*, these models are used to automatically construct large parts of the intended system using transformation and code generation tools.

In general, a model is a goal-oriented description of something. It reduces reality to those parts that are relevant for the goal, and it allows drawing conclusions about the original system. Though (along this definition) code is also a model of computational processes, the community uses the term *code* for programs that are directly executable and the term *model* for more abstract design descriptions.

A large body of knowledge has been accumulated over the last decades. This includes defining modeling languages (in their syntax, their constraints, and their semantics), representing, querying, and transforming models, as well as several powerful additional services to deal with models and meta-models. Given a technological modeling space which supplies all these capabilities, models can nowadays be used as *first-class artifacts* in software engineering like code units.

In his thesis, Mahdi Derakhshanmanesh builds on the state of the art in modeling by proposing to integrate models into running software on the component-level without translating them to code. Such so-called *model-integrating software* exploits all advantages of models: models implicitly support a good separation of concerns, they are self-documenting and thus improve understandability and maintainability, and in contrast to model-driven approaches there is no synchronization problem anymore between the models and the code generated from them.

The thesis elaborates on the foundations of model-integrating software, derives a concept how to realize model-integration for a given component concept, delivers a reference implementation of this concept using TGraph technology and OSGi bundles, and finally describes two case studies as proofs of concept. Thereby it constitutes a considerable step towards understandable and easily evolvable software systems.

Using model-integrating components, software will be easier to build and easier to evolve by just modifying the respective model in an editor. Furthermore, software may also adapt itself at runtime by transforming its own model part.

Jürgen Ebert

Acknowledgements

To work successfully on a dissertation, a solid foundation, an adequate working environment and appropriate supervision are required. In this regard, Prof. Dr. Jürgen Ebert provided me with excellent conditions. Since January 2011, we have worked closely together on a number of publications, on an industrial project as well as on teaching software engineering courses. Dear Jürgen, I deeply appreciate your insightful, encouraging and respectful guidance.

Many thanks also to Prof. Dr. Gregor Engels for providing his valuable feedback on the topic of my thesis during several meetings with him and his working group at the University of Paderborn.

In retrospective, my journey in software engineering research truly started in July 2010 when I visited the working group of Prof. Dr. Ladan Tahvildari at the University of Waterloo (Canada) for six months to write my master's thesis. I learned a lot about scientific publication practices and got to know the joy of research. Dear Ladan, thank you so much for your kind support and for the many insights on self-adaptive software.

In Waterloo, I had the chance to meet Dr. Mehdi Amoui and to work closely together with him on the design and development of a framework for engineering self-adaptive software. We published several papers together over the years. Dear Mehdi, many thanks for the numerous long nights at the lab, fruitful discussions, coffees and jokes. My stay in Canada shaped me quite a bit.

Already during my bachelor's studies, I met Thomas Iguchi. Years later, we had the chance to work together again. Over the course of the past nine months, he supported me as a freelancer during prototyping and with conducting the feasibility studies for this dissertation. Thomas is an excellent software engineer and an awesome friend.

Furthermore, I'd like to give special thanks to my colleagues Andreas Fuhr, Tassilo Horn and Dr. Volker Riediger for the many chats during lunch and coffee breaks. I also like to thank the former colleagues at TRW Automotive for their feedback on various topics related to software engineering in practice during our joint project.

Many more people have supported me with their friendship and kind encouragement over the years. I am afraid I cannot name all of you here. So, in no particular order, many thanks to Dimitri Waganow, Elena Fokina, Sebastian Eberz, Richard Becker, Chantal Neuhaus and Eckhard Großmann.

Finally, I am eternally grateful to my dear mother Sylvia and my father Mahmood for loving me and for carefully shaping my character during the crucial early years. My brothers Hamid and Hadi deserve my sincere thanks for always supporting and understanding me.

                                                        Mahdi Derakhshanmanesh

Abstract

Component-based as well as model-driven approaches have become popular to support the engineering of complex software systems. In model-driven development and especially according to the model-driven architecture, models are step-wise refined using transformations and, at the end of this transformation chain, code is generated. While models are an essential part of development, the final software consists in large part of code. Furthermore, if models are used at runtime, they are usually not treated as software components.

Despite all efforts (e.g., round-trip engineering), the problem arises that over time model and code artifacts may be not aligned. Additionally, valuable design-time knowledge encoded in the models may be lost after code generation, i.e., this knowledge is not part of the final product. Even if models shall be kept inside the deployed system, a guiding realization concept is missing.

To avoid the steadily increasing distance between models and code, we propose the integration of (executable) models and code at the level of software components. By interpreting models directly, redundancy – the source of inconsistencies – is reduced. There is no redundancy between models and code, unless it is introduced willfully.

In this dissertation, we introduce a realization concept for such Model-Integrating Components (MoCos) that is compatible with existing component technologies. Our work is specifically motivated by previous research on self-adaptive software, software product lines and by the use of models in both research areas.

Using MoCos, adaptivity and variability can be managed by applying the services of a technological modeling space (e.g., querying/transforming/interpreting) on the embedded models. Models at runtime can be cleanly encapsulated and used like regular software components with clearly defined interfaces.

The presented research advances the state of the art in software engineering by introducing the systematic combination of models and code as two possible constituents of a software component with equal rights. More specifically, we describe (i) a comprehensive discussion of design considerations, (ii) a realization concept for MoCos, (iii) a reference implementation based on Java, OSGi and TGraphs as well as (iv) two feasibility studies.

Our findings show that integrating models and code in the broader context of component models is feasible. The presented approach opens up interesting new perspectives for developing flexible software systems. The MoCo concept is a first step towards model-integrating development.

Table of Contents

List of Figures

List of Tables

List of Listings

Part I

Introduction and Foundations

1 Introduction

In this initial chapter, we describe the motivation behind the present dissertation. Especially two projects had a major impact:

- developing the Graph-based Runtime Adaptation Framework (GRAF) in cooperation with the University of Waterloo (since, 2009) and
- supporting the COre software development for BRAking (COBRA) at TRW Automotive (2010-2012).

The remainder of this chapter is structured as follows. First, we give some additional *background and motivation* on the related research fields. We describe the two above-mentioned projects because many parts of this work originate from them or are closely related. Afterwards, the *problem statement, research goals* and *research questions* tackled in this dissertation are presented. This chapter ends with a list of *contributions* and an overview of the *thesis structure*.

1.1 Background and Motivation

As requirements change, software shall be changed, too. Developing non-trivial software systems that can be continuously and quickly adjusted to changing requirements (with an adequate amount of effort) is a difficult task, though. Ideally, systems can change themselves autonomously in reaction to changes sensed in their operating environment. This process is at the heart of *managing adaptivity* and it is called adapting.

As systems become more complex, similar core parts shall be reused in multiple variants of the system to reduce costs. In addition, some solutions may need to be tailored even further to suit a set of needs that are very specific to one customer. Ideally, software can be automatically derived from a systematically built repository of "master artifacts" based on a description of the desired software capabilities. This process is at the heart of *managing variability* and it is called tailoring.

Among others, these *visions* drive software engineers to search for improved software construction approaches. Many different directions can be taken, e.g., depending on the personal research background and preferences, community and work domains as well as the chosen technologies and platforms. In this thesis, we focus especially on two research areas: (i) Self-Adaptive Software (SAS) [111, 120] (related to GRAF) and (ii) Software Product Lines (SPLs) [27, 116] (related to COBRA).

While works in the field of SAS concentrate on adapting, SPLs aim at handling tailoring. In both areas, *models* and *components* play a vital role for coping with complexity during all phases of the software's development process and life-cycle. Both can be seen as enabling technologies that are independent from their application domain.

Modeling approaches such as Model-Driven Software Development (MDSD) [18, 125] support building stakeholder- and concern-specific views on software and its environment that can be used for communication, but also for the semi-automatic derivation of parts of the final system (e.g., via code generation).

- In SAS, *models@run.time* [14] can be used to represent a "live-view" of the running system that is suited for its administration (either manual or automated). Furthermore, some models can be executed [48, 105] so they play a role very similar to code. The commonly known *activity diagrams* that are part of the Unified Modeling Language (UML) are an example.

- In SPLs, *feature models* [82] represent variability and these models support the conceptual definition of software variants as an input for tailoring.

Component approaches also known as Component Based Software Development (CBSD) [129] offer a means to develop complex systems by connecting reusable components. These basic building blocks are represented by code written in a programming language such as Java.

- In SAS, components are updated and re-orchestrated at runtime if requirements change or a bug in the system was detected.
- In SPLs, core assets are elementary building blocks that are configured and composed to create a product variant. Depending on the artifact type, these may be components that adhere the rules of a specific *component technology* or are simply a set of files (e.g., XML, image formats, MS Word, MS Excel, ...) stored in a folder.

The facts and impressions described so far led us to the following *hypothesis* as a driver for this research:

Hypothesis

The cooperation of (executable) domain-specific models and code within software components opens up new opportunities for developing and evolving flexible software systems.

Before presenting the research goals, we subsequently describe the research background in more detail. Especially (i) the *evolution of conventional systems towards adaptive software* and (ii) the *adoption of product line engineering* were influencing directions. Afterwards, a summary of related experiences in the form of *motivating factors* is given.

Evolution of Conventional Systems Towards Adaptive Software. In real-world scenarios, software solutions do already exist and engineers have to build on top of them. New solutions need to be compatible with these existing systems. Starting on the *greenfield* is usually not the case in practice, although there are certainly exceptions, e.g., highly innovative projects. We are convinced that this holds true for SAS, as well.

In an initial feasibility study – in cooperation with the Software Technologies Applied Research (STAR) laboratory at the University of Waterloo[1] – we have developed GRAF [37]. GRAF is a Java-based and model-centric framework that can be connected to existing software with minor technical effort and in a mostly non-intrusive way to implement adaptivity [2]. Amoui covered this topic in detail in his PhD thesis [1] and we discussed how adaptivity can be introduced to achieve longevity in software [40]. The detailed design of the technical solution as well as the results of two case studies were elaborated on in further publications [3, 39].

GRAF and its tool set is being continuously extended. It is used as a basis for further research, especially by our colleagues and friends in Waterloo. For instance, preliminary results and thoughts on *ultra-large-scale SAS* were presented at CASCON 2012 and CASCON 2013.

Adoption of Product Line Engineering. The engineering of complex but similar software systems that are sold to different groups of customers requires the *systematic management of variability* across all areas of the producing organization. Especially, economical aspects as well as technical concerns and general management tasks need to be synchronized with each other to achieve good reuse and time-to-market of high quality products that meet the customers' requirements.

Research on SPLs aims at supporting these goals. There is a need to deal with *adopting* Software Product Line Engineering (SPLE) [28, 109] in organizations with existing product lines, too.

In the three years project COBRA[2], we have conducted research on how to adopt SPLE at TRW Automotive's department for Slip Control Systems (SCSs), located in Koblenz, Germany. We published our experiences with a focus on requirements engineering [43, 44], including technical issues and solutions related to (i) *needed tools* and (ii) limits of existing approaches for creating *feature models*, but we also covered (iii) challenges for *project management* and (iv) *social aspects* in engineering teams.

---

[1] http://stargroup.uwaterloo.ca/ (accessed July 6th, 2014)
[2] The author of this thesis was an active part of the COBRA project at TRW Automotive for two full years: from January 2011 to December 2012.

1.1.1 Motivating Factors

Based on the split research background sketched in the paragraphs before, we like to point at some of the critical *motivating factors* that led to parts of this dissertation. For a detailed list of the *lessons learned*, please refer to our individual publications cited above. The following list summarizes essential motivators for conducting research on combining models and code in a modular form to manage adaptivity and variability:

- *The Query/Transform/Interpret (QTI) approach is powerful for realizing adaptivity:* With GRAF, we have shown that techniques from model-based approaches can be used successfully to achieve adaptivity, i.e., to perform changes to software automatically at runtime.

  At the heart of this adaptivity management approach are three techniques: (i) *querying of models* for gathering information on state and structure, (ii) *transforming of models* for making modifications at any point in time during the software's life-cycle and (iii) *interpreting models* to ensure that model changes take effect immediately. No code generation is required.

  We like to refer to the interplay of these techniques as the *QTI approach*. This combination showed to be flexible, even though it comes at the expense of overhead in memory and execution time added by the necessary infrastructure for model handling [39, 70]. Note that in comparison to their application in traditional MDSD, there is a strong shift in focus from development time to runtime.

- *A modular realization concept for software components using model at runtime is absent:* There are various approaches for developing SAS and for engineering SPLs. In both areas, models – computer-processable abstractions of real-life concerns – play an important role for dealing with engineering complexity. The relationship between models and component technology is not generically discussed, though. Instead, models are usually put in the context of the whole (monolithic) software system. Models are not treated as components.

Based on our experiences with GRAF, which also follows a monolithic approach, we are convinced that applying similar techniques in a composable form will be beneficial because engineers can achieve the *separation of concerns* in a cleaner fashion. Furthermore, we are convinced that a well-defined modular concept for cooperating models and code within software components can support establishing adequate *views* on software.

- *Adaptivity and variability are complementary concerns:* Looking at SAS and SPLE, both share complementary properties in their technical nature.

On the one hand, SAS is meant to target an *open-ended world*, where software can adjust itself to meet the ever-changing needs of its users and its execution environment. Hence, software is designed for adaptivity and – ideally – it shall learn new behaviors autonomously. The overall state space is (usually) not explicitly enumerated but it is still encoded implicitly, e.g., using a set of adaptation rules.

On the other hand, SPLs are built on the assumption that all possible allowed combinations of artifacts are anticipated[3] and represented by model types such as feature models. As more and more customization is desired by end-users, features need to be changed or adapted, possibly even after delivery and during operation.

We argue that variability and adaptivity are important abilities of modern software systems and that we need to fully understand them as well as provide a well-defined vocabulary of the main concepts and relationships. In fact, the basic building blocks of

---

[3]Product variants are fixed at least for a certain period of time in which the products are to be sold.

software need to support variability and adaptivity in a uniform way and at an adequate level of granularity.

In Chapter 2, a more elaborate description of related concepts and related work is given to complement the research background described so far.

1.2 Problem Statement

Vision: We want to be able to develop software that can be systematically evolved to face changing conditions. High-level representations of the domain-knowledge in the form of (visual) models that can be developed with existing modeling approaches shall become an integrated part of software without generating code. Changes to the software can be encoded in the form of repeatable well-defined model transformations that can be used both during development as well as at runtime. This approach shall be compatible with existing software component technologies and any modeling language that can be described with a meta-model.

Issue Statement: In model-based as well as in model-driven development, models and code are handled side-by-side which – despite all efforts – is often a source of inconsistencies between both artifacts. Generated code is still the primary artifact when building the shipped software system, even though more and more effort is put into the development of models. Additionally, valuable knowledge such as design decisions, constraints and alternatives as well as further meta-data that may be available at domain-specific levels of abstraction may be not explicitly available at runtime anymore. This data could support system administration and self-adaptation, though.

Method: We will design an architectural blueprint for the realization of software components that can contain (executable) models and code side-by-side and with equal rights. Then, we will implement this blueprint and explore its feasibility by applying it in two non-trivial studies.

1.3 Research Goals and Research Questions

Models and components are two well-accepted concepts in modern software engineering. They support the development, evolution and adaptation of software systems and help to manage complexity of these systems.

In this thesis, the first steps towards a novel *Model Integrating Development (MID)*[4] approach for software systems shall be made. Its foundation shall be the non-redundant combination of models and code in the form of *Model-Integrating Components (MoCos)*[5]. Thus, important knowledge about the software remains accessible during operation and can even be updated. The model part of a MoCo supports flexibility and comprehensibility of the component. The code part allows for more efficiency and supports the use of existing (native) software libraries and enables the connection to middleware.

Models and code are both *first-class entities* of MID. From a long-term perspective, it shall be even possible to move from models to code (freezing) and from code to models (melting) to tackle changed non-functional requirements. Especially, existing component technologies (e.g., OSGi bundles) shall be capable of expressing MoCos to enable the use of existing software on the one hand and to support tailoring and adapting of components, on the other hand. The envisioned solution concept supports a component-based way of developing software systems where users of components cannot differentiate between MoCos or other, more traditional software components.

Fundamental research is required to tackle the challenges that come with this briefly sketched vision. This thesis is a first step in this direction and it builds on top of experiences from research projects presented earlier in Section 1.1. The *research goals* to be tackled here are described subsequently.

---

[4]The first vision of MID has been proposed by Jürgen Ebert.
[5]The term "MoCo" was suggested by Gregor Engels.

RG1: Understanding the Essential Requirements for Model-Integrating Software

We have made initial experiences with applying models at runtime to achieve adaptivity and our colleagues in Waterloo have successfully discussed a part of the involved migration challenges with a focus on (monolithic) legacy systems.

Realizing MoCos shall ideally be possible in most component technologies. The intention is *not* to design "yet another" component model. Hence, it is crucial to clearly state the requirements for MID. Especially the structure and interfaces for MoCos shall be examined and required capabilities shall be well-understood. Conflicting requirements must be enumerated, analyzed and discussed. Resulting design decisions shall be clearly documented. Experiences from prior work on SAS and SPLE shall be considered.

Related *research questions* are:
(RQ1) Which kinds of relationships do exist between models and code?
(RQ2) What are alternatives for designing and formalizing interfaces between models and code?
(RQ3) How can knowledge that is stored in models be accessed from outside of a component?
(RQ4) What kinds of conflicts with existing component models are there?
(RQ5) How to control the joint execution of models and code?

RG2: Defining a Generic and Modular Realization Concept for Model-Integrating Software

The practicability and usability of the MID approach depends significantly on design decisions that govern the structure and behavior of the model-integrating components. A *realization concept* for MoCos in the form of an architectural blueprint shall be the basis for achieving all subsequent goals.

Furthermore, it shall be explored how the models embedded in MoCos facilitate tailoring and adapting the behavior or structure of software. Motivated by our previous work on GRAF, the same ideas shall be applied, but in a more generic way, i.e., independent of the chosen modeling language.

Related *research questions* are:

(RQ6) What is a reasonable blueprint for a MoCo (e.g., regarding: structure, interfaces, connection between model and code)?

(RQ7) How to achieve interaction and composition between MoCos?

RG3: Providing a Reference Implementation for the Realization Concept

Once the MoCo concept has been designed, it needs to be initially implemented and continuously refined. This technical realization of the blueprint for MoCos shall be constructed in such a way that it can be simply used by software engineers. Additionally, tools need to be developed that support the creation and management of MoCos. The concrete implementation shall be done in Java, because the Java Virtual Machine (JVM) is a portable execution platform. The component technology of choice shall be OSGi [134] and models shall be expressed as TGraphs [56].

Related *research questions* are:

(RQ8) What are the necessary technological prerequisites for implementing the MoCo concept?

(RQ9) How can MoCos be implemented to support design, evolution and self-adaptation of software?

RG4: Evaluating the Approach's Potential for Success

The evaluation of the presented work in this thesis shall be done in the form of two *feasibility studies*. The main goal is to examine the MoCo concept regarding applicability with different combinations of modeling languages. In addition, it shall be explored how the concept can be realized with state-of-the-art component technology such as

OSGi bundles and services. Applicability of MoCos shall be analyzed, as well.

Related *research questions* are:
(RQ10) Does the MoCo concept abstract reasonably well from different modeling languages (genericity)?

1.4 Contributions

In line with the research goals, the list of *contributions* of this thesis can be summarized as follows:

- *A comprehensive discussion of design considerations for developing model-integrating software:* Based on our lessons learned from previous research on designing and developing enabling technology for the engineering of SAS, we present a set of common use cases that need to be supported when developing flexible – potentially self-adaptive – software. The design considerations related to providing solutions for these use cases are carefully described and alternatives are discussed. Systematically, a recommendation is given and manifested as design decisions. They may be used as a data set by other researchers, e.g., as a basis to start further discussions and to compare the rationale behind their own decisions made.

  The related chapters are: Chapter 2, Chapter 3.

- *A generic component realization concept for model-integrating components:* An architectural blueprint for the design and development of MoCos is described. This component realization concept does not rely on specific functionality of a component model. Rather, we claim that it can be implemented with existing component technology. The required capabilities are encapsulation and a mechanism for the clear definition of interfaces. Moreover, this MoCo concept is applicable with any modeling language that is described in terms of a meta-model and, optionally, a set of model interpreters that implement execution semantics. A technological space [95] for creating and managing models is a prerequisite.

The related chapter is: Chapter 4.

- *A reference implementation of the MoCo concept:* First, a mapping of the MoCo concept to existing component models (JavaBeans, Enterprise JavaBeans, OSGi) is presented. Then, a realization of the MoCo concept is provided using selected technologies. The programming language is Java, the component model is OSGi[134]. The component technology is either Eclipse Equinox[6] or Apache Felix[7]. The technological space for modeling is provided by jGraLab[8] and TGraphs [56].

  The related chapters are: Chapter 2, Chapter 5.

- *A description and discussion of two non-trivial software systems built with MoCos:*

  The first study is an app for the Android mobile platform that is intended to support insurance sales staff. This insurance sales app (ISA) adapts itself to support the user. For example, based on the user's expertise, only the required set of features is deployed on the mobile device. Additionally, tax computation formulas can be adapted based on sensed geo-location. Involved models are (i) a *feature model* for representing and reconfiguring the app's capabilities, (ii) a *computation model* for encoding the amount of fees to be payed for a certain insurance product and (iii) a *graphical user interface model* that is linked with a computation model for displaying formulas to the user.

  The second study is a simulation of an access control system that protects cyber-physical assets in an organization. The software

---

[6]http://www.eclipse.org/equinox/ (accessed July 6th, 2014)
[7]http://felix.apache.org/ (accessed July 6th, 2014)
[8]http://jgralab.uni-koblenz.de (accessed July 6th, 2014)

system changes access rules to rooms at runtime based on the location of a VIP as sensed by cameras and card-readers. Involved models are (i) a *person model* that describes persons and their roles, (ii) a *room model* for rendering the floor plan, doors and sensors in an organization to be protected, (iii) *event-condition-action rules models* to encode access rules and adaptation rules as well as (iv) a *feature model* that encodes the variability of the dynamic access control product line.

The related chapter is: Chapter 6.

In terms of further contributions, this research has led to fruitful cooperation with the STAR group at the University of Waterloo [2, 3, 39, 40] as well as with Lero - The Irish Software Engineering Institute [45]. In addition, the two-years MoSAiC project funded by the Deutsche Forschungsgemeinschaft (DFG) has been successfully initiated [41, 42] as a joint project between the University of Koblenz-Landau and the University of Paderborn.

1.5 Thesis Structure

So far, we have given the overall *motivation* for MID and especially for MoCos. The envisioned approach is based on the integration of core concepts from variability and adaptivity management using well-defined *models*. Details were described in terms of concrete *research goals* and *research questions*, followed by a list of *contributions*.

The dissertation at hand is structured as sketched in Figure 1.1. A description of each part is given subsequently.

Part I: Introduction and Foundations. After an *introduction* to the research topic, motivation and research goals, *foundations and related work* are introduced. The main topics are self-adaptive software, (dynamic) software product lines, models (at runtime), software languages in general as well as architectural concepts. In addition to the background concepts introduced, implementation-related knowledge is

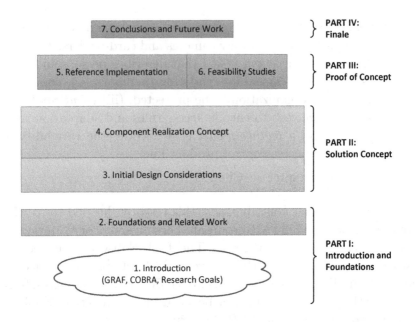

Figure 1.1: Overview of Thesis Structure

described as well. Especially TGraphs [56] and the component model OSGi are covered.

Part II: Solution Concept. In this part, a *solution concept* is described. This is the core part of the thesis where an architectural blueprint for model-integrating components is designed that can especially support variability and adaptivity management for the construction of flexible software.

Based on experience from previous work, *design considerations* are discussed, initially. Afterward, the *MoCo concept* is proposed. It contains a template for implementing components: the *MoCos*. This MoCo template represents a pattern for component realization that combines models and code seamlessly. Among others, embedded models can be domain concept representations, behavioral models, variability models or models of any kind of software asset. Moreover, a description of an abstract execution environment as well as a utility service library are given.

Moreover, there is a domain-independent infrastructure offering a set of *utility services* for engineering MoCos. This architectural concept is based on the balanced interplay between models and code to achieve dynamism throughout the software life-cycle.

Part III: Proof of Concept. In this part, a reference implementation of the developed concept is presented and its capabilities are explored to gain confidence and evidence regarding the MoCo concept's practicality.

Initially, experiences on how to implement MoCos using different existing component technologies are shared. Then, the *MoCo Core API* is described from a user's perspective. The implementation of this Application Programming Interface (API) is based on existing technologies such as Java, TGraphs and OSGi bundles.

In addition to smaller unit tests developed in parallel to the MoCo Core API, the designed and implemented solution approach is tested under various conditions via two different *feasibility studies*. They cover the use of different models (e.g., feature models, requirements models, business process models), different target environments and architectures (Android, PC). Finally, the results of the studies are discussed and the concept for MoCos is analyzed carefully.

Part IV: Finale. In this part, final conclusions are drawn, the essential outcomes of this research are summarized and a list of topics for future research is proposed that can be followed to continue the MID initiative started in this dissertation. Following the concluding chapter, a *glossary* of terms, a list of *acronyms* as well as the *bibliography* can be found. As required, the *curriculum vitae* of the author is attached, too.

2 Foundations and Related Work

This dissertation is related to multiple research and practice areas of software engineering. In this chapter, the necessary *foundations* of these related areas are introduced. We give an overview of the *related work*, as well.

The main goal of this chapter is to provide readers with the essential background knowledge needed to follow the upcoming chapters. The basics introduced here sketch the background of the author of this thesis which shall help to follow some of the decisions made in the remainder of this work. Experts in the field may skip parts, of course.

The topic introduced in this thesis is related to a broad area of research. Accordingly, we introduce (i) *adaptive software*, (ii) *software product lines*, (iii) *modeling*, (iv) *software language engineering* and (v) *software components* in the remainder of this chapter. We define special terminology the first time it is used. A *glossary* of terms (starting on page 293) and a list of *acronyms* (starting on page 305) are attached to this thesis. This chapter ends with a short *summary*.

2.1 Adaptive Software

The main concept and driving idea especially behind *Self-Adaptive Software* (SAS) [96, 111] and likewise behind *Autonomic Computing* (AC) [71, 86] is to achieve the automation of tedious administration and maintenance tasks. Specifically, software shall take active responsibility for its own *robustness* [97] by adapting its own state and behavior at runtime in response to observed changes (i) in its *context* as well as (ii) in its *self*. While the context covers especially the *operative environment*, the self denotes the whole *body of software* as it is implemented (e.g., logically organized into a stack of layers) [120].

Many researchers use the terms self-adaptive, autonomic computing and self-managing interchangeably [76], while some see SAS as the more general area [120]. There is also a community that works on *Organic Computing* (OC) [112, 144]. In the scope of this dissertation, we handle SAS and Autonomic Computing (AC) as two strongly related research areas that target similar goals. Thus, we refer to them collectively as *adaptive software* or "software with adaptivity" (see Definition 2.1) in this thesis.

Definition 2.1: adaptivity

Adaptivity is the ability of a system to make controlled, i.e., meaningful, changes to its own states and behavior to suit changing conditions at runtime.

Adaptivity management (see Definition 2.2) is a very wide and complex topic. The subtopics include *technical* (How to develop adaptive software and its critical parts such as the feedback loop? How to plan and foresee the set of actions that will be most successful in new environments?) and *non-technical* challenges and issues (How to ensure that the adaptive software acts in compliance with the law?).

Definition 2.2: adaptivity management

Adaptivity management is the process of engineering software with adaptivity and controlling its evolution.

The motivation for adaptive software stems from various issues related to engineering *complexity, flexibility, robustness*, continuous *on-time evolution* and the overall desire for *short turn-around times* required to deal with ever changing customer needs. For example, software is commonly built to operate within (strongly) restricted bounds. Components and their interfaces are being developed for *anticipated* use cases and scenarios. Once placed outside of the context it was engineered for, software tends to fail miserably and intervention of humans is required for such *unanticipated* situations.

In practice, it is common to perform necessary maintenance tasks on software *offline* and to deploy a new version, eventually. This time-consuming process results in high costs and also in delays during which the system cannot operate and *Service Level Agreements (SLAs)* [91] are violated. The promise of adaptive software is to provide proven methods, tools and techniques that support the automation of large portions of maintenance tasks *online*, i.e., during operation time (run-time). Furthermore, the vision is that software shall be *fault-tolerant* and stable, with minimal human intervention.

Relying on a mix of *sensing* and *effecting* mechanisms that may be implemented by a combination of hardware and software, an *adaptation manager* (see Definition 2.3) is capable of controlling the coupled *managed software.*[1]

> **Definition 2.3: adaptation manager**
>
> An *adaptation manager* is a subject, e.g., a software component, that performs the process of adapting.

Often, controlling is also referred to as *adapting* (see Definition 2.4).

> **Definition 2.4: adapting**
>
> *Adapting* is a process that operates on a software system to adjust it to varying requirements at runtime by executing adaptations.

> **Definition 2.5: adaptation**
>
> An *adaptation* is a planned sequence of actions that makes a system suitable for a new condition.

---

[1]Autonomic computing names them *autonomic manager* and *managed element*. In control theory, the related terms are *controller* and *controlled plant*.

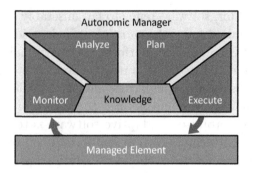

Figure 2.1: IBM's MAPE-K Loop

A common sequence of steps involved is described by the popular *MAPE-K loop* [86]. An illustration is given in Figure 2.1. It consists of (i) *monitoring* changes in the environment, (ii) *analyzing* them for their relevance, (iii) *planning* possible adaptation steps and, finally, (iv) *executing* an adaptation strategy. Additionally, this process is supported by (v) *knowledge*, which is often available in the form of a *self-representation* that can be achieved by following the *reflective architecture pattern* [20].

When designing an adaptation manager, it is common to distinguish between *internal* and *external* approaches [120]. While internal solutions merge the individual steps with the software's (application) logic, external solutions avoid this tight coupling and propose to develop the adaptation manager separately and to connect them with the (existing) application software. This connection is usually established via traditional interfaces, event systems or by injecting code with Aspect-Oriented Programming (AOP) techniques, for instance. Most research seems to focus and rely on the external approach [120, 147].

Most proposed approaches to engineering SAS have in common that they achieve dynamic change by managed, incremental change at the structural level of software, i.e., SAS is also an *architectural challenge* [93]. In Section 2.5, we describe the essentials of software architecture in terms of components and connectors.

2.1.1 Self-* Properties

Software adaptivity is based on a set of properties that facilitate (i) the *observation* of operating state transitions and (ii) the *modification* of the managed application's behavior at runtime [128].[2]

Depending on the domain of the managed software and depending on its requirements, adaptive software needs to possess certain properties to fulfill its requirements, i.e., there are different kinds of adaptivity. This class of properties is widely known as *self-* properties*[3] [6] and can be categorized. Each self-* property focuses on a specific set of system capabilities.

Horn describes eight of such self-* properties that may characterize an autonomic system [71]. In [120], the authors propose a hierarchical view of these properties as illustrated in Figure 2.2. According to this hierarchy, self-adaptiveness and self-organizing are *general* properties of adaptive software. These are further decomposed into *major* and *primitive* properties. This categorization can serve as a starting point for understanding the required and desired properties of adaptive software to be built. In the following, we give an introduction to this hierarchy.

General Level

The *general level* contains global properties of adaptive software such as self-managing, self-governing, self-maintenance [86], self-control [90] and self-evaluating [98]. These terms support the discussion of adaptivity at an abstract level, i.e., without explicitly mentioning concrete capabilities.

Major Level

The *major level* contains all of the four self-* properties introduced in [71]. These were motivated by analogies from biology, where, for

---

[2]The section on self-* properties is partially based on text from the author's master's thesis [37].

[3]The "*" symbol in "self-*" is a placeholder for different properties.

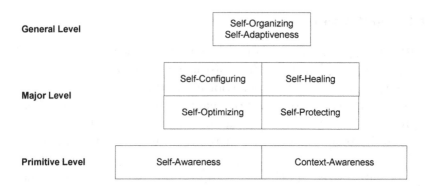

Figure 2.2: Hierarchy of Self-* Properties (Derived from [120])

instance, the autonomous nervous system monitors and controls the heart rate and body temperature [86]. Self-* properties at this level of abstraction can be used to identify and specify the needed adaptivity properties for a concrete software system.

- *Self-configuring* is the ability of adaptive software to adjust its own configuration. Such an adjustment may include installing, updating, integrating, composing and decomposing existing or new software elements.

- *Self-healing* is the ability of adaptive software to discover, diagnose and react to disruptions. Adaptive software with such capabilities is able to detect potential problems and can take proper actions accordingly to prevent failure.

- *Self-optimizing* is the ability of adaptive software to manage performance (e.g., end-to-end response time and throughput) and resource allocation (e.g., CPU and memory consumption).

- *Self-protecting* is the ability of adaptive software to protect itself against threats by detecting security breaches and by recovering from their effects.

Primitive Level

The *primitive level* contains the fundamental properties needed for adaptive software to enable any kind of reasonable adaptation.

- *Self-awareness* refers to the ability of adaptive software to be aware of its *self* (i.e., states and behaviors) based on self-monitoring [68].

- *Context-awareness* refers to the ability of adaptive software to be aware of its *context* (i.e., the operating environment) based on context-monitoring [113].

2.1.2 Selected Publications

The foundations of adaptive software – as needed for this thesis – were described. For a comprehensive list of publications on adaptive software, please check some of the existing surveys [25, 33, 46, 76, 115, 120, 149] and the programs of:

- the International Symposium on Software Engineering for Adaptive and Self-Managing Systems (SEAMS)[4],
- the International Conference on Cloud and Autonomic Computing (CAC)[5] and
- the Self-Adaptive and Self-Organizing Systems (SASO)[6] community.

Subsequently, we give a summary of *selected publications*[7] from different subareas of the field. The idea is to give the interested reader some more details and background by introducing interesting recently published work.

---

[4]`http://www.self-adaptive.org/` (accessed July 6th, 2014)
[5]`http://www.autonomic-conference.org/` (accessed July 6th, 2014)
[6]`http://www.saso-conference.org/` (accessed July 6th, 2014)
[7]Please note that the author of this thesis is "influenced" by the SEAMS community.

Subtopics Related to Applications

Pasquale et al. [114] describe the application of SAS to solve the challenge of protecting valuable assets (physical or virtual) within an organization. This area of research is called adaptive security. The assumption is that a protecting system based on hardware and software exists. Because assets change over time, the appropriate countermeasures against attacks need to be decided on at runtime, too. The contributions are a modeling notation for representing assets, the use of models of security requirements and monitoring functions as well as the description of a set of scenarios in the domain of smart grids.

Pasquale et al. combine a domain-specific *model of assets* (containing rooms, energy, CCTV camera, etc.) with an *extended goal model* [119] that also includes vulnerabilities. Each asset has a value and these are recomputed on change based on defined monitoring functions. Countermeasures are injected into the source code using AOP techniques; in this specific work, the AspectJ [8] is used. Different kinds of countermeasures and their implementation are presented, including one solution that waits for the input of a human administrator ("human-in-the-loop").

Ingolfo and Souza [79] propose to use mechanisms from requirements-based approaches to building SAS in order to achieve *regulatory compliance* for software systems. The challenge is to cope especially with changes and variability in the law. For instance, the allowed age of drivers varies across the US from state to state and assisting solutions must adapt accordingly. Google's driver-less car is taken as an example of an autonomous system that shall comply to applicable law. For example, it shall respect stop signs.

The *Zanshin* approach [124] is used to illustrate how to implement an adaptive system using a requirements model consisting of *awareness requirements* (definition of what should be monitored) and *evolution requirements* (definition of actions to face detected failure).

---

[8]http://eclipse.org/aspectj/ (accessed July 6th, 2014)

Ingolfo and Souza conclude that, based on their preliminary approach, a piece of law (text) can be systematically converted into a model that can be used by a SAS for decision making. Changes in the law are faced in terms of automated reconfiguration of the software. The SAS is able to identify breaches of the law and to search for variations in the law(s) it can fulfill, essentially resulting in a reconfigured system.

Huang and Knottenbelt [74] propose a framework for the realization of *self-adaptive containers* to support software developers building resource-efficient applications. Assuming that an execution environment exists, these low-level containers (e.g., List, Set, Stack, Queue) adapt their use of algorithms to provide an implementation that satisfies a set of Service Level Objective (SLO) [127] best.

These containers consist of two parts: an API and a *Self-Adaptive Unit*. While the first one is subdivided into *configuration interfaces* and *operation interfaces*, the latter consists of an SLO store, observer analyzer, adaptor and an execution unit. They perform a feedback loop. SLOs are defined by using Web Service Level Agreement (WSLA) [85] in XML format and containers are implemented in C++. Internally, a combination of (probabilistic) data structures is used.

Based on a case study where the author's implementation is compared against C++'s standard implementation of the respective containers, Huang and Knottenbelt demonstrate that adaptivity can also support the needs of software developers as the burden of manual optimization of the used algorithms is removed from their shoulders (in this specific example).

Subtopics Related to Architecture

Weyns et al. [147] investigate if the choice of building SAS with an external control loop (in contrast to an internal control loop) really improves software design or not. The claim that an external control mechanism (i.e., an adaptation manager) is the better solution from an engineering perspective was especially propagated by *Garlan et al.* [61] and the proposed Rainbow[9] framework [26].

Weyns et al. present their results from a controlled experiment carried out with 24 final-year Students of a Master in Software Engineering program at Linnaeus University in Sweden. Even though external and internal solutions seem to be roughly the same size, external mechanisms simplify the software's design in terms of its control flow complexity. The outcome of the experiment is that, indeed, external feedback loops are the better choice for engineering SAS.

Cámara et al. [21] report on their findings when integrating the Rainbow framework [61] with an existing industrial-scale software solution for monitoring and managing networks of devices. The primary goal is to investigate if and how new frameworks for adaptivity can be integrated with existing industrial solutions (here called *legacy system*). The associated effort is measured, as well. The overall assumption is that a solution like Rainbow can enhance existing software.

The authors describe the changes necessary for a certain part of the Acquisition and Control Service (DCAS) under inspection and illustrate the newly introduced adaptation mechanisms and their realization using the framework's capabilities of placing probes, effectors and expressing adaptation strategies.

Cámara et al. conclude that the Rainbow-based solution performs adaptation better than the existing solution. Moreover, it was not too complicated to integrate both software systems with the exception of an initial learning effort added. Once the integration has been completed, evolution of the system takes minutes, not hours. This facilitates maintenance which is the primary effort associated with software over its full life-cycle [19].

Subtopics Related to Evaluation

Weyns et al. [146] discuss that no systematic study has been performed to check if the claims associated with SAS are actually valid or not.

---

[9]`http://www.cs.cmu.edu/~able/research/rainbow/` (accessed July 6th, 2014)

The goal of the paper is to gain a representative impression of quality of research carried out in the field, so far. Based on examining 96 papers out of a total of 124, Weyns et al. discover that 90 studies focus on engineering and only 6 of them are related to (concrete) applications. The two most-frequently occurring subjects of the studies in all papers are software architecture (26 %) and models (24 %).

The interest in architecture dropped significantly in publications after 2008. Instead, models became the "hot topic", then. It is guessed that this change is strongly related to the organization of the models@run.time [14] workshop. Weyns et al. state that research on SAS is nearly exclusively related to the enhancement of software quality attributes. Among those, flexibility, reliability and performance are the most popular ones. While 85 % of the works claim that their approach has enhanced the quality attribute(s) aimed at, only little negative influence has been reported. Among the negative reports, efficiency and/or performance seems to be the only one.

All in all, the results presented in [146] lead to the conclusion, that research in SAS is weakly evaluated. Among others, Weyns et al. propose to enhance review processes. For instance, a discussion section shall be mandatory in all papers and there shall be a "hall of fame" for the papers presenting the best studies. The negative outcome of the work by Weyns et al. is in line with the findings published earlier by *Zannier et al.* [150] who analyzed the state of research published in the proceedings of the prestigious International Conference on Software Engineering (ICSE)[10].

2.2 Software Product Lines

A vast amount of different *products* driven by software have been developed to date. As software is flexible in many ways, e.g., it can be copied and modified with little effort compared to physical entities, it is easy to introduce *variability* (see Definition 2.6). This variability usually is meant to add value to a product (line) in terms of

---

[10]http://www.icse-conferences.org/ (accessed July 6th, 2014)

additional functionality or quality properties. Besides the introduction of completely new capabilities, in many cases, *existing* functionality is modified to suit specific customer needs.

In practice, this results in a set of different products that originate from one root product. In that case, the developing organization shall move away from *single system engineering* and to adopt a systematic *product line engineering* approach.

Definition 2.6: variability

Variability is the ability to select from a set of different possibilities that cover the same concern.

SPLs [116] cope with aspects of *reuse* as well as *variability management* (see Definition 2.7) for the construction and maintenance of a group of complex but largely similar software applications. Often, these applications are found in the *embedded software* domain and operate together with hardware like manufacturing machines or other electro-mechanical components. Braking systems in the automotive industry are another example.

Definition 2.7: variability management

Variability management is the process of engineering software with variability and controlling its evolution.

Variability management [22, 24] is a very wide and complex topic. The subtopics include *technical* (How to develop software variants?) and *non-technical* challenges and issues (How to plan and foresee the set of *features* (see Definition 2.8) that will be most successful from a business-perspective?).

The complexity in SPLs stems from the vast number of possible combinations of software and hardware variants that are offered and requested by the market. *SPLE* comprises methods such as *feature modeling* [82] to model variability within a domain for the explicit elicitation of *commonalities* and *differences* among products within a product line. Details on feature models are given in Section 2.3.2.

Definition 2.8: feature

A *feature* is a distinguishable concept of a product that is relevant for at least one stakeholder.

In addition, the variability within *core assets* (see Definition 2.9) is made explicit to achieve a high degree of flexibility for the development of even previously unknown products. Managing these flexible core assets is an essential concern to support reuse.

Definition 2.9: core asset

A *core asset* is "a reusable artifact or resource that is used in the production of more than one product in a software product line" [100].

In Table 2.1, an overview of the major concepts in SPLE is given together with associated processes. These are introduced subsequently.

Domain Engineering is a process to be defined at the organizational level for providing the capabilities to develop the desired products for a product line.

Table 2.1: Overview of SPLE Processes and Main Concepts

	Problem Space	Solution Space
Domain Engineering	Feature Models	Variation Points & Variations
Application Engineering	Product Configuration	Build Procedure

- At the conceptual level (problem space), the *features* supported by products are modeled, together with logical dependencies and restrictions between them.
- At the asset level (solution space), *variation points* (see Definition 2.10) and *variations* (see Definition 2.11) are described within the *core assets* conforming to an overall product line architecture. Domain engineering is *engineering for reuse*.

Application Engineering is a process to be defined at the organizational level for deriving a specific product by describing it in terms of features and its depending variations available from core assets in the platform.

- At the conceptual level (problem space), a product configuration is established by choosing features and resolving conflicts and incompatibilities. Ideally, depending variations are detected automatically, in some cases, manual configuration may be required, though.
- At the asset level (solution space), the product configuration is used to derive a concrete product by instantiating and composing concrete variations according to predefined build procedures. Application engineering is *engineering with reuse*.

Problem Space is a virtual space that denotes the set of all products that can be potentially described in terms of features. The problem space is bounded by the product line *scope*. In practice, this space of possible product variants is described conceptually by features that are identified during domain engineering. By making feature choices during application engineering, the problem space is narrowed down to a single product variant that can be built.

Solution Space is a virtual space that denotes the set of all products that can be potentially built by instantiating core assets with a certain binding of variations at their variation points. The solution space is bounded by the product line *scope* as well as by strategic (e.g., architectural) decisions regarding technical extendability and maintainability of the platform. Such decisions are made during domain engineering. The procedures for deriving concrete products by instantiating core assets to realize a given product configuration is are tweaked and executed during application engineering.

Features are capabilities, functional or non-functional properties that a product may possess or not. The commonalities and differences of all possible products within a product line are described in terms of features and their dependencies. A feature is usually described by a unique, human readable label that is also used to communicate with customers. Feature models describe the problem space and are the basis for product configuration.

Variation Points and Variations denote spots in assets that are engineered for variability. A variation point is the point in an asset at which options are available to choose from. These options are called variations. The process of determining one concrete variation for a specific variation point is called *binding*.

Definition 2.10: variation point

A *variation point* is a point in an asset at which a decision between different but logically coherent functional units can be made.

Definition 2.11: variation

A *variation* is a logically coherent asset fragment that is explicitly associated with at least one variation point.

To automate the build procedure, there are usually mappings defined at a variation point (or per variation) that define which variation is required for the implementation of a certain feature. Variability in assets can be expressed by models that only reference core assets (external approach), as well as by annotating the core assets or by using the language's built-in mechanisms for expressing variability (internal approach).

Product Configuration is a part of application engineering that either denotes (i) the *process of feature selection* to describe a product

variant on the conceptual level, or (ii) the *actual model of a product
variant* as the result of the configuration process. Depending on the
followed approach, the binding of variations at variation points is
computed in parallel or is done later, i.e., as a preparation step of the
build procedure.

Build Procedures are predefined steps that take a product configuration and the actual physical locations of core assets as their input
and derive a (partial) product. This is also called *tailoring* (see Definition 2.12) and usually involves model-driven [125] as well as generative
programming techniques [31].

Definition 2.12: tailoring

Tailoring is a process that operates on a set of artifacts to derive
the variation needed for engineering a specific product variant.

In an ideal world, this derived product can be directly shipped
to the customer and documentation, user guides as well as other
accompanying artifacts are also automatically derived. Depending
on the known scope of the product line and the maturity of this
approach in an organization, complete product generation may be
possible, or not. In many cases, the output of the build procedures
at the end of application engineering is a "hand-over-package" to
application engineering teams for further customization and extension
with previously unavailable functionality [44].

To categorize the available variations, SPLE uses the concept of
binding time to refer to a point in time where variations for certain
variation points are determined. For example, variations can be
assigned to variation points during design, development, deployment
and dynamically at run-time. Nevertheless, the topic of *dynamic
reconfiguration*, i.e., adapting a product during operation, has not
been extensively explored in SPLE [63].

2.2.1 Dynamic Software Product Lines

In traditional SPLE, feature models and product configuration models are heavily used for communication as well as for generative, model-driven development. The focus is set on (one-time) forward engineering, where the knowledge on variability (e.g., stored in models) is usually not explicitly accessible during product operation any more.

The driving idea behind *Dynamic Software Product Lines (DSPLs)* (see Definition 2.13) is to address changes in the user's needs or available resources for a product variant at runtime and is described as *"one among several approaches to building self-adapting/managing/healing systems"* [63]. Similar to adaptive software, product variants, i.e., instances of the DSPL, shall be capable of adapting themselves autonomously. Moreover, *"dynamic software product lines extend existing product line engineering approaches by moving their capabilities to runtime, helping to ensure that system adaptations lead to desirable properties"* [69].

> **Definition 2.13: dynamic software product line**
>
> A *Dynamic Software Product Line* (DSPL) is a software system that achieves adaptivity within a predefined (but not necessarily fixed) state-space by applying and evolving proven variability management techniques as proposed in the field of SPLE.

Although SPLE already distinguishes between different *binding times* including runtime, configuration in a traditional SPL is done as a part of the development process. In contrast, DSPLs focus on managing variability at runtime. From that perspective, even the initial product derivation process may be performed (automatically) as a complex form of *runtime (re)configuration*.

Research in this area is based on topics similar to those in traditional SPLE, SAS and AC. The main focus of the DSPL research direction is on mixing SPLE mechanisms and techniques for variability management with autonomous capabilities to achieve dynamic software variants. This area is still emerging and – in the opinion of the author of this thesis – a final consensus about common DSPL characteristics has not yet been reached within the research community.[11] We also noticed that, in contrast to SPLE, the term *Dynamic Software Product Line Engineering (DSPLE)* (see Definition 2.14) has not been published in the literature, which is another hint at the current lack of maturity of this field.

Definition 2.14: dynamic SPLE

Dynamic Software Product Line Engineering (DSPLE) is a software development approach comprising mature methods, best practices and tools for building and evolving DSPLs.

To give the reader some more background information, we summarize recently published *core principles* of a DSPL [69] subsequently.

- *Explicit Configuration Space Modeling:* The configuration space shall be explicitly represented in any DSPL. This variability model shall express the possible states reachable by reconfiguration at runtime. The description shall be on the level of intended capabilities, not at the technical level.

- *Autonomous System Reconfiguration:* The ability to reconfigure itself shall be supported by any DSPL. Given a desired state to be reached, a DSPL shall adapt itself to reach that configuration. This process of reconfiguration can be triggered by a human administrator. Sensing the environment and subsequent planning of adaptation steps is not a required DSPL capability.

- *Variability Scoping:* Defining the scope of variability shall be part of constructing a DSPL by following a systematic engineering process. This is similar to the scoping step proposed

---

[11]State of discussion at the *Fifth International Workshop on Dynamic Software Product Lines* (DSPL) in Munich, 2011 and the *Sixth International Workshop on Dynamic Software Product Lines* (DSPL) in Salvador, 2012. The author participated actively.

in classic SPLE approaches where the bounds of the product line are defined. In contrast to SPLE though, reuse is not in the focus for DSPLs. Instead, variability scoping shall support the enumeration of possible system states that may especially change during operation. Thus, not only SPLE methods shall be used but other approaches may be feasible, too.

Besides the "principles" mentioned above, Hinchey et al. give further hints that shall help to characterize DSPLs:

- *No SPL Basis Required:* A DSPL does not need to be developed by following an SPL process. This means that variability is fully handled at runtime. Variations in core assets can be developed following other processes, as well.

- *No Analogous or Continuous Models:* For the definition of the adaptation space, only discrete models shall be used. Problems for adaptation that require some form of continuous modeling (e.g., using differential equations) are not in the scope of DSPLs.

- *Not Just Parametrization:* Adaptations that are purely based on parametrization are not sufficient to implement DSPLs. Adaptivitys shall ideally be managed at the architectural level, e.g., by switching components, while the system is executing.

2.2.2 Selected Publications

In this section, we describe some *selected publications* related to the basics of SPLE, but especially on the use of models for tailoring. The topic of DSPLs is covered, as well. The presented subtopics are related to this thesis because, in parts, the motivation for designing MoCos was to support building variable software in a way that can be used during design, development and at runtime in similar ways.

Subtopics Related to Foundations

Capilla et al. [22] present concepts tools and industrial experiences on systems and software variability management. In doing so, theoretical foundations and concepts as well as practical guidelines are described. Furthermore, insights into novel research directions such as service-oriented and dynamic software product lines are given and a survey of (popular) commercial and research tools is provided, too.

Similarly, *Pohl et al.* [116] cover the state of the art in SPLE. Amongst others, ways to document variability in various kinds of artifacts are described. For example, the various approaches of describing requirements with variability are taken into account for textual and visual representations. In addition, implementable guidelines are given with concrete examples such as the realization of variation points and associated variations.

Clements et al. [27] comprehensively describe the foundations of SPLE, including the underlying principles, required skills and involved (standard) activities. The descriptions are based on several industrial projects but also on academic research. This solid expertise is clearly presented in the form of focus areas and related (sub-)patterns to be applied in practice.

Kästner et al. [84] propose a *variability-aware module system*. It supports resolving variability inside a module and its interface at compile-time. In order to solve the problem that variability may strongly influence system decomposition, i.e., its architecture, an approach for variable module composing is proposed that does not rely on a global variability model. The module system is formally defined and an implementation in C is given which is applied to the Busybox product line.

Subtopics Related to Variability at Runtime

Hallsteinsen et al. [63] proposed DSPLs to deal with changes in the users' requirements or in available resources for a product variant at runtime. Explicit variability models are at the heart of this approach that uses SPL techniques to achieve adaptivity. DSPLs are described as "one among several approaches to building self-adapting/managing/healing systems". Similar to SAS, product variants, i.e., specific instances of an SPL, shall be able to autonomously adapt themselves.

In a more recent publication, *Hinchey et al.* [69] provide their updated view on DSPLs. Especially the differences between classic SPLs and DSPLs is described and discussed. The authors stress that the strengths of DSPLs is especially the engineering foundation inherited from the mature field of SPLE. The claim is that, in contrast to other work on constructing SAS, DSPLs can lead to more reliable and predictable systems. A list of research issues is identified and briefly introduced.

Bencomo et al. [12] analyze nine different proposed approaches to the development of DSPLs and systems that support the "late binding" of variations at variation points, i.e., *dynamic variability*. The authors distinguish between *when* to adapt and *how* to adapt and compare all inspected approaches based on their capabilities for the individual steps in the MAPE-K loop. The result is that DSPLs seem to be (too) limited by the specification of design-time decisions and are not as dynamic as desired, e.g., by the SAS (research) community. Recently, Bencomo et al. surveyed the landscape of DSPLs again and provide an updated view [11].

2.3 Modeling

Abstraction is a cornerstone in computer science and software engineering. Thus, the use of *models* (see Definition 2.15) is an important part of the field. Models exist in various flavors with different goals and application areas.

Definition 2.15: model

"A *model* is a purposeful description of a system which, on the one hand, permits similar observations and conclusions as the original system and, on the other hand, simplifies this reality to

> **Definition 2.15: model (cont'd)**
>
> the problem-related aspects by abstraction." [148, Translation from German original].

Two popular *modeling* (see Definition 2.16) approaches are MDSD [18, 125] and Model-Driven Architecture (MDA) [88, 107]. The goal of both of them is to use use models not only for communication (*descriptive models*) but also for the derivation of executable software (*prescriptive models*). From this perspective, models are becoming more and more an essential part of modern software engineering.

> **Definition 2.16: modeling**
>
> *Modeling* is the (creative) process of planning, designing, implementing and evolving models.

Before introducing specific modeling approaches that are related to adaptivity and variability, we describe some of the basic terminology in the next paragraphs. These terms will be used throughout the rest of the thesis.

Modeling languages can be visual, textual or a combination of both. In simple words, the "appearance" of models (including color, layout and size) is called the *concrete syntax*. Models are usually created and rendered by a software tool.

In Figure 2.3, an example for a visual model is depicted. It can be easily understood that this is a room named B118 with an open door named D1. Additionally, there are two persons in it: Alice and Bob.

In contrast, the *abstract syntax* of models describes the pure data structure excluding any additional information that is part of the concrete syntax. No layout information, color etc. is stored – obviously except for the special case that the purpose of the model is actually to represent visual data (e.g., graphical user interfaces). The abstract syntax of models – including additional *constraints* that can

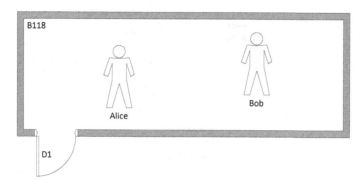

Figure 2.3: Model of a Room Including one Door and two Persons (Concrete Syntax)

be described by a dedicated language – is described by *meta-models* (see Definition 2.17).

Definition 2.17: meta-model

A *meta-model* is a formalization of allowed model elements, their relationships and optional constraints defining the abstract syntax of a modeling language.

We sometimes use the term *schema* (see Definition 2.18), as well.

Definition 2.18: schema

The term *schema* is used as a synonym for meta-model in this research.

Meta-models are described using another modeling language, i.e., UML class diagrams. Concepts are represented as *classes* and relationships are represented by *associations*. In the following, we assume that the reader is familiar with the basics of object-orientation and UML. Otherwise, the publicly available documents [130, 131] provided

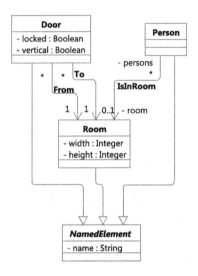

Figure 2.4: Meta-Model of Persons, Rooms and Doors (UML Class Diagram)

by the Object Management Group (OMG) may be a first starting point.

In Figure 2.4, such a meta-model is shown. It declares all concepts used in the model depicted in Figure 2.3. Namely, these are Door, Person and Room. All of these concepts have a name, therefore they inherit a name attribute from the abstract concept NamedElement. Additionally, the dimensions of the room are represented by two integer attributes: width and height.[12]

According to the IsInRoom association and its multiplicities, a person can be in one room and there may be an arbitrary number of persons in a room. Also, there is always one room associated to each door (see From and To associations) and – in this case – a room may even exist without any door. This is required to simulate border cases. Each door can be open or closed as modeled by the Boolean locked

---

[12]In this case, models will store size information as this is a fundamental part of the domain. It shall not be mistaken for concrete syntax.

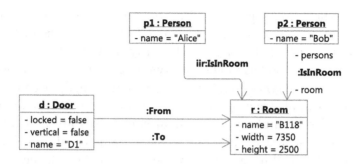

Figure 2.5: Model of a Room Including one Door and two Persons (Abstract Syntax)

attribute and the rough orientation of the door (horizontal or vertical) is represented by the Boolean **vertical** attribute. If a model satisfies all constraints of its meta-model, we say that the model *conforms* to the meta-model.

Schemas can be *extended*, e.g., with attachments and annotations as well as with operations that are necessary and useful for handling instances, i.e., models that conform to the extended schema. We refer to these extensions as *schema extensions* [126] (see Definition 2.19).

Definition 2.19: schema extension

A *schema extension* is "everything that can be added to a base schema that is not a transformation" [126].

Coming back to the model visualized in Figure 2.3 and knowing the meta-model that dictates the structure of the model, we can explain the sample model in abstract syntax. It is shown in Figure 2.5 as a UML object diagram (*objects* are instances of classes, *links* are instances of associations).

The model contains two objects of type **Person**: these are labeled p1 and p2. The actual person's name ("Alice", "Bob") is stored in the respective **name** string attribute. They are situated in room r as shown by the :IsInRoom links with no label.[13] The door is labeled as d here and, as visualized in Figure 2.3, it is not locked and it is horizontally oriented. Its name is obviously set to "D1".

To summarize: models in abstract syntax conform to meta-models. Models in concrete syntax (e.g., diagrams) are (informal) visualizations of the model in abstract syntax. Conformance can be *validated* by tools. In this example, no additional constraints are added. For example, a constraint could ensure that all name attributes shall be non-empty and shall have a string value that is unique in the specific model. OMG's Object Constraint Language (OCL) [110] is a language for defining such constraints for UML (meta-)models.

Subsequently, we describe the foundations of modeling techniques that are commonly applied in SAS and SPLs as these are the two cornerstones of this thesis.

2.3.1 Modeling for Adaptivity Management

The topic of *modeling for adaptivity management* has become especially popular with research on engineering SAS. To achieve adaptivity, different approaches have been proposed and are being applied. Depending on the application domain, the techniques are specific to certain low-level programming languages and very customized hardware (e.g., in mission-critical embedded systems) or make use of general purpose programming languages and modern software platforms, frameworks and hardware (e.g., for application servers). In this thesis, we focus especially on solutions that make use of models in various ways to achieve adaptivity.

It must be noted that in some cases, *existing modeling languages* are used at runtime to support achieving adaptivity. In other cases, existing languages are extended, or *new modeling languages* are designed and developed.

Regarding the use of existing modeling languages, feature models, architectural models (components and connectors) as well as models describing program flow such as UML activity diagrams, state charts

---

[13]In UML, instances do not have to be labeled and may be anonymous.

or Business Process Model and Notation (BPMN) diagrams are usually used. An advantage of this direction is that these languages are already familiar to software engineers and there are tools for creating, editing and viewing them. If software was developed following a model-driven approach, then a set of models is already there to be (re)used.

Regarding new modeling languages, any kind of language that can be expressed by a meta-model may be developed. That is, very specific solutions for an application domain, customer or target platform can be realized. For example, technology-specific architecture models (e.g., for OSGi) that carry detailed development information may be used. An advantage of this direction is that these languages can be smaller, easier to learn and they may possess certain properties that make them well-suited for use at runtime, e.g., regarding memory consumption or required validation effort. Such new modeling languages are also called *Domain-Specific Modeling Languages (DSMLs)*.

Models at Runtime

In order to be able to adapt at runtime, an adaptation manager requires information about relevant parts (e.g., state information) of the managed element, available resources and further information about the operating environment of the SAS. Such models are referred to as *runtime models* (see Definition 2.20). There may be various kinds of such models, including (but not limited to) structural and behavioral models as well as static and dynamic models [9]. The levels of granularity – from coarse to fine-grained – vary, too.

Definition 2.20: runtime model

A *runtime model* is a model that offers "abstractions of runtime phenomena" [59].

Similar to classic *development models* used for communication and code generation, runtime models support (limited) reasoning about the structure or behavior of software. Instead of analyzing systems statically, runtime models can be used to realize state monitoring, for example. Moreover, new or extended artifacts may be generated from these models during execution. According to Blair et al. [14], "a runtime model can be seen as a life development model that enables dynamic evolution and the realization of software designs."

Research carried out in *models@runtime* [14] (see Definition 2.21) aims at applying model-driven techniques to runtime. In particular, the basic definition and usage scenarios for models as proposed by MDSD are accepted and adopted as a basis for investigating the set of possible roles that models may play in a runtime environment.

> **Definition 2.21: model@run.time**
>
> "A *model@run.time* is a causally connected self-representation of the associated system that emphasizes the structure, behavior, or goals of the system from a problem space perspective" [14].

In contrast to runtime models, maintaining a *"causal connection"* between the model and the underlying system is a distinguishing mark of models@runtime. This is similar to earlier work in the field of (architectural) reflection [20]. Despite this similarity, there is a major difference: while reflection is concerned with providing a meta-layer that represents the current state of software as it is implemented (solution space perspective), models@runtime aim at providing information at a higher level of abstraction, ideally up to the level of requirements (problem space perspective).

Blair et al. [14] propose a set of *key dimensions* to describe a model@run.time. These are (i) structure versus behavior, (ii) procedural versus declarative, (iii) functional versus non-functional and (iv) formal versus informal. In the literature, most works seem to be related to the software structure described with procedural models (e.g., software architecture models).

We noticed that the terms model@run.time and runtime model are not used in a consistent manner in the literature or in discussions with colleagues during conferences and workshops. Especially the fact that both kinds of models are "models (used) at runtime" seems to be an issue.

Executable Models

Models in software engineering are used for communication, but also as an essential artifact in early stages of the development process. Code can be generated from these prescriptive models, i.e., the *semantics* of the model is encoded by a code generator that maps the intended meaning (in terms of structure or behavior) to the specified *execution semantics* (see Definition 2.22) of a programming language.

Definition 2.22: execution semantics

Execution semantics is the description of how a valid program or model is executed as a sequence of (computational) actions.

This *intermediate step* of deriving code from models is common in MDSD and the MDA and automates steps that would otherwise have to be done manually. This approach brings a set of challenges, though.

Models and code may become "out of sync", i.e., when either side is changed and no automatic synchronization mechanism is defined, models and code will become inconsistent. This problem is also known in the reengineering community as the "roundtrip engineering problem" [16].

Tackling this challenge for any kind of model and generated program is difficult as (i) a 1:1 mapping of concepts from the model to concepts of the target programming language is a challenge (for the general case) and (ii) information may be lost so additional data needs to be stored on either side to be able to derive the original model from the code and vice-versa. For example, UML's aggregation or composition associations between classes are both represented in the same way as a normal association in Java: as a simple reference, a list or a set. Layout information in diagrams is typically lost, too.

In order to overcome some of these issues, *model execution* (see Definition 2.23) has been proposed, e.g., for the UML under the name of Executable UML (xUML) [105] and its application in an industrial context [48] have been reported as a success. The advantage of this approach is that no further artifacts are generated from a model, but it is directly executed.

Definition 2.23: model execution

Model execution is the process of traversing a model in its abstract syntax representation and thereby invoking specified actions for model elements.

The execution semantics of the modeling language can be encoded in a *model interpreter*[14] (see Definition 2.24).

Definition 2.24: model interpreter

A *model interpreter* is software that executes models based on their Abstract Syntax Graph (ASG) representation. It encodes (parts of) their execution semantics.

In addition to the different approaches that have been reported in the literature, the OMG has also worked on developing standards for executing some of the modeling languages that are part of the UML. Recently, the OMG published Foundational UML (fUML) which specifies the "semantics of a foundational subset" [132] of the UML. The proposed default implementation of the virtual machine for models is extended in the work of Mayerhofer et al. [103] in such a way that some of the hidden state information (e.g., events and execution traces) is explicitly available as a runtime model to support the development of SAS.

---

[14]In this thesis, we assume that execution semantics for models is always encoded by a model interpreter but there are other possibilities such as model compilation (including just-in-time-compilation), too.

2.3.2 Modeling for Variability Management

The topic of *modeling for variability management* has become especially popular with research on engineering SPLs where related (engineering) concerns are split into two virtual spaces: the *problem space* and the *solution space*. We covered related terminology in Section 2.2. In each space, different requirements need to be met by the models.

- In the problem space, the purpose of variability models is especially (i) to provide a *structured vocabulary* of terms for communication about product *features* (see Definition 2.8) (similar to a domain model), (ii) to support *managing the product line scope* and (iii) to provide a machine-processable basis for the *description of product variants* from a customer's perspective.

- In the solution space, the purpose of variability models is especially (i) to provide a *structured vocabulary* of terms for the description of variation points and variations in core assets as well as (ii) to provide a machine-processable basis for the *description of artifacts* for realizing product variants from a developer's perspective.

The most prominent way of modeling variability is *feature modeling* in the form of a rather simple "and-or tree" structure plus additional constraints. This was initially proposed by Kang et al. [82, 83] as a part of the *Feature-Oriented Reuse Method (FORM)*. In their first paper on the FORM approach, the authors talk about *feature space* (today: problem space) and *artifact space* (today: solution space). Both spaces are connected with each other by a mapping relationship.

Variability in the feature space is defined by *feature models* (see Definition 2.25) at four levels: capabilities, operating environment, domain technologies and implementation technologies. These feature layers are especially useful to document *commonalities and differences* among products explicitly. Especially the commonalities indicate *opportunities for reuse*.

> **Definition 2.25: feature model**
>
> A *feature model* is a model that captures stakeholder-visible variability in the problem space in terms of features (with unique identifiers) as well as their relationships.

In Figure 2.6, an excerpt of an example feature model is illustrated.[15] In their purest form, feature models have the following notation:

(A) Each *feature* is represented by a box with a unique name. Naming conventions such as for classifiers in UML class diagrams are useful. Here, the root feature is the **Smartphone**. It is related to the sub-features **Camera** and **Internet**. The root feature is, by convention, *mandatory*.

(B) *Optional* feature relationships are marked with a line and the outline of circle shape at the end. The meaning in this special case is that if the **Smartphone** feature is part of a product (which it always is in this case), then it is possible to chose the **Camera** feature or not.

(C) *Mandatory* feature relationships are marked with a line and a filled circle shape at the end. The meaning in this case is that if the **Smartphone** feature is part of a product, then the **Internet** feature is also part of any product variant.

(D) *Exclusive Or* (XOR) feature relationships are shown as the outline of a triangle shape with one "rounded" side and at least two outgoing lines. The meaning in this special case is that if the **Camera** feature is selected as a part of the product, then *exactly one* of its associated sub-features shall be selected: for example the **LiveStreaming** feature. The box with ... in it symbolizes a set set of further features or a sub-tree in this particular example.

(E) *Inclusive Or* (OR) feature relationships are shown as a filled triangle shape with one "rounded" side and at least two outgoing lines. The meaning in this special case is that if the **Internet**

---

[15]The letters in capital case and in braces are not part of the modeling language but are introduced to ease referring to its parts.

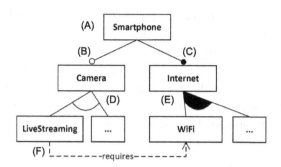

Figure 2.6: Sample Feature Model for the Mobile Domain

feature is part of a product, then *at least one* of its associated
sub-features shall be selected: for example the WiFi feature and
one of the other (not visualized) sibling features.

(F) *Cross-tree-relationships* between features are shown as a labeled
dashed lines with an arrow. The meaning in this special case
is that if the LiveStreaming feature is part of a product, then
WiFi needs to be part of it, too. As one can easily see, having
many of such cross-tree-relationships make a feature model more
complex.

Kang et al. propose *engineering principles* that are centered around
the design and development of different kinds of models and their
(inter)relationships. They shall guide the construction of artifacts with
variability. Besides the rather common principles such as *separation
of concerns* and *localization* (of function, data and control) the rather
novel principle – at the time of publication – was the *parametrization
of artifacts with features*: features from the feature model are used
as instantiation parameters for software components. These "feature
parameters" are instantiated when design decisions are made during
the course of application development time.

Additionally, it must be noted that a certain amount of effort needs
to be put into the development of a *reference architecture* to support

reuse and automated product derivation as well as into the use of *flexible component connector technology* to reduce coupling.

Automation, is primarily achieved based on a *feature configuration* (see Definition 2.26) that is validated against the feature model. Despite both being models, feature models act as meta-models for feature configurations. A partial configuration still has a *"meta-model character"*, so to speak: The more features are selected, the narrower the configuration space gets, i.e., less choices are available.

Definition 2.26: feature configuration

A *feature configuration* is an instance of a feature model.

Usually, tools support the creation of feature configurations by automatically updating it where possible based on a changed feature selection by selecting and deselecting associated features. A feature configuration can be invalid, e.g., when a mandatory feature is not part of it.

2.3.3 TGraph Technology

Besides manually drawn models with "pen and paper", software models are developed using software tools. This requires a *technological space* [95] for models, i.e., a formal basis for defining meta-models and models as well as tools, best practices and a common glossary of terms that are known by the community members working within this technological space.

There are various technological spaces for modeling; among them the currently popular solution is Eclipse Modeling Framework (EMF)[16]. In this thesis, we work in the technological space of *TGraphs* [52, 53] (see Definition 2.27). The class of TGraphs has been proposed, developed and maintained by Prof. Dr. Jürgen Ebert and his working group at the University of Koblenz-Landau in Germany. TGraphs can be used to implement many common algorithms and data structures.

---

[16]http://www.eclipse.org/modeling/emf/ (accessed July 6th, 2014)

Definition 2.27: TGraph

The *TGraph* class of graphs, i.e., typed, attributed and ordered directed graphs, is a general graph class for graph-based modeling.

In this dissertation, we develop models, meta-models as well as queries and transformations in the technological space of TGraphs, i.e., we *apply* this technology. Therefore, we introduce the four main properties of TGraphs only informally[17] here and do not repeat the related formal definitions.

A TGraphs is:

- *typed*, i.e., all vertices and edges are typed,
- *attributed*, i.e., all vertices and edges may carry a type dependent set of attribute-value pairs,
- *ordered*, i.e., there is a global order of all vertices and edges as well as a local order of the incidences at each vertex and
- *directed*, i.e., all edges are directed.

This TGraph representation can be used to represent many kinds of graphs which are equal or poorer in their modeling expressiveness simply by ignoring some of the TGraph properties. The expressiveness of TGraphs is between Essential Meta Object Facility (EMOF) and Complete Meta Object Facility (MOF) (CMOF). Both are parts of the OMG's[18] MOF, a standard for model-driven engineering that has its roots in the UML and its meta-model.

The types of vertices and edges of a TGraph represent the domain-specific characteristics. The structure of incidences as well as associated attributes are defined by a *TGraph schema* (see Definition 2.28). It can be expressed using *Graph UML (grUML)*, which is a sublanguage of UML class diagrams. Such a schema specifies the possible types and the overall structure of a class of TGraphs that conform to this schema.

---

[17]The interested reader can obtain details on the formal basis as well as mathematical definitions from Ebert et al.'s papers [52, 53].

[18]http://www.omg.org/mof/ (accessed July 6th, 2014)

> **Definition 2.28: TGraph schema**
>
> A *TGraph schema* is a meta-model in the technological space of
> TGraphs.

The technological space of TGraphs is supported by a comprehensive and versatile Java library called *JGraLab*[19]. It provides an API for creating and managing meta-models and models. Additional functionality includes a dedicated *query language* called the Graph Repository Query Language (GReQL) [55], model validation capabilities and much more. With the Graph Repository Transformation Language (GReTL) [54] and with FunnyQT [72], there is ongoing research on *transformation languages* for TGraphs, too.

Subsequently, we describe the foundations needed to follow topics related to implementation such as those that are discussed later on when presenting the feasibility studies in Chapter 6.

Typical Workflow With TGraphs

There are various ways to work with and to use TGraphs. The exact workflow depends on a couple of factors. The following questions are an attempt to characterize the sort of decisions to be made when starting: Is a meta-model already available as a TGraph schema? Is there a (visual) modeling tool for the specific class of models to be created based on the given meta-model? Shall the model be used in-memory or is it persisted?

When developing models with TGraphs, a couple of steps need to be taken. The most essential and commonly carried out ones – in the scope of this dissertation – are as follows:

(1) *Develop TGraph schema:* Usually, we model TGraph schemas using the IBM Rational Software Architect (IBM RSA) tool [20]

---

[19]https://github.com/jgralab (accessed July 6th, 2014)
[20]http://www-03.ibm.com/software/products/en/ratisoftarch (accessed July 6th, 2014)

and its UML class diagram facilities but there is support for
ArgoUML[21], too. A class diagram (such as the one shown in
Figure 2.4) is created. Note that it must follow certain conventions
as the class diagram editor is used to model a schema in grUML.

(2) *Add Constraints to TGraph schema:* Similar to the use of OCL for
UML class diagrams, it is possible to add constraints to a TGraph
schema, too. They are written using GReQL expressions inserted
into a UML constraint model element. Constraints can refer to an
arbitrary number of meta-model elements. A typical example for
a constraint is to limit the allowed values for an attribute: a `name`
: `String` attribute shall never be null and shall never contain only
the empty string "".

(3) *Generate a Schema-specific Java API:* Once the TGraph schema
is ready, it is exported to an XML Metadata Interchange (XMI)
file containing only the abstract syntax representation of the
meta-model without any visual information. Using JGraLab tools,
e.g., triggered from an ANT build file, this XMI-representation is
processed and a Java API is automatically generated. For each
meta-model element, i.e., for each class (vertex type) and for each
association (edge type), a Java interface and an implementing
class is created.

(4) *Use the Java API:* Based on the generated schema-specific API,
software engineers can (i) *create and manage models* programmatically[22], e.g., instantiate, save, load and plot, as well as (ii) *create
software for processing models*, e.g., visual modeling tools and
model interpreters.

Next, the basics of GReQL, the query language for TGraphs, are
introduced by giving some examples. Thereafter, an example for using

---

[21]`http://argouml.tigris.org/` (accessed July 6th, 2014)

[22]We use the adverb "programmatically" to refer to actions on models that are carried out by writing source code instead of using some tool offering a (graphical)
user interface.

a generated schema-specific Java API is given, too. The running example is based on the meta-model for rooms and persons as already introduced in Figure 2.4.

GReQL: Graph Repository Query Language

GReQL is a schema-sensitive *expression language* used for retrieving data stored as TGraphs (queries) as well as for defining Boolean expressions on them (constraints). It was developed in the Generic Understanding of Programs (GUPRO) project [55]. The value of a GReQL expression is precisely defined [52]. A typical GReQL expression (i) specifies the range of free variables in terms of vertices and edges, (ii) poses conditions on them and (iii) describes the desired output set.

The most powerful concept in GReQL are *regular path expressions*. A path expression describes the set of all paths that match a given pattern. Path expressions can be used to test if pairs of vertices in a model are connected via the specified path. Moreover, a path expression can be used to obtain the set of vertices that can be reached from a starting vertex.

Given the extended sample TGraph schema visualized in Figure 2.7, we illustrate the use of GReQL exemplarily. It is the schema introduced earlier, now with a constraint added to the NamedElement.

In a grUML diagram, constraints consist of three parts: (i) a *textual description* of the constraint, (ii) a *Boolean expression* formulated in GReQL that shall be satisfied and (iii) a *query expression* formulated in GReQL that returns the set of model elements that do not satisfy the constraint (for reporting).

In this specific example, the purpose of the constraint is to ensure that all models that conform to the meta-model, i.e., to this TGraph schema, have model elements of type NamedElement that carry a valid name. Here, *valid* is defined to be a name that is not null – it may be the empty string, though. This is also expressed by the textual description.

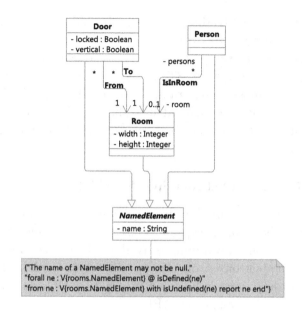

Figure 2.7: Meta-Model of Persons, Rooms and Doors (grUML Diagram)

The Boolean expression uses the forall quantifier expression (GReQL also supports an exists quantifier) and refers to all vertices of type NamedElement. Vertex types are referred to by using the V{} expression and passing a fully qualified name of a meta-model element. Here, the NamedElement is located in a package called rooms.

The @ letter marks the beginning of a constraint on the set of vertices and the ne variable is bound to one instance of type NamedElement, i.e., to a Room, Door or to a Person (NamedElement itself is abstract). During evaluation of the constraint (e.g., by the model validator class offered by JGraLab), ne is bound to one model element at a time and the helper function isDefined is executed to check if the variable is valid or not.

In case that the Boolean expression does not hold, model validation can return a report with the set of model elements that do not satisfy the constraint. The query expression as the third constituent of a constraint in the grUML diagram computes this set using an *From-With-Report (FWR) expression*.

In the from part, vertices or edges are declared using vertex : V{VertexType} or edge : E{EdgeType} constructs, respectively. The with part expresses constraints and report describes the output set (output can be also defined as a list, bag or table). In this example, the set of all elements is returned that have an undefined name attribute.

Programming With a Schema-Specific API

At the lower level of software development, models can be created programmatically. This is especially useful when a new meta-model has been created and no tooling is available for visualizing, creating and editing models based on this specific meta-model. Therefore, an API-based approach is followed in practice. JGraLab offers the generation of a schema-specific API.

We assume that such an API was generated for the sample meta-model depicted in Figure 2.7. The goal here is to create a model, i.e., a TGraph, illustrated in Figure 2.3 and Figure 2.5. The full source code to create the model is shown in Listing 2.1.

In line 1, the package for our class is declared. The required imports are not shown here (see comment in line 3) to avoid clutter. The actual class is declared in line 5 and in line 6, a static method is declared that returns a RoomsGraph, i.e., the model to be created. All operations for creating this model are offered by an empty model object. This root type is instantiated in lines 7-8 using the factory method offered by the meta-model representative RoomsMetaModel. Afterwards, the code is more or less straightforward. The model reference is used to invoke create_* methods where * denotes a placeholder for any vertex or edge type defined in the TGraph schema. Note, how all identifiers here are named as given in the meta-model shown in Figure 2.7.

The two persons Alice and Bob are represented by Person vertices created and initialized in lines 11-15. The Doortype is also instantiated and its attributes are set as described earlier. The same goes for the Room instance (width and height attributes are set in millimeters).

```
1   package de.uni_koblenz.ist.manesh.phd.samples.rooms_model_creator;
2
3   // Skipping imports...
4
5   public class RoomsModelCreator {
6       public static RoomsGraph createModel() {
7           final RoomsGraph model = RoomsMetaModel.instance().
8               createRoomsGraph(ImplementationType.STANDARD);
9
10          // Create vertices.
11          final Person p1 = model.createPerson();
12          p1.set_name("Alice");
13
14          final Person p2 = model.createPerson();
15          p2.set_name("Bob");
16
17          final Door d = model.createDoor();
18          d.set_locked(false);
19          d.set_vertical(false);
20          d.set_name("D1");
21
22          final Room r = model.createRoom();
23          r.set_name("B118");
24          r.set_width(7350);
25          r.set_height(2500);
26
27          // Create edges (demonstrate different ways).
28          @SuppressWarnings("unused")
29          final IsInRoom iir = model.createIsInRoom(p1, r);
30          r.add_persons(p2);
31          model.createFrom(d, r);
32          model.createTo(d, r);
33
34          return model;
35      }
36  }
```

Listing 2.1: Java Code for Creating the Sample Model

These vertices are not connected at this point, i.e., no edges have been instantiated. This is done throughout lines 29-32 where we demonstrate two different ways offered by the API. In line 29, an edge type is explicitly created[23] and its starting (also called "alpha") and ending points (also called "omega") are passed to the createIsInRoom method, returning a reference to this newly created edge instance. This reference is not used, though.

Another way is to use role named and to call the also provided add_* method where the * denotes a role name. This is shown in line 30. The associated IsInRoom edge between p2 and r is instantiated internally. Finally, the created model is returned in line 34 and it can be manipulated, traversed, stored to disk or plotted using functionality offered by the JGraLab library.

2.3.4 Selected Publications

The presented subtopics are related to this thesis because the primary motivation for designing MoCos was to mix models and code within one executable reusable and possibly adaptive software component. The topic of modeling is cross-cutting, i.e., models are used in SAS and SPLs. We introduce a few *selected publication* in the following.

Subtopics Related to Modeling for Adaptivity

Angelopoulos et al. [4] compare the use of two different kinds of models for achieving adaptivity: *architectural models* and *requirements models*. As a representative for the architectural approach, the Rainbow framework [61] is taken. It uses a model of the software architecture in terms of components and connectors written in the ACME language [62]. The representative for the requirements approach is the *Zanshin* approach [124]. It uses a model of the requirements in terms of goals.

Besides the differences in the realization of adaptations, the main difference in both approaches is in the use of different models. Angelopoulos et al. state that architectural models seem to be well-suited for development as they can capture properties and the structure of the software. Adaptation in Rainbow automates steps that would

---

[23]In TGraphs, edges are first-class entities.

be performed by human administrators, otherwise. In contrast, requirements models – in the way encoded in the presented work of Angelopoulos et al. – provide means to apply well-founded principles of control theory.

Angelopoulos et al. conclude that each model has its advantages and drawbacks and they suggest that architectural models and requirements models shall be combined to capture mode details of SAS. Given that more information is available, an adaptation manager may be able to make better decisions.

Vogel and Giese [140, 141] describe a language for feedback loops. Their approach is based on *megamodels* [13] that can be executed at runtime [142]. The goal is to offer a domain-specific modeling language for capturing adaptation logic that consists of various domain- and application-specific runtime models, their relationships, operations on them as well as the control flow between these operations. Multiple feedback loops are supported and may interact with each other, e.g., they may be arranged hierarchically. The ExecUtable RuntimE MegAmodels (EUREMA) [141] language proposes a visual notation for feedback loops, too. The implemented solution is based on Java, EMF and the Java Compiler Compiler (JavaCC) [24].

Subtopics Related to Modeling for Variability

Kang et al. [82] proposed the Feature-Oriented Domain Analysis (FODA) method which is based on the identification of distinctive *features* of software systems. Features describe characteristics of products from the customer's perspective. The goal of the approach is to systematically manage variability and to enhance *reuse*. This is achieved by explicitly modeling commonalities and differences of products via *feature trees*, which are essentially "and-or trees" with the addition of cross-tree relationships and global constraints. This modeling technique have become an accepted part of modern SPLE. Whenever the term "feature model" is used, immediately this (or a quite similar) structure comes to mind.

---

[24]https://javacc.java.net/ (accessed July 6th, 2014)

Sinnema et al. [121] describe *COVAMOF*, a framework for modeling variability. Its design is based on experiences gathered from three case studies on developing software with variability in industrial projects. COVAMOF supports a uniform representation of variation points, hierarchical modeling of variability and simple as well as complex dependencies. The specification of relations among these dependencies is possible, too. A detailed description of the application of the framework and its concepts is given, together with a visual concrete syntax for variability modeling.

Czarnecki and Wąsowski [32] inspect the notion of feature models as proposed by Kang et al. [82] and describe an algorithm for deriving such a feature model from a given *propositional formula*. In doing so, redundancies in the representation are minimized, i.e., the formula is simplified. The algorithm is implemented using the open-source libraries JavaBDD (for representing binary functions) and GraphViz (for visualization of feature models).

Bosch and Capilla [17] discuss the topic of *dynamic variability* in software-intensive embedded system families. Besides giving a comprehensive motivation and covering recent trends that are targeted at a *unique customer* that demands continuous evolution of the purchased products and their interaction and dynamic binding to (new) services. A sidebar description in this article introduced the *Common Variability Model (CVL)*[25] [65] as one possible solution to deal with runtime variability. CVL can enrich other Domain Specific Languages (DSLs) with variability information.

Subtopics Related to Executable Models

Mellor and Balcer [105] introduced xUML to enable the early simulation and testing of models before code generation. The authors claim that this approach can accelerate development projects and reduces costs by enhancing reliability. Code generation remains a major part of software development to create the final product.

---

[25]`http://www.omgwiki.org/variability/doku.php` (accessed July 6th, 2014)

Crane and Dingel [29] describe the implementation of a model interpreter for UML 2 actions and activities in detail. This work is based on a three-layer architecture for encoding semantics and is an initial step towards a UML virtual machine.

Recently, the OMG published the fUML specification [132], i.e., semantics of a foundational subset for executable UML models. fUML defines a virtual machine for UML. *Mayerhofer and Langer* [102] introduce *Moliz*, an execution framework for UML models to be used for quality assurance, i.e., for that is based on fUML but extends it with various services, such as debugging.

2.4 Software Language Engineering

In this section, we describe the basics of managing *software languages* (see Definition 2.29). The emerging field of research is called *Software Language Engineering (SLE)* (see Definition 2.30). Here, we adopt the definition given on one of the related conference websites.

Definition 2.29: software language

"The term "software language" refers to artificial languages used in software development including general-purpose programming languages, domain-specific languages, modeling and meta-modeling languages, data models, and ontologies." [122].

Definition 2.30: software language engineering

"*Software Language Engineering* (SLE) is the application of systematic, disciplined, and quantifiable approaches to the development (design, implementation, testing, deployment), use, and maintenance (evolution, recovery, and retirement) of these languages." [122].

From our perspective, programming languages can be seen as modeling languages, too. Therefore, many of the basics are similar but there are also some differences. For instance, when comparing the formalisms for describing a language's syntax, textual languages are usually described by grammars and (visual) modeling languages are described by meta-models.[26] A somewhat similar perspective is shared by the SLE community and it is manifested in their given definition of a *software language*:

Different aspects of a software language are [51]:

- *Layout:* The *layout* defines the positioning of language elements when defining an instance, i.e., a program or a model. For instance, in textual languages, the use of space characters, line endings or line feeds impacts the layout of source code. In visual languages, the position of elements in a diagram is layout. Depending on the language, the layout may be relevant, or not.

- *Lexis:* The *lexis* defines the basic building blocks of the language. In a textual language, these can be predefined symbols (e.g., type names) as well as identifiers (e.g., method names). In visual languages, modeling constructs are offered in the respective editor's menu bar.

- *Syntax:* The *syntax* defines the structure of language elements as well as their relationships. For example, the context-free syntax of programming languages is usually described by an EBNF-grammar. There may be additional rules defined in natural language to define the language's context-sensitive syntax, as well. In visual languages, meta-models describe the abstract syntax, optionally including context-sensitive constraints.

- *Semantics:* The *semantics* defines the meaning of instances of the language. While the specification of semantics can be done in different ways, it is usually implemented by a compiler or interpreter.

---

[26] In related work [87], the use of meta-models is even recommended for creating DSLs.

- *Pragmatics:* The *pragmatics* defines a set of best-practices for using the language. All kinds of additional knowledge, e.g., regarding the style of comments, names of variables as well as the use of standard APIs and design patterns are to be documented and supported by an Integrated Development Environment (IDE).

Due to the many different possible languages, the methods, tools and processes that are subject to research and practice in SLE are related to various application areas. Amongst others, these are the development of compilers and interpreters, the development of textual and visual DSL as well as the generation of programs. More generally speaking, SLE teaches us ways to design, develop and maintain software languages.

Subsequently, we focus on sub-topics of SLE that are immediately related to the topic discussed in this thesis. Especially the foundations of (i) *compilers and interpreters* as well as (ii) *multi-language development* are presented. Moreover, (iii) *selected publications* extend this introduction and shall be a starting point for the interested reader who likes to dive deeper into specific topics.

2.4.1 Compilers and Interpreters

Software languages need to be processed by computers for automation, in contrast to natural languages or sketches of diagrams on a whiteboard. The most common need for processing is to prepare an instance of a software language, i.e., a program or a model, for execution.

The processing of textual languages is subject to the mature discipline of formal languages and *compilers* [138] (see Definition 2.31). This knowledge is usually described for a general purpose programming language. When developing any kind of textual DSLs, the same principles apply, too. Today, the steps in processing and handling visual DSLs are influenced by the experiences and knowledge from processing textual languages.

In contrast to the processing of textual languages, visual DSLs usually are based on diagrams and have a graph-like structure. Hence, their abstract syntax is described using meta-models and not grammars.[27] In result, the ASG is not created in a parsing phase but it is created and manipulated in an editor during modeling.

Definition 2.31: compiler

A *compiler* is a computer program that translates an instance of one software language into an instance of another (possibly lower-level) software language.

Definition 2.32: interpreter

An *interpreter* is a computer program that systematically traverses an instance of a software language and, thereby, executes specific actions.

To *execute* an instance of a software language, its semantics must be clearly specified. There are two common ways, using compilers (see Definition 2.31) and interpreters (see Definition 2.32):

- *Compilation:* The *compilation process* is a translation of a program or model into a lower-level representation that can be executed by a computer, e.g., machine code. This yields a well-performing solution, but changes to the program or code require recompilation prior to execution.

- *Interpretation:* The *interpretation process* is a direct execution of a program or model by traversing its data structure (in abstract syntax representation) and executing (predefined) associated actions. This yields a flexible solution where no additional steps are required, in comparison to compilation. Yet, execution is often slower compared to compilation.

---

[27]It is also possible to express a grammar with a meta-model.

Advantages and Disadvantages

In this thesis, we assume that mostly, code is compiled and models are interpreted. In traditional MDSD, models are also compiled, i.e., code in some (general purpose) programming language is generated, first. Obviously, both directions have their advantages and drawbacks and they have been also discussed in the code generation community by den Haan [36]. While we confirm the points discussed by den Haan, we mix them with our own experiences and briefly summarize them in the following paragraphs.

When generating code, it is possible to protect the implementation in the sense that only the application- and even customer-specific code is deployed. This code has a clearly defined set of functionality, as opposed to a generic model interpreter that can execute arbitrary models of the specific DSL. The customer may get more than he paid for, but the model interpreter is also only a software component to be added to the existing software architecture, while generated code can be created in a way that conforms to the target architecture.

Moreover, generated code may be understood better by programmers who can check only the portion of code required. Depending on the structure of the model interpreter it may be required to understand a larger part of the generic implementation related to the whole modeling language, which is time-consuming. In addition, when changing the model interpreter, it does not become immediately clear what parts of the executable models are affected. When code is regenerated, any differences can be compared using existing "diff tools".

Still, model interpretation has many advantages, too. The primary reason why we intend to mix code and models in this thesis is that executable models do not require an additional code generation step. This facilitates adaptivity as models can be changed at runtime, e.g., using an editor, an API or a transformation language.

Furthermore, given that a model interpreter can be executed on a specific platform, no additional changes are needed and portability is ensured. In contrast, if the target language of code generation is not compatible with all supported platforms, different code generators may be required. Given a language like Java, this issue may be less important, though, because the generated intermediate (byte) code is created for a generic virtual machine that abstracts from platform- and operating-system-specific details.

To summarize, compilation and interpretation have their advantages and drawbacks and the choice depends on the application domain, use cases, available technologies and expertise of the involved software engineers.

2.4.2 Multi-Language Development

As software projects evolve over time, different languages are used. For example, some languages may be no longer used because they are not supported anymore and some new languages may be introduced to use novel technologies. Additionally, organizations may develop their own domain-specific languages to solve their issues specifically well. Hence, there are many different reasons for *multi-language development*.

While some languages are more concise, others require more programming effort. For instance, there are established general purpose programming languages like C, C++, C# and Java that are compiled to machine code or to an intermediate format and are then executed. In contrast, there are scripting languages such as JavaScript, Lua and Python that can be edited during operation because they are (usually) interpreted. That way, the need for flexibility can be satisfied by using Python for encoding business rules that need to change often or simply shall not result in a down-time of the overall system.

The idea to combine different programming languages on an *intermediate format* can be identified in different areas of software languages. For instance, *virtual machines* that execute standardized bytecode, such as the JVM, are used to execute a multitude of programming languages[28] with different syntax and paradigms such as imperative programming (e.g., Ada), object-oriented programming (e.g., Java) and functional programming (e.g., Closure).

---

[28]http://en.wikipedia.org/wiki/List_of_JVM_languages (accessed July 6th, 2014)

Furthermore, the Common Language Infrastructure (CLI) is another example for a standard that specifies systems which shall enable application development and execution independently from a specific language and platform. The most popular implementation of this specification is Microsoft's *.Net* framework for Windows operating systems, but there are variants for Linux and Mac OS X, too. The CLI not only defines an architecture concept, but, amongst others, a virtual execution system that can run programs in the Common Intermediate Language (CIL), an intermediate format for .Net languages[29].

The Case of Scripting Languages

The use of dynamic *scripting languages* is the state of the art in developing flexible software that can be easily changed and potentially even be adapted at runtime. For this purpose, scripts can be simply reloaded which enables faster turnaround times. Especially parts of the application logic that change frequently or need to be tweaked to determine a "best fit" are typical candidates for scripting.

For example, in game development, the parameters for simulated cars such as speed, torque or weight are tweaked by playing and continuously editing the attributes until one is content with the results. This is possible in Crytek's *CryEngine*[30] (a full game development platform) by using the *Lua*[31] extension[32] programming language, for example.

Most scripting languages have been developed as a means to extend an existing host application. This is also referred to as *embedding*. In some cases, there are interpreters provided that support the stand-alone-execution of scripts, e.g., from a console as in the case of Python. In general, scripts are meant to support *rapid prototyping*.

---

[29]http://en.wikipedia.org/wiki/List_of_CLI_languages (accessed July 6th, 2014)

[30]http://cryengine.com/ (accessed July 6th, 2014)

[31]http://www.lua.org/home.html (accessed July 6th, 2014)

[32]Lua is designed to be embedded and requires a host programming language to run as it does not support a "main" entry point by itself.

To give a more concrete example for code/script relationships, we exemplarily list the possible relationships between Java as the host programming language and JavaScript as the dynamic scripting language. This information was gathered from the *Java Scripting Programmer's Guide*[33] available online. In fact, there is at least a tendency towards duality between code and script, i.e., each side may provide similar mechanisms and capabilities.

Java can interact with JavaScript in different ways. Java can:

- provide data (variables) in different scopes/contexts (default, others).
- invoke scripted behavior (also passing values to invocation).
- invoking scripted behavior on a script object or some other entity instance.
- provide interfaces to be implemented by the script part.
- invoke a specific interface implementation provided by a script.

JavaScript can interact with Java in different ways. JavaScript can:

- implement interfaces defined in Java.
- support different contexts of execution (i.e., the variables can be bound to values from different contexts).
- import packages and classes from Java (it may be needed to allow importing code only in a certain scope of the scripts).
- choose which existing overloaded method from Java code to call.

In this work, some of the use cases for integrating models and code overlap with the motivation for the use of scripting languages.

2.4.3 Selected Publications

Some of the foundations from SLE were introduced so far. In this section, we describe a set of *selected publications* from the field as a starting point for further reading and inspiration.

Völter [143] provides an up-to-date and practical discussion on the design, development and use of domain-specific languages. Based on a detailed motivation for DSLs, including case studies and examples,

---

[33]http://docs.oracle.com/javase/7/docs/technotes/guides/scripting/
programmer_guide/ (accessed July 6th, 2014)

the terminology and challenges to be tackled are introduced. Besides fundamental concept and process issues, a core topic in this book is DSL implementation in a practical way, i.e., with examples using existing tools. These are namely *Xtext*[34], *Spoofax*[35] and *MPS*[36]. Amongst others, the realization of interpreters and required IDE services are covered. Völter also discusses the application of DSLs in different application areas like software architecture and product lines.

Kleppe [87] gives a detailed description of how to develop domain-specific languages. She gives an introduction to many related fields and brings them together under the umbrella of SLE. The different roles of the language user and the language engineer are distinguished and related processes are introduced. The core of the book deals with language specification and the use of meta-models for this purpose. Further topics such as language semantics and code generation are covered, as well as the combination of multiple languages.

Klint et al. [89] propose to gather knowledge on developing software languages using grammars, i.e., *grammarware*. They claim that an engineering approach to the design and development of grammars is missing and lay out an agenda to guide and promote research in this field. A substantial list of challenges is provided to be tackled. Today, related topics are researched under the more general topic of SLE.

Thomas [137] informally discusses some thoughts on *programming with models* and *modeling with code*. He argues that, sometimes, it is the best way to "model" using a programming language to really understand what is to be built. In his eyes, this is not premature hacking. The underlying assumption is that the only truth of a software system can be found in the code: "All models lie a little; some lie a lot!". Thomas tends to be code-focused in his article, i.e., he proposes to model using code and the available powerful IDE without using UML. The possibility of executing models is not mentioned, which is a contrast to the approach presented in our thesis.

---

[34]http://www.eclipse.org/Xtext/ (accessed July 6th, 2014)
[35]http://strategoxt.org/Spoofax (accessed July 6th, 2014)
[36]http://www.jetbrains.com/mps/ (accessed July 6th, 2014)

2.5 Software Components

As systems become more and more complex, techniques for handling larger parts of software become even more critical. The principles of separation of concerns, the divide and conquer approach to solving complex problems as well as the goal to develop reusable parts are all motivations for *software components*[37] (see Definition 2.33). Multiple components can be *assembled* and to build a complex software system and they communicate via *connectors* (see Definition 2.34).

Definition 2.33: component

A *component* is "a unit of composition with contractually specified interfaces and explicit context dependencies only" [129].

Definition 2.34: connector

A *connector* is a communication link between at least two components.

Especially object-oriented programming languages were aimed at providing practical solutions, but they did not quite succeed. In traditional software development based on *libraries*, i.e., (structured) collections of source code artifacts, usually multiple layers of software are stacked on top of each other and form the final software system.

In case that the library needs to be extended or bugs need to be fixed, the whole library needs to be recompiled and deployed. Additionally, changes to interfaces used within the system may require a certain effort to change all depending parts. On the positive side, this system it is still under control of the software developer who is usually informed by compilation errors before deployment (depending on the changes and programming language used).

---

[37]We use the terms "software component" and "component" interchangeably.

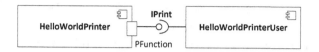

Figure 2.8: Two Assembled Components With Provided/Required Interfaces

In contrast, modern approaches to Component-Based Software Engineering (CBSE) support components that can be dynamically started, stopped and replaced at runtime. This allows for *incremental updates* of software and, thus, supports a means for "spot-repair", i.e., the correction of mistakes in only an isolated part of the software without the need for touching the rest.

In fact, many fixes can be applied at runtime without the need for a full redeployment of the whole software system. Changes to interfaces may require special treatment, though, because parts of the own (or third-party) systems may rely on their availability and defined contracts at runtime. The explicit versioning of interfaces while keeping all older versions is one solution applied in practice.

Moreover, the documentation of the structural design of software architecture in terms of "components and connectors" is usually done by using *component diagrams* such as those proposed by the UML [80]. A small example is given in Figure 2.8.

The diagram shows two components. As their names suggest, the first component (HelloWorldPrinter) offers printing the familiar "Hello World" message, while the second component (HelloWorldPrinterUser) uses this functionality, i.e., it executes it. HelloWorldPrinter has a *port* (see Definition 2.35) named PFunction.

Definition 2.35: port

A *port* is a structural element that marks an interaction point between a component and its environment via provided and required interfaces.

HelloWorldPrinter *provides* a single interface: IPrint. Provided
interfaces are represented by a *ball*, sometimes also called "lollypop".
HelloWorldPrinterUser *requires* the IPrint interface as represented
by the open *socket*. The connected ball and socket together represent
an *assembly connector* [80].

It must be noted that the mapping of the presented concepts to a
specific *component model* (see Definition 2.36) and *component technology* (see Definition 2.37) needs to be done. Wang and Qian [81] discuss
this topic extensively under the umbrella of Component-Oriented
Programming (COP) and provide detailed examples of how to realize components and connectors in JavaBeans, Enterprise JavaBeans,
Common Object Request Broker Architecture (CORBA), .Net, OSGi
and web services.

Definition 2.36: component model

A *component model* is a specification that defines standards and
conventions for the structure and composition of components that
conform to it.

Definition 2.37: component technology

A *component technology* is a concrete and utilizable implementation of a (formal) component model.

In this dissertation, we use the *OSGi framework* [134] and its
specified component model for realizing prototypes and feasibility
studies. An introduction is given subsequently.

2.5.1 OSGi: Dynamic Components for Java

The OSGi framework is the essential part of the OSGi specification.
The framework aims at providing a general-purpose, secure and managed Java technology for the engineering of software that can be
dynamically extended as needed.

The functionality provided by the OSGi framework is organized into five layers: (i) security layer, (ii) module layer, (iii) life cycle layer, (iv) service layer and (v) actual layer. The security layer is orthogonal to the other layers (security is a cross-cutting concern) and it is optional.

While Java's platform-independence is a major advantage of OSGi, this is also a limitation: a JVM and an implementation of OSGi for the target device is a prerequisite. Moreover, there are multiple implementations of the OSGi core specification. Here, we use the reference implementation called *Eclipse Equinox*[38] in a desktop environment and *Apache Felix*[39] in a mobile environment.

In this work, we focus mostly on the *module layer* as well as the *service layer*. Hence, we describe the needed terms and structures in the following. Please, refer to the comprehensive *OSGi Core Release 5* document [134] for a detailed introduction and specification.

Module Layer

The basic "building block" of software developed in OSGi is the *OSGi bundle* (see Definition 2.38), or simply *bundle*, that can be added and removed on demand. This is especially useful when developing software for devices with limited memory. Obviously, this *dynamism* at the level of components is an ideal basis for the development of adaptive software as well as DSPLs.

Definition 2.38: OSGi bundle

An *OSGi bundle* (or simply: *bundle*) is the basic building block, i.e., a modularization unit, in the OSGi component model.

An OSGi bundle contains compiled Java source code (classes) as well as all other resources that are required for realizing an application,

---

[38]http://www.eclipse.org/equinox/ (accessed July 6th, 2014)
[39]http://felix.apache.org/ (accessed July 6th, 2014)

such as image files, text files or the like. OSGi bundles are deployed as Java ARchives (JARs)[40]

In contrast to normal Java programming, class types cannot be accessed globally. Instead, dependencies among OSGi bundles need to be made explicit and the OSGi framework can *resolve* them automatically. In this process, additional constraints such as version numbers and manually defined constraints on further meta-data elements of OSGi bundle can be taken into account, too.

OSGi bundles clearly define what packages they *export* and what packages they *import*. The export of packages allows to *provide* functionality in the form of Java class types (including interfaces, of course) and the import of packages represents a *required* dependency to a set of Java types. The OSGi documentation also refers to bundles as an *importer* bundle or an *exporter* bundle, respectively. In practice, a bundle can play both roles simultaneously.

Each OSGi bundle has a META-INF/MANIFEST.MF file. This is a structured text file contains meta-information such as the definition of imported and exported packages. Additionally, there are mechanisms for defining *capabilities* offered by a namespace of a bundle and requiring bundles can define *requirements* by naming the needed capabilities. Optionally, constraints can be defined using the concrete syntax of *LDAP filters* [73]. An overview of all possible entries, called *bundle manifest headers*, is given in [134, Section 3.2.1].

The *life cycle* of bundles is managed, i.e., each OSGi bundle is always in a specific state. There is a comprehensive life cycle concept provided and enforced by the OSGi framework. Some of the typically used states a bundle can be in are: installed, started, stopped and uninstalled. Each bundle may have an entry point at which actions can be defined, e.g., especially when the bundle has been started or stopped. This class is usually named `Activator` and implements the `org.osgi.framework.BundleActivator` interface. There may be at most one activator class per bundle.

---

[40]A JAR is essentially a compressed archive in the well-known *.ZIP* file format.

Service Layer

In addition to dependency management based on packages, OSGi also support a *service approach*, also referred to as "publish, find and bind model" [134, p. 123] to stress its supported dynamism. OSGi bundles may search for service and register services themselves; in fact, *OSGi services* (see Definition 2.39) "live" inside OSGi bundles.

Definition 2.39: OSGi service

An *OSGi service* (or simply: *service*) is a Java object that is registered under at least one interface with the service registry specified by the OSGi component model.

Additionally, OSGi bundles receive notifications in case that the registration state of services change. Such events are sent: for instance whenever a service is registered, modified or unregistered.

Given the sheer size and complexity of OSGi, we introduce the most essential part from a programmer's point of view subsequently as used in this thesis. Two steps are critical: *registering* an OSGi service in a "provider bundle" and *retrieving* an OSGi service in a "requirer bundle".

The listings given below are based on the example components introduced in Figure 2.8. We assume that each component shall be represented by an OSGi bundle. Hence, there are two bundles, one named HelloWorldPrinter and the other one is named HelloWorld-PrinterUser.[41]

Service Registration. The Activator located in the HelloWorld-Printer is shown in Listing 2.2. After the common package declaration in line 1, the code in lines 3, 4 and 5 imports types from the OSGi framework:

---

[41]There are recommended naming conventions for OSGi bundles that propose to include a reversed domain name and a version number. Here, we simplify a bit.

- The `BundleActivator` is the basic interface to be implemented by any activator class.
- The `BundleContext` interface represents data about the execution context of the bundle and serves as an intermediate object (i.e., as a proxy) to the OSGi framework.
- The `ServiceRegistration` interface encapsulates access to a successfully registered OSGi service intended for use only *within* the owning bundle.

In line 7, the *service declaration*, i.e., the `IPrint` interface, is imported. An implementation of this interface named `PrinterImpl` will be the actual OSGi service.

```
1  package de.uni_koblenz.ist.manesh.phd.samples.hello_world_printer;
2
3  import org.osgi.framework.BundleActivator;
4  import org.osgi.framework.BundleContext;
5  import org.osgi.framework.ServiceRegistration;
6
7  import de.uni_koblenz.ist.manesh.phd.samples.hello_world_printer.ports.
      function.IPrint;
8
9  // Skipping further imports...
10
11 public class Activator implements BundleActivator {
12   private ServiceRegistration<IPrint> printServiceRegistrationRef;
13
14   @Override
15   public void start(BundleContext bundleContext) throws Exception {
16     printServiceRegistrationRef = bundleContext.registerService(IPrint.
        class, new PrinterImpl(), null);
17   }
18
19   @Override
20   public void stop(BundleContext bundleContext) throws Exception {
21     printServiceRegistrationRef.unregister();
22   }
23 }
```

Listing 2.2: Java Code for Registering an OSGi Service

This registration is done when the bundle starts and the service is removed from the OSGi service registry once the bundle is stopped.

The Activator class starting in line 11 implements the start and stop methods of the BundleActivator interface accordingly.

Once the bundle has been asked to start, start is automatically invoked by the OSGi framework. The bundleContext parameter allows to register an OSGi service as shown in line 16. IPrint is the *service declaration* and a new PrinterImpl instance is passed that represents the *service implementation*. No additional properties are used here, so the third parameter of registerService is assigned null. the printServiceRegistrationRef field declared in line 12 holds a handle for cleanup (not the actual service object).

Once the bundle has been asked to stop, the previously registered service is removed from the service registry by using the printServiceRegistrationRef field in line 21.

Service Retrieval. The code for retrieving the freshly registered service is sketched in Listing 2.3. An Activator class is created and acts as the entry point for reacting when the HelloWorldPrinterUser bundle is started or stopped.

Note that this time a IPrint-typed field, i.e., the printerService, is created. The actual service is retrieved in lines 16 and 17. First, the service registry is asked for an implementation of the IPrint interface (in this case there is only one). Based on the ServiceReference and the bundleContext, the actual service object can be obtained. It is used exemplarily in line 19 and set to null in line 24 (optional step) when the bundle is stopped.

```
1   package de.uni_koblenz.ist.manesh.phd.samples.hello_world_printer_user;
2
3   import org.osgi.framework.BundleActivator;
4   import org.osgi.framework.BundleContext;
5   import org.osgi.framework.ServiceReference;
6
7   import de.uni_koblenz.ist.manesh.phd.samples.hello_world_printer.ports.
        function.IPrint;
8
9   // Skipping further imports...
10
11  public class Activator implements BundleActivator {
```

```
12     private IPrint printerService;
13
14     @Override
15     public void start(BundleContext bundleContext) throws Exception {
16         final ServiceReference<IPrint> printLoaderServiceRef =
           bundleContext.getServiceReference(IPrint.class);
17         printerService = bundleContext.getService(printLoaderServiceRef);
18         // Invoke the print method (''Hello World!'').
19         printerService.printWelcome();
20     }
21
22     @Override
23     public void stop(BundleContext bundleContext) throws Exception {
24         printerService = null;
25     }
26 }
```

Listing 2.3: Java Code for Retrieving and Using an OSGi Service

2.5.2 Selected Publications

In this section, we describe some *selected publications* related to the basics of CBSE. The presented subtopics are related to this thesis because the motivation for designing MoCos was to establish a realization concept for software components that consist of models and code with equal rights.

Szyperski et al. [129] give an extensive introduction to software components and cover the fundamental concepts, properties and methods of *CBSD*. Components support the modular development of complex software systems and enable reuse at the architectural level. Therefore, component models provide standardized ways for expressing the essential building blocks for creating modular software systems.

Crnkovic et al. [30] identify and discuss the basic principles of component models and provide a *classification framework* for them. A wide range of existing component models is discussed in detail. The authors also clarify that existing modeling languages like xUML [105] (a language derived from the UML) may be translated to executable components, but "...do not operate with components as first-class citizens...".

Modern dynamic component models such as *OSGi* [134] enable the development of flexible systems that can be adapted at the granularity of components (architectural reconfiguration). This is achieved by supporting the loading, unloading and updating of components at runtime. *Müller et al.* [108] discuss how to represent formal component models in OSGi. Their motivation was that the capabilities of (formal) component models are usually not reached by existing component technologies. Along the example of OSGi, shortcomings (e.g., the lack of composite components) are described and a list of enhancements is proposed.

Usually, the topics of models and software components have not been mixed. The work of *Ballagny et al.* [7] is an exception to this where a state-based component model for self-adaptation is introduced that is based on components that carry models at runtime. In contrast to our generic approach, these models are always UML state machines.

2.6 Summary

In this chapter, we introduced the basic terminology and concepts of different research areas that are directly related to this dissertation. Namely, these areas are Adaptive Software, Software Product Lines, Modeling, Software Language Engineering and Software Components.

The cornerstones of this work are *adaptivity management* and *variability management*. The latter term has been established for quite some time now, while – in our personal experience – the term adaptivity management has not been used often. Both areas provide powerful approaches, techniques and tools for targeting challenges in their respective field. In some areas, similarities become immanent.

For example, both SAS and SPLs follow an iterative and incremental approach to software development. In both cases, a repository of base artifacts is maintained and adjusted to face changes in the system's operating environment and customer requirements. The focus is set on different phases of the software's life-cycle, though. While research in SPL aims at managing variability in terms of features and the

variations in implementation during the (early) stages of software
development, research in SAS aims at managing adaptivity in terms
of the actions to perform in reaction to sensed environmental changes
or in itself.

Either way, based on some information input (customer feature
requests, sensor data) a plan for making changes (to artifacts or to
runtime objects) is developed and executed. While the execution of
this plan yields a new product variant in SPLE (artifact-level), an
adapted software system is obtained in SAS (runtime-level). Indeed,
variability and adaptivity are related: variability opens a state space,
adaptivity describes transitions within this space. Partially motivated by this observation, research on DSPLs attempts to use SPLEs
approaches to achieve adaptivity.

In software development, *software languages* and *components* are
used to face complexity. In the scope of this thesis, the chosen
programming language is Java and the technological modeling space
is provided by JGraLab. We selected OSGi for realizing dynamic
components. Since we assume that the reader is familiar with Java
(or a similar object-oriented programming language) it was skipped
in this foundations chapter.

Part II

Solution Concept

3 Initial Design Considerations

In this chapter, we discuss the potential ways to get from the vision of MoCos to a solution concept and discuss a set of related *initial design decisions*.

The main goal of this chapter is to sketch and to communicate our way of thinking towards the solution concept. The idea is to clearly document our assumptions and decisions as a basis for future discussion. We do not intend to present a complete solution here and not all sketched ideas will be part of the initial MoCo concept, i.e., some parts are subject to future work.

The remainder of this chapter is structured as follows. First, we introduce four *exemplary use cases* for MoCos. We selected them based on our SAS and SPL background as introduced at the beginning of this thesis. A list of *identified issues* is provided per use case, together with a list of carefully elicited solutions. Then, we systematically *revisit the identified design issues* and elaborate on possible design options. For each design issue, one of the alternative solutions is selected and the rationale is clearly documented. This chapter ends with a short *summary*.

3.1 Exemplary Use Cases

In order to achieve a largely generic, reusable and flexible solution to the vision we sketched initially, the most common *use cases* for MoCos need to be well-understood. To start, we give examples taken from application areas we are familiar with: (i) creating frameworks for adaptive software (to target adaptivity) and (ii) creating a solid platform for a software product line (to target variability).

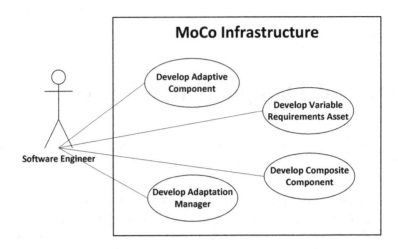

Figure 3.1: Excerpt of Use Cases for the MoCo Infrastructure (UML Use Case Diagram)

The goal of this section is to elicit an initial set of *design choices* for a corpus of identified issues, guided by relevant use cases[1]. These use cases are illustrated in Figure 3.1 and each of them is discussed in detail subsequently.

3.1.1 Develop Adaptive Component

Context

Assume, software engineers need to develop a component that implements different features or the same feature in different variations. These features shall be partially bound during an initial build process (tailoring), but the component shall be monitored and evolved during runtime (adapting), as well.

---

[1]We are aware of the fact that the choice of these use cases is influenced by our research background. We are convinced that the presented approach targets a subset of relevant software engineering issues, e.g., as discussed in [34, 75].

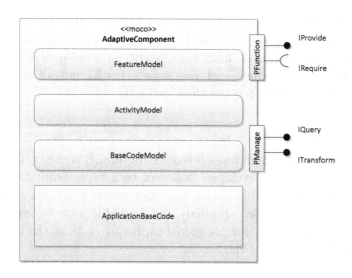

Figure 3.2: Draft of an Adaptive Component MoCo

We assume that software engineers are familiar with Java programming and modeling or cooperate with colleagues who have solid modeling skills. By modeling conceptual variability in terms of feature models and the most critical behavior in terms of UML activity models, the engineers create a foundation for communication within the team and for defining the possible variations of the component to be created (*variability scoping*).

Based on an estimation of in-house domain experts and by analyzing the customer's feedback, critical features and depending behavioral variations are identified that may be subject to frequent changes (*adaptivity scoping*). Those behaviors that require change, either for tailoring or for adapting, are developed as models and the more stable rest is realized in code. The output is a MoCo as sketched in Figure 3.2.

Note that this and subsequently shown MoCos serve illustrative purposes to communicate the idea by example. A detailed architectural blueprint for MoCos is introduced later in Chapter 4.

The AdaptiveComponent is a fictional MoCo implementing a specified functionality in different variations. Such a component can be seen as a description of a set of components in a broader sense.[2] In SPLs, it is common to have such *core assets* that include all variations needed to produce different product variants.

Structural Description

The AdaptiveComponent has a layered structure. It consists of (i) the *application base code*, developed in source code representation implementing core functionality, (ii) a *base code model* reflecting selected parts of that source code (optional), (iii) an *activity model* representing behavior and (iv) a *feature model* capturing at least the internal conceptual variability of the MoCo.

- *Application Base Code:* A part of the functionality to be provided by the AdaptiveComponent is developed in source code which is also the basis for the rest of the MoCo. In terms of control flow, we assume a *primary/secondary relationship* (widely known as "master/slave") between the code and the models here. This means that the main flow starts (and ends) in the code. This must not be the case for all MoCos in general, as the control flow could also start and end in a behavioral model that invokes functionality present in the source code, essentially using it like a library.

- *Base Code Model:* In order to bridge the *technological spaces* of the models and code [95], a model representation, i.e., the BaseCodeModel, acts as an intermediate layer between the code and other, more abstract models. The BaseCodeModel is technically a model that contains (all) details about the ApplicationBaseCode. Not in all cases this layer may be needed, but

---

[2]Since the same component contains different variations and integrates all of them to reduce redundancy, the single AdaptiveComponent actually represents the set of all derivable components that can be configured via the internal feature model.

whenever fine-grained information about the code's structure
shall be processed or behavioral models need to link to functionality existing in code, such a model of the code can be useful.
Obtaining this model is a reverse engineering task.

- *Activity Model:* Assuming that a part of the behavior shall be
  variable and adaptable, the composition of the main control
  flow is defined by a UML-style ActivityModel. Its visualization
  (even if only in parts) can help to understand the big picture
  of the MoCo's behavior. Being a model, it can be queried and
  transformed at all times. Therefore, similar techniques can be
  used for creating variants of the MoCo, either for the purpose
  of *tailoring* (pre-runtime) or for *adapting* (runtime). In the
  first case, the changes on the ActivityModel will be manifested
  via code generation (using the BaseCodeModel), while in the
  second case, a *model interpreter* executes orchestrated sequences
  of actions in activity models at runtime.

- *Feature Model:* Variability within the MoCo is encoded in the
  form of a feature model. It describes the functionality of the
  AdaptiveComponent in an abstract form and contains all kinds
  of dependencies that may exist at a conceptual level. Features
  are mapped to implementing elements of the ActivityModel.
  Hence, the FeatureModel can be used to describe subsets of the
  MoCo's capabilities (views) in terms of feature configurations
  and linked variations.

The AdaptiveComponent MoCo has two ports: PFunction and
PManage. These ports and their interfaces serve as clearly defined
starting or ending points for communication between instances of
MoCos and other software components.

- *PFunction:* This *function port* groups an IProvide and an IRequire interface. They symbolize the set of interfaces so the
  MoCo can fulfill its functional requirements.

- *PManage:* The *management port* groups the IQuery and ITransform interfaces. IQuery provides functionality for accessing the
  internal models of the MoCo, such as the feature model and
  the activity model in a read-only mode. Information can be
  provided by means of a predefined set of methods provided
  by the interface or by a generic implementation that allows
  arbitrary complex queries using an expression language. ITransform provides functionality for accessing and modifying the
  internal models. This interface is used to realize tailoring and
  adapting via external adaptation managers as well as human
  administrators.

The distinction between pure domain functionality and technical
management capabilities seems reasonable. In [92], a similar splitting
between a *functional interface* and a *control interface* is discussed
for the topics of component control and component management.
Moreover, in [74], the authors distinguish between *operation interfaces*
and *configuration interfaces* in their presentation of the architecture
for self-adaptive containers (e.g., List, Set, Stack, Queue). In practice,
this distinction may not be always as clear as described here, though.

Behavioral Description

The control and data flow in this MoCo is dominated by the ApplicationBaseCode. Parts of ApplicationBaseCode can be executed as
usual, e.g., by the JVM. All models can remain available at runtime
as a part of the MoCo. The BaseCodeModel is optional as it does
not influence the MoCo's behavior.

At predefined spots in the code, the control flow is redirected to
one of the models, e.g., to the ActivityModel. This model is then
traversed and executed by a *model interpreter* (not visualized here).
We have shown the feasibility of this approach to model interpretation
and adaptation in earlier work [39], motivated by the application of
model interpretation for the engineering of flexible meta-case tools for
visual modeling languages [57]. A model interpreter can be embedded

in the MoCo, it can be required by the MoCo's interfaces and it may
be provided by the MoCo Infrastructure.

In the presented case, the MoCo contains an additional model: the
FeatureModel. It captures the variability of the domain (problem
space). The structural and behavioral variations implemented in the
MoCo (solution space) are mapped to these features. At runtime,
a *feature configuration* based on this FeatureModel is maintained.
Depending on whether a feature is part of the given configuration,
its depending variations – implemented in models or code – may be
enabled and disabled. Hence, the component's behavior depends on
its current configuration at the time of execution.

To support this way of making changes to a component, the MoCo
Infrastructure provides a set of fundamental services on MoCos and
on its contained elements, i.e., models and code. Based on Create,
Read, Update and Delete (CRUD) operations [101, p. 381], more
complex changes can be realized. These operations can be used
(i) by *software engineers* via an API (development, tailoring), (ii) by
adaptation managers for autonomous reconfiguration (adapting) and
(iii) by *administrators* via a control panel (maintenance).

Identified Design Issues

In this section, we describe an initial set of *identified design issues* that
need to be solved when developing a MoCo Infrastructure that can
support the described AdaptiveComponent MoCo. For each issue,
considered solutions are enumerated.

Issue 1: How to represent feature configurations for an Adaptive-
Component?

1. The configuration is stored separately as a model (but still
   within the MoCo) that conforms to the feature model, with
   the addition of markers at feature nodes to represent a feature
   selection.
2. The feature configuration and the feature model are stored as
   one model.

Issue 2: How to represent the full feature model (i.e., the system feature model) within a single MoCo?

1. Each MoCo holds the variability information of the whole system, even if itself only requires a small part of it.
2. A view on the full system feature model can be obtained by communicating with another MoCo that holds this information.
3. No global system feature model exists explicitly, as it can be constructed from the network of all linked MoCos and their internal partial feature models.

Issue 3: How to expose the internal variability information to other MoCos?

1. The raw feature model and its configuration data is exposed completely to the outside world for read/write access.
2. An API exposes only parts of the feature model and, possibly, in a read-only fashion.
3. The model schema contains annotations, e.g., the elements that shall be visible are marked (e.g., public, private, protected), and access rights are checked and enforced at runtime by the MoCo Infrastructure, in particular by the MoCo Execution Environment.

Issue 4: How to realize different views on MoCos to only show its parts needed for certain concerns?

1. There is generic support for access profiles in the MoCo Infrastructure that can be implemented for each MoCo (e.g., via queries that define the elements accessible for a certain profile).
2. A set of application-specific interfaces is defined for each group of concerns.

Issue 5: How shall model semantics be encoded?

1. Semantics is partially encoded in additional code fragments that logically extend a schema so models can execute themselves.
2. Semantics is fully encoded in a stand alone model interpreter.
3. Semantics is described using another model that is fed into a generic model interpreter.

Issue 6: Where does the semantics description for executable models belong to?

1. All needed model interpreters ship with the MoCo Infrastructure.
2. Each model schema comes with a model interpreter.
3. There is a set of schema-specific model interpreters for each MoCo that contains an executable model.
4. A set of MoCos with similar models shares a model interpreter (that may be realized as a MoCo, too).

Issue 7: How shall variability and other parts of the MoCo be exposed to its environment, e.g., to users?

1. Models in a MoCo are accessible via (predefined) queries and there are generic as well as schema-specific rendering components for MoCo visualization (concrete syntax).
2. There are profiles for a set of identified roles that need to interact with a MoCo, including access rights (e.g., for privacy and security concerns [58]) and visibility implications.

Issue 8: How to deal with CRUD operations on embedded models and their impact on other model and code parts of the MoCo at runtime?

1. Operations on the model can be performed via an API that is derived from the schema.
2. Traceability links to other models are taken into account (e.g., "on delete cascade" effects).

3. Changes on the model are reflected back into the (compiled[3])
   code when requested.
4. All CRUD operations follow a predefined reference implementation with customizable steps (e.g., via template methods) to be
   provided by the software engineer.

Issue 9: What kinds of views are needed for working with MoCos?

1. Analogous to the commonly known *ANSI 3-layer architecture
   for databases*, it is possible to represent a MoCo from three
   perspectives: (i) *external layer* (user view), (ii) *conceptual
   layer* (logical view) and (iii) *internal layer* (physical view).
2. Analogous to the *4+1 views architectural view model* [94], it is
   possible to represent a MoCo from five perspectives: (i) *logical
   view* (ii) *development view*, (iii) *process view*, (iv) *physical view*
   and (v) *scenarios*.
3. An existing architecture model is used and (if required) is extended for describing MoCos with a special focus on tailoring
   and adapting.

3.1.2 Develop Adaptation Manager

Context

Assume, software engineers need to develop a component that can
adapt the behavior and/or structure of other components during
runtime. This adaptation manager shall be rule-based and the
adaptation rules shall be developed in a customizable language.

We assume that software engineers have experienced that encoding
variable parts in models is feasible and, hence, they encode adaptation
rules in the form of a model that can be processed (i.e., interpreted)

---

[3]Research prototypes like *JavAdaptor* [118] showed that patching Java bytecode
at runtime is technically feasible (with limitations for the general case).

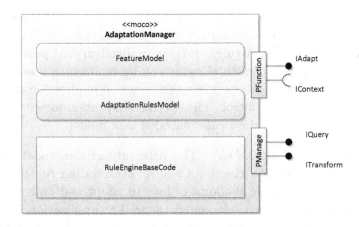

Figure 3.3: Draft of a Rule-Based Adaptation Manager MoCo

and visualized in a simplified manner for non-technicians and administrative staff. Since the MoCo shall be reused among different products with varying subsets of features, the adaptation rules are mapped to a feature model, too.

Essentially, a "master" adaptation manager is developed as an SPL that can be tailored to the specific needs by selecting only the adaptation management capabilities needed. The output is a MoCo as sketched in Figure 3.3.

The AdaptationManager is a MoCo that is capable of controlling other MoCos that are connected to it. Being a MoCo itself, it can be adapted, too.

Structural Description

The AdaptationManager consists of (i) a *rule engine*, developed in source code representation, (ii) a set of *adaptation rules* represented by a model and (iii) a *feature model* that covers variability in the controlling capabilities of the adaptation manager.

- *Rule Engine Base Code:* The RuleEngine is implemented in source code to be more efficient in terms of execution performance. The basic strategies as well as the low-level functionality for handling adaptation rules (we assume Event-Condition-Action rules (ECA-rules) [47]) is realized in this part of the MoCo. In fact, the RuleEngine can be realized as a *model interpreter* that is independent of the actual application domain of the MoCo to control. The specific adaptation logic is added by a set of *adaptation rules* encoded as a model.

- *Adaptation Rules Model:* The AdaptationRulesModel allows for quick and easy changes to rules, even during runtime. As these rules include the logic of how to adapt and under which conditions, they encode generic as well as application-specific (or at least, the domain-specific) parts. Because the AdaptationRulesModel may need to be changed during runtime as well, it is appealing to store them as a model that can be queried and transformed, too. Additionally, this allows for the design of a specific (textual or visual) modeling language that enhances the development and comprehension of rules in a given domain by providing a suitable concrete syntax.

- *Feature Model:* The FeatureModel MoCo captures the variability in the MoCo and specifically in the set of generic adaptation rules. Hence, there are links from the AdaptationRulesModel to the features in the FeatureModel. This information can be used for tailoring as well as for adapting the AdaptationManager. Variability is explicitly encoded and physically stored with the MoCo.

This AdaptationManager MoCo has two ports: one for its essential functionality (PFunction) and one for managing the component – especially the models (PManage).[4] Their responsibilities are as follows:

---

[4]This is a concrete case where the distinction between the two MoCo ports is controversial.

- *PFunction:* The *function port* serves as a grouping element for the IAdapt and IContext interfaces. IAdapt provides functionality to adapt a connected MoCo. IContext requires an implemented interface for receiving sensing information it shall react to.

- *PManage:* The *management port* holds a set of interfaces for managing, i.e., observing and changing, the runtime model via the IQuery and ITransform interfaces. IQuery provides functionality for exposing parts of the adaptation rules. It is a matter of encapsulation and manual *scoping decisions* that need to be made during system design to decide which fragments of which models shall be exposed to the MoCo's environment. ITransform provides functionality for adapting the internal AdaptationRulesModel, in this specific example.

In this sketched setup, the AdaptationManager's design borrows characteristics from existing scripting technologies, where a static (i.e., a compiled) host application – often written in a general purpose programming language – is extended with flexible scripts that are written in a domain-specific syntax and interpreted at runtime. Such scripts can also be modified and then reloaded at any point in time. From that perspective, the code and model in this example have a *complementary relationship*, where the AdaptationRulesModel serves as an extending input to the RuleEngine, developed in code.

Behavioral Description

The AdaptationManager receives data from outside, e.g., from another MoCo that needs to be controlled, and applies actions according to (i) general *strategies* encoded in the rule engine and (ii) a set of *adaptation rules* in the form of ECA-rules.

Whenever a change is observed (e.g., via the IContext interface), the RuleEngineBaseCode starts to analyze the situation and to plan actions accordingly by using the available set of rules that are encoded in the AdaptationRulesModel. After rule selection and the composition of a chain of actions, the rule engine executes them. In brief, the *MAPE-K loop* [77] is executed.

This rule engine can be realized as a special variant of a model interpreter. Moreover, the illustrated MoCo is adaptable itself, i.e., especially its rules can be changed whenever needed.

Identified Design Issues

In this section, we describe an initial set of *identified design issues* that need to be solved when developing a MoCo Infrastructure that can support realizing the described AdaptationManager MoCo. For each issue, considered solutions are enumerated.

Issue 10: How can data be provided to an adaptation manager by an adaptable MoCo?

1. The adaptation manager defines the required interfaces in its PManage port and connected adaptable MoCos need to implement them.
2. The adaptation manager receives full access to the internals of a MoCo.
3. The adaptation manager receives a model representation of the MoCo to be controlled, i.e., there is a generic schema that defines the core information to be passed to any AdaptationManager.

Issue 11: What kinds of interfaces must a generic adaptation manager provide to other MoCos?

1. The adaptation manager requires query interfaces for sensing and provides transformation interfaces for effecting.
2. There is a predefined way of adapting other MoCos where the communication between adaptation manager and adaptable MoCos is encoded in a generic base model (protocol) that can be customized to suit individual needs and that is shipped with the AdaptationManager.

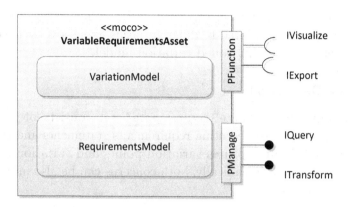

Figure 3.4: Draft of a Variable Requirements Asset MoCo

3.1.3 Develop Variable Requirements Asset

Context

Assume, software engineers need to develop a container that can hold a set of requirements with variability. These requirements shall be tailored based on features, and multiple sets of requirements shall be composed into one comprehensive and consistent set of requirements.

We assume that software engineers intend to allow the isolated configuration of parts of a large requirements document via features, but they also need to prevent redundancy among the resulting set of special feature models. They design a MoCo that can hold requirements statements as a model including variability information that is needed to configure the given subset of requirements. Full requirements documents can then be configured in terms of composing MoCos. A single MoCo is illustrated in Figure 3.4.

The VariableRequirementsAsset is a MoCo that holds requirements statements in the form of a model. This MoCo's primary goal is to provide requirements data in various different configurations, i.e., the whole MoCo can be tailored to different needs expressed by means of a configuration of an embedded variation model.

Structural Description

Conceptually, the VariableRequirementsAsset consists of (i) the *requirements model*, representing requirements statements and (ii) the *variation model* that captures variation points and variations in the requirements model. Technically, both concerns can be also integrated into a single model.

- *Requirements Model:* In this example, the MoCo represents an encapsulated, self-contained set of structured requirements statements to enable automated data modification and analysis. At this point, we do not make any restrictions on the concrete syntax of the RequirementsModel – it is certainly possible to work with a textual representation and with a table-like visualization to mimic commercial requirements management tools like DOORS[5].

- *Variation Model:* The VariationModel encodes the variation points and variations present in the RequirementsModel. Importantly, the VariationModel is coupled with the RequirementsModel, either via trace links or via Boolean expressions (e.g., using a constraint language).

  A common way to encode variability in assets is to use feature models. That said, feature models are not expressive enough to encode technical details that may be needed to configure assets at a fine level of granularity (e.g., at the level of parameters) [8]. In this example, we do not strictly define the VariationModel's syntax but highlight that its purpose is to model variability in the solution space, as opposed to feature models that aim at variability in the problem space.

---

[5]http://www-01.ibm.com/software/awdtools/doors/productline/ (accessed July 6th, 2014)

The two ports of the MoCo, i.e., PFunction and PManage, are introduced subsequently.

- *PFunction:* The *function port* groups the IVisualize and the IExport interfaces. IVisualize requires functionality to display the requirements. This needs to be implemented by another component. IExport requires functionality to export the stored data from the models into other formats (such as PDF) for reporting in a human-readable format.

- *PManage:* The *management port* groups the IQuery and ITransform interfaces. IQuery provides functionality (i) to view a subset of the requirements according to a given configuration in the VariationModel and (ii) to query the requirements similar to a database.

  ITransform provides basic CRUD operations on the contained models. These can be used by an external service to generate a tailored variant of the MoCo, thereby tightening the runtime configuration space (e.g., we can imagine a *generic copy service* provided by the MoCo Infrastructure). Such a transformation has a severe impact, i.e., it means information loss. The result of tailoring is a partial copy of the MoCo as a result of transformations. Additionally, an undo stack may be maintained for the case of adaptation if some of the earlier dropped variations are required unexpectedly during operation.

Behavioral Description

This MoCo does not carry application-specific behavior, but it represents a data container that holds requirements statements. Essentially, it acts like a *data store* with the addition of utility functionality to perform operations on the data encoded as a model (here: requirements statements). Other MoCos need to be developed to establish a full requirements management tool – this is just an example for a MoCo that holds data.

In contrast to the other two examples of MoCos presented so far, immediate adapting to environmental changes is not primarily in the focus. It is the *tailoring* of the provided requirements data to the given feature configuration, a process that is done before design and development of software. Since "only" data is changed that is not executable, the behavior of software does not change automatically. Tailoring and adapting can be handled in the exact same way, i.e., tailoring consists of adapting plus serialization of the MoCo and its transformed model.

Identified Design Issues

In this section, we describe an initial set of *identified design issues* that need to be solved when developing a MoCo Infrastructure that can support the VariableRequirementsAsset. For each issue, considered solutions are enumerated.

Issue 12: How must the PManage port be designed such that adapting and tailoring are handled similarly?

1. An adaptation manager can be temporarily connected to a MoCo for tailoring, i.e., an adaptation manager is reused as a part of the traditional SPLE build process for tailoring.
2. The functionality for making changes to a MoCo and for persisting them – as needed for tailoring – are clearly separated.

Issue 13: Can a MoCo exist without (an application-specific) code part?

1. A MoCo is always a combination of model and code parts (i.e., the MoCo Infrastructure itself enforces this by construction/definition).
2. Forms of MoCos are allowed where only models are embedded into the MoCo container, i.e., the code part may be empty.

Issue 14: What if data is already present in an external database or tool?

1. A model representation of the data is derived, embedded into a MoCo, and changes are synchronized with the original data source.
2. A model representation of the data is derived during a one-time migration phase and replaces the original data source completely.
3. A MoCo just acts as a *facade* to the original data, i.e., its model is simulated by an intermediate code layer (wrapper).

Issue 15: How can persistency of MoCos be realized?

1. The MoCo Infrastructure provides a generic way of saving models and code in a predefined format.
2. Each schema ships with custom extensions that define the saving of the model that is then handled generically by the MoCo Infrastructure.
3. The MoCo Infrastructure provides interfaces to be realized using the specific mechanisms of the chosen technology for serialization and deserialization.

3.1.4 Develop Composite Component

Context

Assume, software engineers need to develop a software system by composing existing components and newly developed special components. In addition, the composition mechanisms shall support tailoring and adapting.

We assume that software engineers are familiar with CBSE [66] which supports the development of rather complex systems from pre-built,

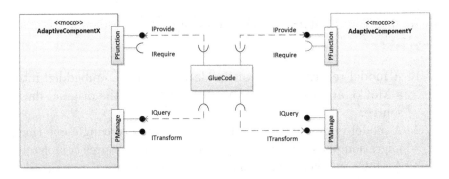

Figure 3.5: Sequential Composition of two MoCos

self-contained pieces.[6] This *separation of concerns* enhances reuse and allows the parallel development of system parts that are then used and composed in a black-box fashion, i.e., based on interfaces and not based on knowledge about the components' internals.

Structural Description

According to [123, p. 453-454], there are three patterns of component composition, namely (i) *sequential*, (ii) *hierarchical* and (iii) *additive* composition. Obviously, software development using MoCos shall support all of these cases, too, as they have shown to be needed in theory and in practice. Hence, we discuss the composition of MoCos according to these structural patterns as a basis for further elaboration.

- *Sequential Composition:* Two MoCos can be composed *sequentially* by means of some glue code that invokes provided functionality, either from the PFunction or the PManage ports. In fact, the glue code invokes provided functionality of other MoCos in sequence, which gives this type of composition its name. The

---

[6] An initial vision of components for software development (and to some extend, a vision of software product lines) was described earlier by [104].

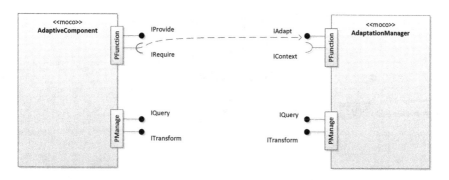

Figure 3.6: Hierarchical Composition of two MoCos

invoking code *uses* the other components but there is no other form of coupling. An example is illustrated in Figure 3.5.

- *Hierarchical Composition:* Two MoCos can be composed *hierarchically*, i.e., there is no intermediate glue, but there is a parent-child relationship directly between one (the parent) and a non-empty set of other components (the children). That this structure does not imply containment in any way, even though the term "hierarchical" may imply this. An example is illustrated in Figure 3.6.

- *Additive Composition:* Multiple MoCos can be composed *additively*, i.e., a subset of the interfaces of a set of MoCos forms the boundary of a new component. This resulting MoCo then contains the set of selected components and additional glue code, e.g., for delegating service requests. The glue is responsible for merging the interfaces of the *inner* components and for exposing them. This new composite MoCo acts like a container and it offers its own PFunction and a PManage ports that are both based on ports of the inner components.

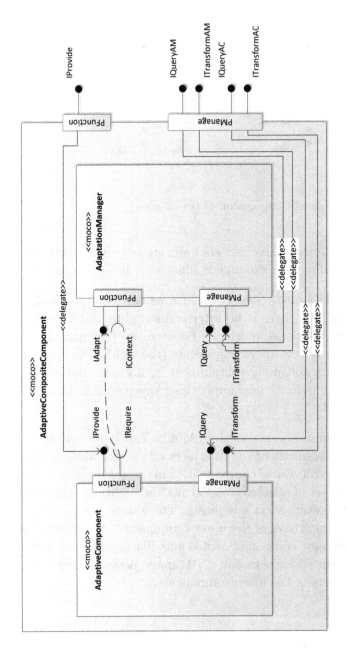

Figure 3.7: Additive Composition of two MoCos

In practice, a mixture of these pure composition patterns is used. Some of these patterns can be used in more high-level architectural patterns [20], such as *layered architecture* (hierarchical composition) or *pipe-filter architecture* (sequential composition). Please note that there are other established ways of component interaction. For example, common structural design patterns such as adapters or wrappers can be applied to MoCos, too.

In this thesis, we decided to leave out additive composition because a clean concept for such components is a whole topic on its own. For instance, questions related to the life-cycle of contained MoCos and their models need to be answered. Clearly, this is a direction for future work.

Behavioral Description

For demonstrating the three composition patterns, we used MoCos that we introduced earlier. Hence, it is not needed to repeat their individual behavior. Instead, we focus on the new behavior that can be potentially achieved by composition and we aim at describing the flow of the previously illustrated examples case by case.

- *Sequential Composition:* As illustrated in Figure 3.5, AdaptiveComponentX and AdaptiveComponentY are used by some third part that we refer to as GlueCode. This glue is not a reusable component by any means, but it realizes the entry point for the application's flow. The core functionality is then realized by composing (i.e., by sequentially calling) provided interfaces of AdaptiveComponentX and the AdaptiveComponentY. Internally, these MoCos consist of models and code, but the user (here: the GlueCode) is not aware of this technical detail.[7]

---

[7]Because we aim at designing a realization concept for MoCos that supports the incremental evolution of existing systems into MoCo-based software, it is important to stick to the black-box principle for components and to achieve interoperability between MoCos and existing technologies.

- *Hierarchical Composition:* As illustrated in Figure 3.6, the AdaptiveComponent satisfies one of its required interfaces (IRequire) by connecting it to a provided interface (IAdapt) of the AdaptationManager. Whenever a part of the AdaptiveComponent requires adaptation, the connected AdaptationManager is triggered to fulfill this task.

- *Additive Composition:* As illustrated in Figure 3.7, the AdaptiveComponent and the AdaptationManager are encapsulated, i.e., their functionality shall be hidden from users. The resulting AdaptiveCompositeComponent is now truly adaptive as it covers functionality for reacting to changes. In this example, the behavior of the AdaptiveCompositeComponent is executed when using its IProvide interface. Calling users do not notice the encapsulated AdaptationManager, which does its job silently. Some management capabilities can be invoked, too. For instance, one can imagine that additional adaptation rules may be added (details of PManage, not illustrated in Figure 3.7).

Identified Design Issues

In this section, we describe an initial set of *identified design issues* that need to be solved when developing a MoCo Infrastructure that can support the development of composite MoCos. For each issue, considered solutions are enumerated.

Issue 16: Shall additive composition imply visibility between the container's code and its inner components?

1. No, accessibility between the container's (glue) code and the inner components shall obey the restrictions/possibilities given by provided interfaces without exceptions.
2. Yes, the container's code can inspect the inner components and can fully modify them (especially their models).
3. Yes, the inner components can use and invoke code of their container to extend their own functionality.

4. Each MoCo can optionally mark other MoCos as "friend" (similar to the concept in C++[8]) to allow exceptions for access to its models and/or code.

Issue 17: Shall additive components always expose the complete set of their inner interfaces?

1. Yes, the PFunction as well as the PManage port of the new MoCo consists of all interfaces offered at the corresponding ports of the inner MoCos, possibly including additional interfaces.
2. No, the offered interfaces are a subset of all interfaces available from the inner MoCos, possibly including additional interfaces.

Issue 18: Shall MoCos share their model interpreters?

1. No, each MoCo comes with its own instance of a model interpreter.[9]
2. Yes, each MoCo registers its models with the MoCo Infrastructure, which in return instantiates one model interpreter per meta-model and this instance is reused for execution of different MoCos.

Issue 19: Shall all three composition types be changeable during tailoring and adapting?

1. No, system composition shall not be changed at runtime, because there is a fixed system architecture.
2. Yes, because components are the basic building blocks for SPLs, DSPLs and SAS and making changes to them shall be done in the same ways at development-time and at runtime.

---

[8] In the C++ language, the keyword **friend** can be used to state that a class is a *friend* of another class and hence, may access its private fields and methods. C++ supports **friend** classes and methods.

[9] Model interpreters are realized for each meta-model.

Issue 20: Shall MoCos composition be represented in a reflective model?

1. No, architectural reflection must not be an integrated part of MoCos.
2. Yes, there shall be a generic solution for architectural reflection (maybe in the MoCo Infrastructure).
3. Yes, but this is an optional functionality that can be implemented using MoCos and can be added to an existing system.

Issue 21: Which patterns of component composition are most suitable when using MoCos?

1. The composition shall entirely depend on the intended design to meet non-functional requirements and not on the used component technology. The presented "pure" composition approaches can be combined as needed.
2. Especially for adapting, sequential and hierarchical composition seem to be more suitable due to looser coupling in comparison to additive composition.
3. The essential internals of MoCos (especially models) can be re-embedded dynamically into new/evolving structures at all times and as needed to satisfy varying (non-functional) requirements.

3.2 Design Issues Revisited

In this section, we cluster the issues identified in Section 3.1 and discuss the listed alternatives and design options. The goal is to derive the most important design characteristics, decisions and rationale in a distilled form as a foundation for the definition of the MoCo concept to be presented in Chapter 4.

Figure 3.8 shows main topics and sub-topics which we defined (subjectively) based on the previously established issue list. Each issue is related to at least one topic.

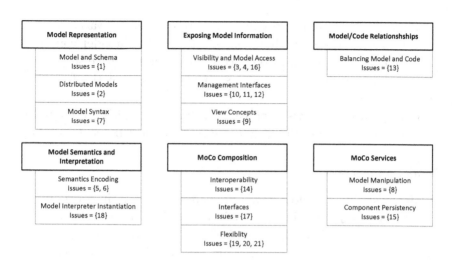

Figure 3.8: Clusters of Issues by Topic and Sub-Topics

Subsequently, the *design decisions* are presented according to a template that links each introduced *issue* to a *decision* and the *rationale*. Additionally, more background information is given on each topic because the main goal of this section is to document and communicate a part of our way from the selected set of issues to a solution.

We like to highlight that the clusters of issues are model-focused, because the embedding of models in components and related services on them is one of the major differences in comparison to other component (realization) concepts. Where we see significant differences on the code-related parts of MoCos, we point them out.

3.2.1 Model Representation

The MoCo concept designed in this research shall be a *generic concept*. Still, there is a need for clear guidelines.

Along the concern of variability (feature models and variation models), we discuss the individual concrete issues in a broader context.[10] The application of the MoCo concept to a representative set of modeling languages and application scenarios is part of the feasibility studies.

Subsequently, we revisit the issues 1, 2 and 7, which are related to (i) *model and schema*, (ii) *distributed models* and (iii) *model syntax*.

Model and Schema

A MoCo shall be a closed well-defined software unit consisting of models and code. In the scope of this thesis, code is defined to be developed in Java and the focus is set on the model side. If models are to be the driving force for achieving variability, adaptivity and evolution throughout the software's life cycle (especially including runtime), then all of the data that defines a model needs to be accessible at all times, i.e., not only the instances of models but also its schema. Optionally, visualization procedures, utility services and an encoding of execution semantics for some modeling languages may be present.

Depending on the modeling language, the relationship between model and meta-model can be more complex. For instance, in the case of feature models, there is a slight difference regarding the distinction of model and schema. On the one hand, there is a feature model schema and there are instances, i.e., the feature models with concrete feature nodes. On the other hand, there is the relationship between the feature model and its potential set of configurations – each of them can be seen as an instance of the feature model. In that sense, the feature model as well as all feature models with selected features that do not yield a configuration, have a *schema character*.

Given that such knowledge shall be available in a MoCo such as the exemplary AdaptiveComponent presented in Section 3.1, the

---

[10]We are aware of the fact that we cannot strictly generalize from so few special cases, but we are convinced that inspecting concrete issues supports the identification of practically relevant issues and design decisions.

question of an adequate representation strategy arises (Issue 1). In the special case of the feature model, the same information (features, dependencies, constraints) can be stored with a configuration, i.e., in the same model, or separately.[11]

Design Decision 1

Issue: How to represent feature configurations for an **Adaptive-Component**?

Decision: The feature configuration and the feature model are stored as one model.

Rationale: Splitting feature and configuration data – not conceptually, but technically – results in redundancy, which is a well-known source for inconsistency. In addition, making changes to a configuration requires the knowledge that is encoded in the underlying feature models, so information on features and made choices shall be kept closely together.

Distributed Models

The MoCo approach intends to support the modular development of various kinds of software with adaptive properties. Encapsulation and modularization also means to follow the principles of *separation of concerns* as well as *locality* which are also discussed in software architecture in terms of *coupling* between components and *cohesion* within components [117].

By inspecting the case of feature models, it becomes clear that modularization can be difficult, i.e., it may introduce redundancy as similar branches of a feature model may be required in multiple

---

[11]In commercial tools such as *pure::variants* (http://www.pure-systems.com/ – accessed July 9th, 2014), there is the option to save a configuration in a *slimmed form*, i.e., containing only the features resulting from the provided selection input and automatically resolved dependencies.

MoCos. In that regard, the models in MoCos share properties of data in *distributed databases* [23]. A distributed database consists of a collection of information units that are distributed on different computers and that are connected to each other via a communication network. Each node in this network can process data locally and autonomously, i.e., it can execute applications and tasks without using other stations, yet, each node contributes to a global goal.

Analogously, the models in MoCos-based software are queried, transformed and interpreted locally, i.e., within each component to carry out their (atomic) tasks. In addition, a complete system usually consist of a set of composed MoCos and the different models contribute to goals to be completed by the system as a whole. Knowledge about a certain part of the configuration may be needed in various MoCos (Issue 2). The complete feature configuration of a system can be seen as the aggregation of all local feature configurations.

Design Decision 2

Issue: How to represent the full feature model (i.e., the system feature model) within a single MoCo?

Decision: A view on the full system feature model can be obtained by communicating with another MoCo that holds this information.

Rationale: It is important to make data explicit, for manual inspection as well as for machine-processing. Hence, there shall be one single place in the MoCo-based software that is responsible for gathering and representing information on variability – similar to a registry or central repository. This repository could be created manually and it could be possibly generated from the individual feature models of all MoCos, as well.

Models in MoCos shall be self-contained and parts of them, i.e., views on models, can be shared between MoCos via a communication network. Moreover, views on models could be created dynamically, e.g., to construct the full feature configuration of the whole system from the single configurations that are local to various MoCos. Furthermore, the proposed central repository could be a *virtual repository*, i.e., an access point, that functions like a wrapper of models that are encapsulated in different MoCos. Such details shall be invisible to the user of MoCos.

Although this is certainly an interesting idea, we consider the distribution of models and the dynamic creation of integrating views on them as future work.

Model Syntax

Working with MoCos must be as convenient as possible for software engineers. Especially models promise to support dealing with complex situations through abstraction. To maintain this property, the way of visually presenting models to users of a MoCo must be kept simple and adequate. Achieving this goal is not simple, because the needed presentation of (parts of) the models depends not only on the *concrete syntax* initially chosen by the modeling language's designer, but also on the potentially new and unforeseen requirements of the model and MoCo user.

Based on our experience in engineering SAS and SPLs using models, a balance between (i) the model's defined *concrete syntax*, (ii) different *views* and (iii) an overall *visibility concept* is desirable.

For the special case of presenting variability information to the environment of MoCos (Issue 7), one can imagine different approaches. Since feature models and configurations can be queried, software engineers can write queries to select the subset of the model to be rendered. Visualization mechanisms could be implemented as a schema extension, or by stand-alone utility libraries. Furthermore, to improve practicality, a set of predefined views for various roles of users may be provided that use the more generic query/render services underneath.

Design Decision 3

Issue: How shall variability and other parts of the MoCo be exposed to its environment, e.g., to users?

Decision: Models in a MoCo are accessible via (predefined) queries and there are generic as well as schema-specific rendering components for MoCo visualization (concrete syntax).

Rationale: Obviously, it is possible to write a visualization component for any kind of model data available, but a user of a MoCo shall be provided with a default presentation service that is assumed to be adequate for at least the most basic use cases foreseen by the schema designer. Hence, some core visualization algorithms shall be provided, e.g., as a schema extension if technically suitable. The MoCo Infrastructure may then provide a generic service for realizing different views on arbitrary MoCos– especially on the contained models – by using their associated rendering services.

3.2.2 Exposing Model Information

Technically, models in a MoCo can be seen as pure data. Existing component concepts handle data encapsulation and the exposing of information in a systematic way. These concepts, such as visibility of data fields in object oriented programming languages and static interfaces, are usually realized in a way that they can support a fixed way of controlling data access. For instance, private data remains private if the code is not changed, recompiled and redeployed.[12]

Since models in MoCos can represent more than plain data, i.e., they can even be executed, changes in these models can be performed

---

[12]Mechanisms like reflection and language extensions like AOP can be used to "break" the visibility levels assigned during development. In most cases, the use of such a technical workaround is a sign for inadequate design, though.

to adapt the software system's behavior at all times. Hence, it is reasonable to expose this data only to a defined set of user roles, while hiding and protecting them from others.

In this section, we discuss concerns related to *exposing model information*, revisiting the issues 3, 4, 9, 10, 11, 12 and 16, which are related to (i) *visibility and model access*, (ii) *management interfaces* and (iii) *view concepts*.

Visibility and Model Access

The topic of exposing selected parts of a model is also related to the topic of model and MoCo representation in general. Subsequently, the focus is set on the ways of exposing the pure data in the form of models.

Assume, information about the internal variability of a MoCo is needed by another connected MoCo (Issue 3), e.g., by an adaptation manager. The simplistic way is to expose the raw model such that it can be queried in arbitrary ways. Although this approach works technically, it clearly violates the principles of encapsulation and data-hiding. A common approach is to design an interface that controls the access rights, but then this is a rather static solution. All kinds of queries to the model need to be known at design time to develop the interfaces.

In contrast, we imagine a solution where the models carry a visibility attribute (e.g., defined with their schema) that is used by a generic implementation of visibility checks in the MoCo Infrastructure. Even though a customization of this access layer seems to be desirable for specific situations, access to models would be handled uniquely across all MoCos– independently from the actual model(s) they hold.

Design Decision 4

Issue: How to expose the internal variability information to other MoCos?

Design Decision 4 (cont'd)

Decision: An API exposes only parts of the variation model and possibly in a read-only fashion.

Rationale: To stay compatible with the existing way of thinking about components as having clearly defined interfaces, it seems obvious that the internals of a MoCo– especially its models – shall be only accessible via interface methods (i.e., the API to work with the MoCo). Exposing the raw models is still allowed that way if the component designer chooses to do so. Although we can imagine a visibility concept for exposing models of MoCos that works based on schema annotations, we believe that the basic MoCo concepts shall be kept simple.

In addition, visibility and accessibility may be relative to a certain concern (Issue 4) like the role of a user. For instance, an adaptation manager MoCo needs different access rights to a MoCo it shall control, than another MoCo that cooperates with the managed MoCo by using it in a black-box manner.

On first sight, supporting such *multi-role access* to models in MoCos seems complex, but we believe that it can contribute to robustness of engineering adaptive software because encapsulation and data-hiding can be adjusted on a case-by-case basis, i.e., for each MoCo and for each user role if really necessary. Tackling this cross-cutting challenge is out of the scope of this thesis.

Design Decision 5

Issue: How to realize different views on MoCos to only show its parts needed for certain concerns?

Decision: There is generic support for access profiles in the MoCo Infrastructure that can be implemented for each MoCo (e.g.,

---

Design Decision 5 (cont'd)

via queries that define the elements accessible for a certain profile)

Rationale: Default mechanisms for viewing MoCos shall be available in the MoCo Infrastructure. Domain and model-specific users of the MoCo Infrastructure can always develop external viewing mechanisms, but the MoCo technology shall support developers by offering the possibility to define views on the same subset of MoCos for various concerns such as roles and technical aspects. A comprehensive access control mechanism for MoCos needs to be fitted into the chosen component model MoCos shall be realized with and it is a crosscutting concern. Hence, we see this topic as future work.

When composing components, the main reasons are reuse of existing, proven functionality as well as the further encapsulation or adjustment of implementation details.

In general, one could argue that code of an enclosing component shall be capable of accessing the internals of its inner components. Such rather invasive composition of components may lead to solutions with hard-wired code breaking encapsulation, which may result in further errors if such usage was not foreseen by the designers of the original components.

In the case of MoCos, we aim at being able to change compositions for tailoring and for adapting. Hence, hard-wired solutions are not suitable, even though they may perform better in some cases due to direct and unprotected data access.

Design Decision 6

Issue: Shall additive composition imply visibility between the container's code and its inner components?

Design Decision 6 (cont'd)

Decision: No, accessibility between the container's (glue) code and the inner components shall obey the restrictions/possibilities given by provided interfaces without exceptions.

Rationale: Although we have taken ideas such as C++'s "friend" mechanism into account, we believe that MoCos shall be as simple as possible. Moreover, MoCos shall be implementable in any given component model and language, so we strictly adhere to the concept of encapsulation. If a MoCo needs to grant access to some other MoCo, its interfaces may need to be changed. This may be achievable by means of adaptation, too. Note, that additive composition of MoCos is subject to future work.

Management Interfaces

As a special case of exposing models to the environment of a MoCo, the PManage port (illustrated earlier in Section 3.1) is revisited in this section since adaptation is a crucial aspect of MoCo-based software.

There is an *external* and an *internal* approach to the development of adaptation managers [120] and each of them has advantages and disadvantages. The external approach has been favored in most cases, because it allows for reusable adaptation managers and clear separation of concerns between the application and the adaptation logic [147]. On the downside, the external adaptation manager does not have full access to the adaptable software and communicates with it via clearly defined interfaces, instead.

In GRAF [3, 39], we developed a management interface that was part of the framework and which allowed to control (i) the *core* parts of the framework, (ii) the *runtime model* and (iii) parts of the *adaptation rules*. We used UML-style activity diagrams at runtime with management interfaces specifically written for this case. In MoCo-based software though, *arbitrary kinds of models* are allowed.

Thus, we need a more flexible solution for managing runtime models that is not hard-wired to any specific modeling language.

Moreover, adaptable MoCos must provide the required information (Issue 10) in a form that is compatible with what an adaptation manager defines as its required input to perform controlling (Issue 11). An adaptation manager may even reject controlling, in case of dynamic binding to a MoCo if it detects insufficient management capabilities.[13]

Design Decision 7

Issue: How can data be provided to an adaptation manager by an adaptable MoCo?

Decision: The adaptation manager defines the required interfaces in its PManage port and connected adaptable MoCos need to implement them.

Rationale: This decision is a direct result of applying the principle of separation of concerns to the set of potentially available interfaces of any MoCo. Hence, we introduce the PFunction and PManage ports at the core of the MoCo concept. Other approaches have successfully applied a similar two-level splitting of interfaces for functionality and control [74, 92].

Determining or strictly defining the generic set of interfaces to be provided or required for adaptation of any type of MoCo is not feasible as they will most likely require and provide too much data. Even though we are convinced that collecting a set of fundamental operations on MoCos for adaptation is practical, we aim at providing

---

[13]We believe that adapting makes sense within clearly defined bounds and that there are limits to what can be achieved, given (i) a specific adaptable software, (ii) a concrete adaptation manager and (iii) other factors such as development time and costs. In some cases, human intervention (maintenance) will be inevitable.

a flexible solution that can be applied consistently across all kinds of
MoCos, but may be (even remotely) adjusted as needed – especially
during operation.

Design Decision 8

Issue: What kinds of interfaces must a generic adaptation
manager provide to other MoCos?

Decision: The adaptation manager requires query interfaces for sensing and provides transformation interfaces for
effecting.

Rationale: This decision is a direct result of applying the
concepts of CBSE to the set of potentially available interfaces of
any MoCo. Because domain-specific information may be required
for adapting, we favor the design of specific interfaces in contrast
to very generic interfaces that, for instance, simply reveal all
available data like the raw model. We have successfully shown
the feasibility of following a similar approach with GRAF [3].

Communication between a managed MoCo and an adaptation manager MoCo shall be defined via interfaces. Additionally, these interfaces may allow the remote access to managed MoCos over a network,
e.g., using HTTP, for manual and automated adaptation.

Finally, tailoring and adapting processes need to be unified and this
means especially that the very same technical solutions can be used
to achieve both. This may not be possible or meaningful for all tasks
that are involved in these processes but we aim at unification where
possible (Issue 12). A key area is the careful design of the PManage
ports of MoCos that need to support tailoring and adapting.

Design Decision 9

Issue: How must the PManage port be designed such that adapting and tailoring are handled similarly?

Decision: An adaptation manager can be temporarily connected to a MoCo for tailoring, i.e., an adaptation manager is reused as a part of the traditional SPLE build process for tailoring. In addition, the functionality for making changes to a MoCo and for persisting them – as needed for tailoring – are clearly separated.

Rationale: One of the motivations behind this research is to find a unified way of dealing with tailoring and adapting, because we believe that it will lead to more flexible (and potentially longer-living) software. It seems natural to merge these key areas of SPLE and SAS and to reuse same techniques. Benefits and drawbacks of this idea need to be explored.

View Concepts

In engineering and design disciplines – not only in software – it is well-established and proven knowledge that complex issues can be better understood and handled, once they are viewed from different viewpoints. Each viewpoint stresses a certain aspect of interest and hides unimportant information.

In software engineering and architectural design of systems, various different approaches have been proposed. The most popular ones being the ANSI-SPARC three-level architecture [5] and the 4+1 views architectural view model [94]. Moreover, the IEEE Recommended Practice for Architectural Description of Software-Intensive Systems [78] discusses the meta-level of software architecture.

Potentially, these guidelines could be applied to software developed based on MoCos, as well. We believe that it is important to provide a set of well-known ways for describing MoCos that are also compatible with existing view-based approaches to architectural design (Issue 9).

Design Decision 10

Issue: What kinds of views are needed for working with MoCos?

Decision: An existing architecture model is used and (if required) is extended for describing MoCos with a special focus on tailoring and adapting.

Rationale: The description and documentation of architectures must be concise and describe only the aspects required for a certain role. The set of views depend on the individual developer's needs and will also be influenced by the type of software to be developed with MoCos. Additionally, the MoCo concept shall be as compatible as possible with existing ways of software development.

In this thesis, we follow a light-weight solution and usually present MoCos in terms of its use cases, structure and behavior with a focus on the (optionally) embedded models to keep descriptions short and concise. In the context of a full software development project, we prefer Kruchten's 4+1 architectural views model [94] because we are familiar with it and because it proposes a good number of orthogonal perspectives on software.

3.2.3 Model/Code Relationships

The conceptual relationship between runtime models and code can be different, depending on the model semantics and the overall behavior of the MoCo. In this section, we revisit issue 13, which is related to the topic of *balancing model and code*.

Balancing Model and Code

One of the novelties in MoCos-based software is the deep integration of models and code within one component. From a technical point of view, this integration allows for enhanced flexibility, and – if the concepts are well-supported by tools – complexity can be managed by means of individually definable abstractions.

For users of the MoCo technology though, this extra room for choice (to develop either code, models or both) means that they need to decide carefully which way to go during system design and implementation. Ideally, concrete guidelines and patterns for using MoCos are provided to the software engineers.[14]

In fact, one may even debate about whether a component with only code or only models is still a MoCo. Not in all cases, one may see the need for developing both parts, especially, in cases where existing technology shall be mixed with MoCos. Finding the *right balance* between the use of models and code is essential for the practicality of MoCos (Issue 13).

In the future, it seems to be desirable to be able to project a logically coherent subset of models into code space (freezing) and vice versa (melting). This topic is strongly related to the *round trip engineering problem* known from research on software reengineering and Computer-Aided Software Engineering (CASE) tools.

Design Decision 11

Issue: Can a MoCo exist without (an application-specific) code part?

Decision: Forms of MoCos are allowed where only models are embedded into the MoCo container, i.e., the code part may be empty.

---

[14]Providing guidelines requires long-term experience with applying the MoCo concept and, hence, is an ongoing iterative and incremental process.

Design Decision 11 (cont'd)

Rationale: The embedded models make the MoCo different from existing approaches, even though there are some
similarities with components that make use of databases or read
XML files at first sight. In contrast, even a component that just
includes code can be a MoCo if it follows a minimum set of
(structural) design guidelines.

3.2.4 Model Semantics and Interpretation

A novel part of this research is the combination of a modularization
approach for software units that integrate models and code with the
requirements for building software that can be tailored and adapted.
The adaptation technology relies on the interpretation of (behavioral)
models at runtime. Therefore, the semantics of these models must be
clearly defined and encoded.

In this section, we revisit the issues 5, 6 and 18, which are related
to (i) *semantics encoding* and (ii) *model interpreter instantiation.*

Semantics Encoding

We decided to encode semantics in terms of model interpreters and
there are different ways of doing this (Issue 5). In this research, the
focus is not set on developing a novel way of semantics encoding, but
we need to provide an effective approach that fits the other MoCo
concepts and can be used in practice. Hence, we intend to develop an
approach that has a formal basis, but at the same time, is sufficiently
easy in application.

In GRAF [3], we followed a monolithic approach and the model
interpreter was completely hard-coded for the case of UML activity
models. Assuming that MoCos shall be usable with new modeling
languages quickly, it is certainly reasonable to invest some effort into
providing a basic infrastructure for realizing model interpreters. In

an ideal solution, model interpreters could be (partially) generated from a simple to write specification.

In either case, an underlying assumption is that model semantics can be encoded in a way that is driven by the modeling language's abstract syntax. The idea is that it is possible to "align" the syntax and semantics of used languages, i.e., the syntax elements, their associations and names are related to the intended modeling language's meaning. For example, a sequence of actions is represented by "Action" classes and connecting "Flow" associations in the meta-model.

Design Decision 12

Issue: How shall model semantics be encoded?

Decision: Semantics is fully encoded in a stand alone model interpreter.

Rationale: The idea behind this decision is that there shall be a systematic way of developing of model interpreters that is not tightly integrated with the meta-model of their respective language. Although model interpreters could be developed in the form of schema extensions, i.e., code snippets that are linked to meta-model elements, integrating multiple interpreters with the same meta-model seems tedious (e.g., using AOP). This is not a "hard" design decision, though, and it shall be read as a recommendation. We assume and allow that a model interpreter can be developed in different ways using MoCos, depending on available base technologies and their benefits.

Besides the different technical approaches to how semantics can be encoded, it must be decided *where* the description shall be stored and in which format (Issue 6). Providing all possible model interpreters with the MoCo Infrastructure is not possible, because the MoCo concept is meant to be extended and customized for various user-specified modeling languages and application scenarios. Storing the model interpreter with the single MoCos cannot be feasible either, because the same model interpreter may be required and reused in various MoCos.

Design Decision 13

Issue: Where does the semantics description for executable models belong to?

Decision: Each model schema comes with a model interpreter.

Rationale: As a schema encodes the abstract syntax of a modeling language, there is still a need for formalizing semantics. This is done in a model interpreter and there shall be at least one for each executable modeling language. That way, the same meta-model and conforming models can be embedded into various MoCos. Syntax and semantics are packaged in a logically coherent way.

At first sight, only behavioral models need an interpreter but there are cases in which a model interpreter may be useful to execute actions based on a purely structural model, too.

For instance, *architectural reorganization* can be achieved by interpreting a model of components and connectors and by adjusting the deployed and potentially operating components accordingly. The visualization of any type of model by means of an interpreter that traverses the abstract syntax graph and plots a visual representation for each meta-model element is another example for interpreted non-behavioral models.

Model Interpreter Instantiation

It is certainly possible that various components use the same types of models internally, e.g., feature models as well as behavioral models such as UML statecharts or UML activity models. The question arises whether to instantiate one model interpreter for each MoCo, or, if it is sufficient to share a model interpreter among several components, e.g., among those that are additively composed (Issue 18).

Design Decision 14

Issue: Shall MoCos share their model interpreters?

Decision: Yes, each MoCo registers its models with the MoCo Infrastructure, which in return instantiates one model interpreter per meta-model and this instance is reused for execution of different MoCos.

Rationale: We discuss the single-threaded case here, in which we assume that there is only one MoCo being executed/interpreted at a specific point in time. Additionally, model interpreters need to be stateless or need to save and restore their state when switching models before an execution pass finished. State information could be stored in the respective models, too. Ideally, the MoCo Infrastructure is aware of the models it can interpret and this can be achieved by a (central) registry of supported modeling languages and model interpreters.

It needs to be shown that sharing of model interpreters can work as expected, as there will be state information specific to each model, for instance. Working out these details will be part of the full concept for MoCo-based software and the development of prototypes.

3.2.5 MoCo Composition

Single components can be developed and tested individually and they can be used in a black-box manner to develop large systems by composing these building blocks. As the level of granularity for components can be chosen by developers, tailoring as well as adapting can be performed mostly at the level of components by recomposing and changing these components and their connectors. MoCo composition is hence one of the most important enablers for flexibility, but this technology must be interoperable with existing (legacy) software parts, too. From the outside, *composite MoCos* cannot be distinguished from atomic ones.

In this section, we revisit the issues 14, 17, 19, 20 and 22, which are related to (i) *interoperability*, (ii) *interfaces* and (iii) *flexibility*.

Interoperability

Nowadays, software cannot be developed from scratch in most cases and even if this is done, the new system must be capable of communicating with other, already existing systems that may hold needed data, for instance (Issue 14). Different paths can be followed to approach this issue.

In case of pure data, it can be migrated into the new technological environment, but this is a rather complicated and potentially error-prone task that needs to be automated for large amounts of legacy data. This approach also assumes that the data and its hosting software system is under control of the developer of the new system.

Furthermore, when working with MoCos, data may be required to be available in the form of a model. In this context, it remains questionable if a one-time migration can be performed, or if data needs to be incrementally re-imported and updated in case the old system is still receiving changes.

Design Decision 15

Issue: What if data is already present in an external database or tool?

Decision: A MoCo just acts as a *facade* to the original data, i.e., its model is simulated by an intermediate code layer (wrapper).

Design Decision 15 (cont'd)

Rationale: We aim at achieving at least basic communication (e.g., using existing APIs) and data exchange with legacy software. Other options like one-time-conversion of existing data may be suitable in some cases, too, but we prefer solutions that do not introduce redundancy. Hence, we believe that a wrapper-based approach is a suitable default solution.

Interfaces

When composing components, either their interfaces are combined and glued together in some way (sequential and hierarchical composition), or a new component is formed (additive composition). Especially in the latter case, one may ask if there should be a rule according to which the interfaces of the inner components shall be used to create the interfaces of the composite MoCo (Issue 17). Technically, this issue is not specific to MoCos, since it is at the heart of building software using components.

Design Decision 16

Issue: Shall additive components always expose the complete set of their inner interfaces?

Decision: No, the offered interfaces are a subset of all interfaces available from the inner MoCos, possibly including additional interfaces.

Rationale: While there may be situations in which a one-to-one mapping between all interfaces of the inner components and the interfaces of the composite component may be required, we see this as a special case. When composing MoCos, the

Design Decision 16 (cont'd)

resulting component usually is meant to hide details of the internal implementation and may also add functionality or (self-)management capabilities. Thus, it remains under the control of the component designer to specify the interfaces of the composite MoCo. The outer component acts as a wrapper.

At this point, we like to add that – depending on the specific application area of the desired system design – we can imagine that software engineers may limit the composition further and may actually define patterns according to which, for instance, all inner interfaces are exposed by the composite MoCo, too.

As mentioned earlier, we do not cover the additive composition of MoCo in detail here but this topic needs to be taken into account for long-term evolution of the MoCo concept.

Flexibility

The composition of components must be considered across the whole life-cycle of components [99] and more flexibility requires the ability to change composition at runtime (architectural reconfiguration). Examples for such dynamically composable components are plug-ins as realized by using an implementation of the OSGi framework.

In other cases, for instance when Java classes are directly used to represent components, the composition is often rather static, e.g., when Java interfaces are imported, implemented and compiled. In the context of MoCos, we need to decide if such static compositions shall be allowed or not (Issue 19).

Many existing solutions for achieving adaptivity are (not surprisingly) based on component technology, because this allows the fragmentation of a larger system into smaller, manageable units that can be tested and replaced individually. That way, the impact of adapting can be managed and at least some properties such as syntactic compatibility of two components can be checked statically (i.e., in terms of their provided and required interfaces). MoCos shall support these development approaches, too.

Design Decision 17

Issue: Shall all three composition types be changeable during tailoring and adapting?

Decision: Yes, because components are the basic building blocks for SPLs, DSPLs and SASs. Thus, making changes to them shall be done in the same ways at development-time and at runtime.

Rationale: We argue that the essential operations on components need to be applicable at any times and in all kinds of situations, including design time, development time and runtime.

In most approaches related to SAS or AC, not only external changes are monitored. There is also a need for the adaptation logic to access the system's own state. The pattern of *architectural reflection* [20] has shown to be a feasible technical solution. Some existing programming languages already incorporate similar techniques, so the question arises whether MoCos shall include reflective capabilities per default or not (Issue 20).

Design Decision 18

Issue: Shall MoCos composition be represented in a reflective model?

Decision: Yes, there shall be a generic solution for architectural reflection (maybe in the MoCo Infrastructure).

Rationale: Being capable of introspection, i.e., to access

Design Decision 18 (cont'd)

and to analyze the current system state, is an essential prerequisite for realizing adaptivity. Modern programming languages such as Java or C# support reflection as a means to access and to even change the runtime behavior of programs. By adding models as an essential part of MoCos, similar mechanisms need to be available for them, too.

We introduced three basic composition patterns as discussed in literature [123]. These are fine-grained and can be used to create higher-level patterns at the architectural level. Assuming that reflection is available and the composition patterns are well-understood, it must be decided which mechanisms to use in which cases as pure technical availability by itself is insufficient for their application. Hence, one may ask if the MoCo concept shall come with strict guidelines that force the use of certain patterns (Issue 21).

Design Decision 19

Issue: Which patterns of component composition are most suitable when using MoCos?

Decision: The composition shall entirely depend on the intended design to meet non-functional requirements and not on the used component technology.

Rationale: Although we see indicators for using one or the other pattern in various cases, the core concept of MoCos shall not influence the use of these patterns. Instead, software engineers shall be able to realize any pattern in their software with the MoCo concept.

3.2.6 MoCo Services

The MoCo Infrastructure needs to provide *MoCo services* to work smoothly with MoCos. Developers need to be supported with a set of fundamental operations that ease the engineering and handling of components. Again, we slightly focus more on the model side, as there are already stable tools available that are mature and well-established for dealing with code.

We see a need for services that enable the manipulation of models in terms of CRUD operations, as well as for services that support working with MoCos as essential building blocks in a way that hides the complexity of its embedded models and code altogether.

In this section, we revisit the issues 8 and 15, which are related to (i) *model manipulation* and (ii) *component persistency*. This is only an excerpt and a starting point for collecting the needed services. These will be elicited and described in detail as a part of the complete concept for MoCo-based software.

Model Manipulation

Since models are an essential part of MoCos and shall be used together with code to build components, there needs to be a set of operations to handle these models in a generic manner. Usually, an API[15] can be generated for a schema. Additionally, developers of modeling languages shall receive a technical solution for extending these in order to include more complex operations in a reusable form as an equal part of the modeling language's definition (Issue 8).

Software engineers shall not be prevented from developing custom solutions for working with models. If possible, meta-models shall ship with the services that are expected to be useful when working with its instances (models) in a MoCo-based software development context.

---

[15]For example, generation of a schema-specific API is implemented by JGraLab (https://github.com/jgralab – visited July 9th, 2014) and EMF ((http://www.eclipse.org/modeling/emf/ – visited July 9th, 2014).

Design Decision 20

Issue: How to deal with CRUD operations on embedded models and their impact on other model and code parts of the MoCo at runtime?

Decision: All CRUD operations on models follow a predefined reference implementation with customizable steps (e.g., via template methods) to be provided by the software engineer.

Rationale: All complex operations on models can be implemented based on a set of atomic CRUD operations. Especially adapting and tailoring shall use the same mechanisms in our unified approach. To support consistency in the way these CRUD operations can be provided and invoked, there shall be a predefined set of implementation patterns, paired with (abstract) base implementations that software engineers can use as a starting point.

Component Persistency

Since tailoring and adapting of MoCos shall use the same underlying mechanisms, users of the MoCo technology can think of tailoring as a sequence of adapting and serialization steps. From this perspective, the mechanism for serializing adapted components is crucial for tailoring. Thus, persistency of MoCos– and hence, persistency of embedded models and code – plays a vital role (Issue 15).

Design Decision 21

Issue: How can persistency of MoCos be realized?

Decision: The MoCo Infrastructure provides interfaces to be realized using the specific mechanisms of the chosen technology

Design Decision 21 (cont'd)

for serialization and deserialization.

Rationale: For realizing tailoring, we envision the combination of adapting and serialization techniques. Nevertheless, these will be strongly technology-dependent. Although we may still provide such functionality for the chosen technologies in the prototypical implementation for this research, it shall be the responsibility of software engineers to provide an implementation of serialization and deserialization for MoCos that suits the used technologies for models, code and the chosen component technology.

3.3 Summary

In this chapter, we presented some of the expected needs of software engineers when using MoCos to build flexible software that can be tailored and adapted. Among these were the cases of developing (i) adaptive components, (ii) variable requirements assets, (iii) adaptation managers and – more generally – (iv) composite components.

From these use case, a non-prioritized list of 21 issues was collected and possible directions for tackling them were carefully described in the form of 21 decisions for 6 clusters of issues. That way, the introduced vision of software development using MoCos has been sketched in detail.

Please note that we have implicitly made some fundamental design decisions already, i.e., we have made the assumption that the integration of models and code in the form of MoCos (using an architectural blueprint) is a feasible solution. Testing the validity of this assumption is the primary goal of this dissertation.

Based on the set of initial design considerations presented so far, we introduce the MoCo concept in the next chapter.

4 Component Realization Concept

In this chapter, we describe the *component realization concept* for MoCos. It does not rely on any specific capabilities of existing component models. Instead, it is meant to be implemented by using an existing component technology of choice and already developed (legacy) components can be mapped to the new structure. The MoCo concept describes a *design strategy* for developing flexible software components.

The main goal of this chapter is to define the conceptual foundation for flexible, model-integrating software components that – when instantiated for a specific application context – meet the requirements and use cases described earlier in Chapter 3. The defined terms can be also looked-up in the attached *glossary*, starting on page 293.

The remainder of this chapter is structured as follows. First, the *big picture* of the MoCo concept is given. Then, each of the three main constituents, i.e., the *MoCo Template, MoCo Execution Environment* and the *MoCo Service Library* are described with their related concepts. This chapter ends with a short *summary*.

4.1 Big Picture

Before defining the details of the MoCo concept, we introduce the *big picture* first. It supports achieving the required component capabilities motivated by the previously introduced use cases. Especially the *rationale* behind each single part of the concept is documented and relationships to the exemplary use cases are summarized. This section is an introduction that is refined step-by-step throughout the rest of this chapter.

In Figure 4.1, the *top-level concepts* of MoCo-based software and relationships among them are shown. The main parts are: (i) the MoCo, (ii) the MoCoExecutionEnvironment and (iii) the MoCoServiceLibrary. All other ones are closely related to one of these.

4.1.1 MoCo

The central concept is the MoCo. It denotes a closed unit of functionality and/or data that possesses certain key characteristics: it supports *tailoring processes* to support variability and *adapting processes* to support self-adaptation. In the broader sense, we use the same term for referring to (i) a *template* for software components that can be realized in various component technology as well as to (ii) the concrete *instances* of this template for a given application area.

All MoCos communicate with each other via specific Ports that groups various Interfaces. There can be one PFunction port encapsulating core functionality and one PManage port that supports the configuration, tailoring and adapting of a MoCo.

The key characteristics that distinguish MoCos from existing ones is that each MoCo may consist of an MoCoModel module[1] and an MoCoCode module. Both are first-class entities of the component and each one is executable by the MoCoExecutionEnvironment. Hence, behavior and data can be represented as models or as code – the full spectrum from (i) *code-only* to (ii) a *mixture of models and code* to (iii) *model-only* is supported [41].

The Mediator is an important module of the MoCo that glues the MoCoModel and MoCoCode together. Essentially, it is responsible for bidirectional data transfer and for the "remote" invoking of behavior from either side: model elements can invoke code and code elements can invoke modeled behavior.

---

[1]In this context, a *module* is a structured and logically coherent group of software elements. Its concrete representation is an implementation decision.

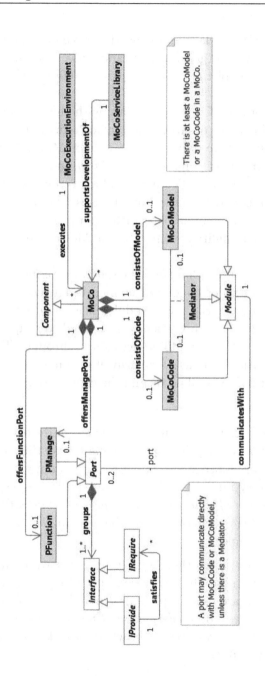

Figure 4.1: Meta-Model Illustrating the Main Concepts of MoCo-Based Software

The Mediator may also filter data and convert between a common range of data types if they diverge in models and code. The role of this module follows the idea of the *mediator pattern* [60] to achieve loose coupling.

By design, the ports of a MoCo communicate with the Mediator which delegates received calls to to either the MoCoCode or the Mo-CoModel. In border cases where only a MoCoCode or MoCoModel exists without a Mediator, direct communication between a port and the respective module is allowed. For expandability, the use of a Mediator is also recommended in these border cases, though. Additionally, the Mediator can communicate with the ports to obtain an implementation of functionality specified by the MoCo's required interfaces.

The MoCo is our proposal of a *template* for software components that are made of models and of code that cooperate harmonically. Component users do not necessarily notice a difference to more traditional software components. It is only when tasks related to adapting or tailoring are carried out that the differences shine through. The MoCo concept is not a static construct. Primarily, it communicates an idea that shall be fitted to individual needs and the chosen component model.

- *Rationale:* The need for more flexible approaches for developing new systems and for systematic ways of changing existing software has been already motivated. Existing solution approaches rely on a few but very fundamental engineering principles, especially on the *separation of concerns* and on *encapsulation*. CBSE and existing component technologies can be used in practice to adhere to these principles.

  Moreover, *abstraction* is another key factor in software engineering. Adequately simplified representations of real-world phenomena (models), are used to plan, design and develop complex systems. The area of *models at runtime* [10, 14] is an emerging and growing field of research, where models are used during execution of software.

Yet, we are convinced that models are still not being treated appropriately, i.e., they are somewhat seen as "second class" entities that are mainly used to design and to manage the "real" product: code. We believe that models need to become an *integrated part* of software components to fully leverage the performance of code but also the flexibility and abstraction capabilities of models. Ideally, both sides shall be capable of fulfilling identical tasks (non-functional properties may vary).

- *Motivating Use Cases:* The MoCo is a key-part of the solution concept. In fact, all of the presented use cases described in Chapter 3 can be seen as motivators for the MoCo, but the driving force is the case *"develop adaptive component"* (presented in Section 3.1.1).

The MoCo and its immediately related concepts are presented and discussed comprehensively in Section 4.2.

4.1.2 MoCoExecutionEnvironment

The MoCoExecutionEnvironment denotes a software system that abstracts away from low-level and hardware-specific computing processes. It is capable of instantiating and executing MoCos. Intuitively, one could imagine the MoCoExecutionEnvironment to be a somewhat extended variant of the JVM.

The execution of software with the help of a virtual machine is state of the art due to its proven benefits (e.g., platform-independence, dynamic optimization). Software components can be executed in a technical environment which may vary depending on the chosen programming languages and underlying hardware at the deployment target. Besides immediate execution of *low-level instructions* that can be sent more or less directly to hardware, there are also virtual machines and interpreters that work on top of an operating system. For now, we do not make any technical assumption about how exactly this environment could be implemented.

- *Rationale:* Given that each MoCo can contain models, there is the need for an extension of the execution environment that is not only capable of running code, but can also execute models. The feasibility of model interpretation and related performance concerns has been discussed in related research papers, e.g., in [49, 70]. Advantages w.r.t. flexibility have been also covered by others, e.g., by [140], as well as by some of our own previous work [3, 37, 39].

- *Motivating Use Cases:* The MoCoExecutionEnvironment is the second key-part of the solution concept. Without an adequate execution environment, a MoCo cannot be instantiated and executed. This concept originates mostly from technical requirements and not so much from the actual use cases described earlier in Chapter 3.

  The requirement for carrying models and for executing them together with code is the driving factor here. All exemplarily described use cases need such an execution environment. In the simplest case, only code is executed as usual.

The required properties of an execution environment for MoCos need to be understood and well-designed if models shall be *on par* with code at all stages of the software lifecycle. The MoCoExecutionEnvironment concept is presented and comprehensively discussed in Section 4.3.

4.1.3 MoCoServiceLibrary

The MoCoServiceLibrary is a collection of *services* that support the development and maintenance of MoCos. In this context, a service is a group of operations for handling MoCos. Multiple application areas need to be considered. To name a few, there are services for the *administration* of components and running software, the *rendering*, *configuration* and *generation* of the MoCo Template in a specific component technology as well as the *derivation* of model interpreter skeletons. Especially the needed boilerplate code is hidden from software engineers to simplify development in most common scenarios. Additional services deal with the most elementary actions required for *tailoring* and *adapting*. Furthermore, there is support for *component persistency* such that details for storing and loading models is mostly hidden. A set of tools for *managing models* is covered, too. Similar to the other parts of the solution concept, this abstractly specified service library needs to be developed initially for a concrete set of technologies (programming languages, modeling languages and component technologies).

- *Rationale:* We are convinced that even excellent concepts cannot be applied – let alone be broadly adopted – in practice if adequate tool-support is lacking. Thus, key tasks that need to be performed in most common application scenarios need to be well-covered by documentation but also by an accompanying set of software utilities that work smoothly and produce expected results. Indeed, we advocate the iterative development and application of this library in early prototypes.

- *Motivating Use Cases:* The MoCoServiceLibrary is the third key-part of the *solution concept*. It is not purely a technical necessity but actually required to enhance the user-experience, i.e., to support software engineers in using MoCos in practice. Since the most essential tasks to be performed with or on MoCos need to be covered, the related exemplary use cases are especially *"develop adaptive component"* (presented in Section 3.1.1) and *"develop composite component"* (presented in Section 3.1.4).

The MoCoServiceLibrary is introduced and discussed comprehensively in Section 4.4.

4.2 MoCo Template

The *MoCo Template* (see Definition 4.1) is an architectural blueprint. Some of its constituents are mandatory and need to occur in every MoCo while others are optional.

Definition 4.1: MoCo Template

The *MoCo Template* is a specification of the possible constituents of concrete MoCos (instances). This template describes all concepts and possible relationships among them abstractly. It must be configured and instantiated for a specific context of use.

Subsequently, details are given in terms of a structure-focused perspective. More concretely, we differentiate between an *external view* (black box), an *internal view* (white box) and a *variability view*.

4.2.1 External View

Judging from the outside, all MoCos show a similar structure to their users. Conceptually, MoCos can have two types of ports: (i) the PFunction port and (ii) the PManage port. These are the major contact-points between a MoCo and its environment such as other components and software engineers. This *external view* is illustrated in Figure 4.2 and it is elaborated on subsequently.

PFunction. The PFunction port represents a logical grouping of all *core functionality* that is either required or provided by the MoCo. There are no special restrictions for the design of this port and no detailed interfaces can be illustrated here because the set of required and provided interfaces depends on the concrete application domain. Interfaces at this port shall not reveal internal realization details such as model-related information unless this belongs to the MoCo's core functionality.

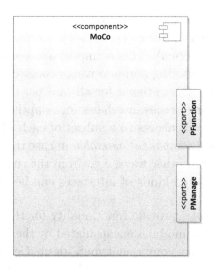

Figure 4.2: External View on the MoCo Template

The PFunction port is *optional* for all MoCos.[2] Components that automatically start their task without any dependencies to other components do not require PFunction (e.g., a "Hello World!" sample).

PManage. The PManage port represents a logical grouping of all *management functionality* that is either required or provided by the MoCo. To manage a MoCo, we rely heavily on applying techniques and mechanisms that were developed and are being successfully applied in the more general domain of MDSD [18, 125]. Already early in the beginning of the GRAF project, we showed the feasibility of this direction in terms of case studies [37].

Moreover, processable information on the available ports and interfaces is an essential part of each MoCo's *meta-data* (not illustrated

---

[2]We can imagine that the *visibility* concern may be covered by an extension of the presented solution concept here, where each MoCo can be set up to hide some of its interfaces for certain users in a specific role and, ideally, in a context-sensitive manner.

here). This information must be accessible not only by software engineers and by other software systems (*inspection*) but also by the MoCo itself (*introspection*). This is important to ensure a baseline of capabilities for all tailoring and adapting processes.

The **PManage** port is *optional* for all MoCos. It is required, if the component designer foresees interfaces for adaptings or tailoring the component. Moreover, access to a subset of each MoCo's meta-data may be provided for *component assembly* in case that this information cannot be obtained in other ways, e.g., from the runtime environment. The subsequently listed kinds of interfaces can be provided:

- *Query interfaces* provide functionality for the *inspection* of the model and code modules encapsulated by the MoCo. It may also provide arbitrary component meta-data. Component designers can specify a wide range of possible access methods, for example including: (i) a *querying API* and (ii) a single *generic querying service* that accepts a string written in a specific query language. Essentially, a designer can fine-tune which parts of the MoCo to expose for read-only access.

- *Transformation interfaces* provide functionality for the *modification* of the MoCo, especially for the embedded model. In fact, most adapting and tailoring activities will be performed at the model-level which allows the application of similar techniques for both categories of tasks. Modifications of code may be supported as well (if technically reasonable) but the focus of modification operations is actually the MoCo's model.

  Similar to query interfaces, the designer of the component has the choice to provide either (i) a *transformation API* or (ii) a single *generic transformation service* that accepts a string written in a specific transformation language. Hence, a designer can fine-tune what parts of the MoCo's internals may be transformed by its users and which not. While revealing more parts for

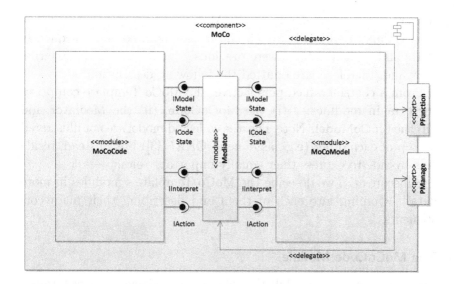

Figure 4.3: Internal View on the MoCo Template

transformation can result in better flexibility[3], it also includes the risk that an external user may bring the MoCo into an incorrect state.

We like to point out that, in this conceptual view, querying and transforming interfaces are described separately. In fact, model transformation languages need to use querying as a part of their transformations, e.g., to select the subset to be manipulated first. As more and more experience with the MoCo concept is gained, a long-term goal will be to provide standardized interface types for PManage.

4.2.2 Internal View

The encapsulated details are not so much of interest for the users of MoCos, but component designers need to be familiar with the

---

[3]We implicitly assume that the more parts of a MoCo's internals are modifiable, the more likely it is that one can react to unforeseen conditions the component may need to operate under.

concepts that are similar among all MoCos. A coarse-grained *internal view* is illustrated in Figure 4.3 and it is elaborated on subsequently. Ports and their interfaces were previously introduced in the external view and, therefore, are omitted the following description.

From a coarse-grained perspective, the MoCo Template comprises three main modules: (i) the MoCoCode, (ii) the Mediator and (iii) the MoCoModel. Note, how the code and model are not illustrated on top of each other (e.g., as done in GRAF [3]) but, instead, reside side-by-side to express their equally important roles.

Subsequently, we describe the MoCo Template's modules in more detail, zooming into each of them and describing their main constituents.

The MoCoCode Module

The MoCoCode is a module that holds stable, efficient and well-tested core functionality. Parts of the provided services of the MoCo can be implemented in code like in all traditional ways of building software components. Not every MoCo needs to implement its application behavior in plain code, though. Models can be used to realize similar functionality, as well.

The realization concept does not require the code to be structured in a predefined way. In cases where the MoCoCode shall cooperate and interact with the MoCoModel module, standardized ways of implementation are proposed.

Obviously, this *standardization* has the advantage that the boilerplate share of any MoCo is similar and, hence, can be better understood by different software engineers. In addition, the connection between model and code within a MoCo can be derived systematically which paves the way for generative and use-case-specific approaches for the instantiation of the MoCo Template.

The internals of the MoCoCode are sketched in Figure 4.4 and each part is introduced in terms of its responsibilities in the following.

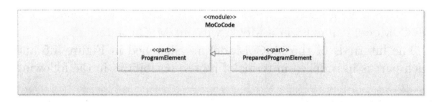

Figure 4.4: Essential Parts of the MoCoCode Module

ProgramElement. The ProgramElement represents any kind of element offered by a programming language. No restrictions are made to the way source code shall be written. MoCos can include arbitrary complex logic or state represented by code (depending on the chosen programming language). In a migration context of legacy software towards SAS, such as described in our earlier works [2], these program elements are also referred to as *original elements*.

PreparedProgramElement. The PreparedProgramElement is a special kind of ProgramElement that supports interfacing with the Mediator module. For example, some of the data fields need to be exposed for read/write access and methods may need to be marked as replaceable with modeled behavior. Hence, it is required to *prepare* some of the code to allow communication with the Mediator. This shall be realized consistently among all components, i.e., very same mechanisms shall be applied. The MoCo service library described later in Section 4.4 supports related (instrumentation) activities.

The MoCoModel Module

The MoCoModel module primarily contains and manages the actual model data that contributes to the functionality of the MoCo. Each model conforms to a *meta-model* that describes its abstract syntax. Moreover, *constraints* may be defined and stored with the schema as needed. Model semantics is described via *model interpreters* that can execute (parts of) models that conform to a specific meta-model. It is up to the designer of a component to plan and decide what kinds of modeling languages to use in the specific application domain. The MoCoModel can exist in a MoCo without MoCoCode.

The internals of the MoCoModel are sketched in Figure 4.5 and each part is introduced in terms of its responsibilities in the following.

Model. The Model is the actual data that represents state information, structure and behavior in an adequate form, i.e., as an ASG. The concrete data structure to be used depends on the technological space chosen for modeling. In this thesis, it is represented as a special kind of graph, i.e., a TGraph. A Model conforms to a Schema (a.k.a. meta-model) and can be created during development, but also during load-time or at runtime. Moreover, the model can be queried, transformed and interpreted (QTI). Flexibility of the MoCo-based software development approach primarily stems from exactly these capabilities.

Schema. The Schema is a structured formal description of the possible concepts and their relationships allowed in instances[4] of this meta-model. Commonly, it is possible to attach further _constraints_, e.g., in the form of Boolean queries using a suitable expression language offered in the technological modeling space. The Schema describes the _abstract syntax_ of the modeling language. The visual notation, i.e., the _concrete syntax_, is not defined here. A Schema is shared between multiple MoCos that keep a reference to it.

The topic of _co-evolution_ of meta-models and models [54, 67] is excluded from this thesis, but it is an important related field of research that deserves special attention.

SchemaExtension. The SchemaExtension is a structured formal description of additional executable _services_ that can be useful when working with models that conform to a certain Schema. Hence, these

---

[4] We usually refer to instances of a meta-model as "models". In the broader sense, and in the context of MoCo-based software, we sometimes refer to the whole MoCoModel module as "model", too.

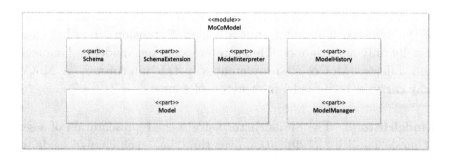

Figure 4.5: Essential Parts of the MoCoModel Module

extensions are developed in code and can be seen as small libraries that are defined together with a schema and the model element types it defines. Depending on the needs of the modeling language's users, a multitude of different tasks can be performed. More generally, functionality that is very specific to a modeling language and that cannot be reused for other modeling languages can be stored as part of the SchemaExtension, as well. An example would be "semantic snippets" for certain model element types to realize a model interpreter that is *woven* into the Schema. More background information on the topic of *schema extensions* can be obtained in related work [126].

ModelInterpreter. The ModelInterpreter can execute a subset of the Model, e.g., by walking along a path in the underlying graph structure, and executing associated operations for visited model elements. Each executable model needs one or more interpreters. A ModelInterpreter is suited for a specific Schema. Note, how the separation between the *abstract syntax* of models (defined by a Schema) and the *semantics* of models (defined by a ModelInterpreter) is achieved.

We considered two directions for developing model interpreters. First, a *stand-alone interpreter* can fully encode the modeling language's semantics. This is the common solution. Second, an interpretation algorithm can be designed and realized as a *woven interpreter*, i.e., each model can execute itself. This is achieved by associating semantics in the form of "semantic snippets" with executable elements of the Schema. This solution is a SchemaExtension. In either case, usually only a single model interpreter exists per modeling language and different MoCos share references to this interpreter. A MoCo may carry its own model interpreter, of course.

ModelHistory. The ModelHistory stores the representation of a set of models and its modification over time, i.e., each change made to the Model can be stored in the ModelHistory, similar to a version control system. With the help of this information, incorrect adaptation steps can be rolled-back when needed. This data can be also used to monitor the development of a component over time with regard to its adaptable parts. In addition, data mining or information retrieval approaches may offer suitable post-processing steps for detecting hidden knowledge or patterns of model states. Ideally, this knowledge can be used for the automation of adapting and tailoring processes in the future.

ModelManager. The ModelManager controls access to the Model. It can be seen as a facade to the critical data to be accessed via queries and transformations. It can also cover further utility functionality, such as the triggering of a rollback to an earlier model state by using the ModelHistory or the checking of access-rights before query or transformation activities.

The Mediator Module

The Mediator provides the technical means for connecting the MoCoCode and the MoCoModel so they can cooperate, i.e., exchange data as well as mutually trigger the invocation of behavior. Moreover, it acts as a *proxy* that receives calls from the MoCo's ports and redirects them to an implementation in the MoCoCode or MoCoModel.

Based on our previous work on combining models at runtime with legacy systems [3], we estimate that at least five cases will occur naturally during software development with MoCos. The *MoCo*

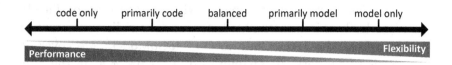

Figure 4.6: Spectrum of MoCos

spectrum [41], i.e., the different configurations of the MoCo Template, is illustrated in Figure 4.6. In each case, the Mediator plays a slightly different role.

It must be noted that the spectrum of MoCos can be seen as describing all different kinds of configurations of the MoCo Template, but it is also a spectrum between non-functional properties of the resulting components. While MoCos that are written only in code are assumed to be most efficient in terms of execution or use of memory, MoCos that consist of models only are assumed to be less efficient but more flexible.[5]

Next, each illustrated configuration of the MoCo Template and the respective purpose of the Mediator are described.

(C1) *Code Only:* The MoCoCode module exists, but the MoCoModel is excluded. The component's interfaces need to be implemented strictly in code. Management capabilities may be realized with the programming language's reflection capabilities, if supported. In this case, the Mediator is optional. Still, it may act as a proxy between the ports and the MoCoCode. Advanced forms of the Mediator may be even able to systematically choose between different variations of the same functionality at runtime (e.g., based on a priorities) to support adaptivity.

(C2) *Primarily Code:* The MoCoCode is the primary module (e.g., w.r.t. the control flow) and it is extended by the MoCoModel,

---

[5]Depending on the available technology, this claim may no longer hold in the future though, e.g., when more efficient model interpreters are available or further progress in fine-grained adjustments to code at runtime are made.

the secondary module, in places which need to be specifically flexible. In this case, the Mediator needs to redirect the control flow from the MoCoCode to the MoCoModel. Moreover, it needs to support all capabilities of a Mediator as in the *code only* configuration.

(C3) *Balanced:* A combination models and code shall be used equally within the same MoCo. For example, data needs to be synchronized bidirectionally between the MoCoCode and the MoCoModel and each side invokes behavior implemented in the counterpart. In this case, the Mediator needs to provide full functionality and it is intensively wired to both sides.

(C4) *Primarily Model:* The MoCoCode module is rather a library of functionality and the main flow is dictated by the MoCoModel. Actions implemented in MoCoCode are used (e.g., orchestrated) for this purpose. The MoCoModel can be seen as the primary module, whereas the MoCoCode is the secondary module. In this case, the Mediator especially needs to support efficient access to parts of the functionality offered by MoCoCode.

(C5) *Model Only:* The MoCoModel module exists but the MoCoCode is excluded. In this case, the Mediator is optional. Still, it may act as a proxy between the ports and the MoCoModel as described for the *code only* configuration.

To summarize, the Mediator module plays the roles of (i) a *proxy* that (smartly) delegates between the ports and the MoCoCode and MoCoModel, (ii) a (bidirectional) *data synchronizer* between them and (iii) a *behavior provider* to the MoCoCode and the MoCoModel, respectively. This is reflected by the internals of the Mediator which are sketched in Figure 4.7. Each part is introduced in terms of its responsibilities in the following.

DataSynchronizationAdapter. The DataSynchronizationAdapter is responsible for (i) synchronizing data from the code to the model and

Figure 4.7: Essential Parts of the Mediator Module

(ii) vice-versa. In its most simple form, this part allows for realizing the *reification* of the code's state to the model as well as the *reflection* of changes made to the model into the actual code state. In addition to such 1 : 1 mappings, the DataSynchronizationAdapter can be configured to *filter* the processed data, e.g., it may aggregate a series of data sources into one by computing an average value for a given time-frame.

Generally speaking, data synchronization between models and code may be conditional and it is optional. Only in cases where redundancy is introduced "by design", e.g., as introduced by the reflection pattern, the DataSynchronizationAdapter is needed.

CodeInvocationAdapter. The CodeInvocationAdapter is responsible for invoking behavior available in the MoCoCode module. If different variations of the same behavior are available, this adapter is also capable of resolving such variability by following an associated resolution strategy.

ModelInvocationAdapter. The ModelInvocationAdapter is responsible for invoking behavior available in the MoCoModel module. In case that type conversions are required, these can be made by this adapter. Similar to the CodeInvocationAdapter, the ModelInvocationAdapter can attempt to resolve available behavioral variations based on a (predefined) strategy.

The Internal Interfaces

A set of interface types is foreseen in the MoCo Template to realize the connection between the MoCoCode and the Mediator as shown in Figure 4.3. In a concrete implementation, each of these conceptual interfaces may be realized by multiple concrete interfaces. Subsequently, each kind of interface is listed and its responsibilities are described.

IModelState. The IModelState interface provides fine-grained functionality to access the model in a read and write manner.

Core functionality of this interface is to select subsets of model elements, according to some defined Boolean condition or pattern described by a query language.

Moreover, the IModelState interface provides fine-grained functionality to modify a subset of the model (transformations are usually done "in-place"). Modifications may be recorded by the ModelHistory. The exact capabilities and performance offered by the IModelState interface depend on the chosen technological space for modeling.

Note that there may be a *technological gap* between MoCoModel and MoCoCode in terms of data types used, so information gathered from the model may need post-processing before it can be used in code. The required filtering of data can be done by the Mediator. In this research, we assume that types used in models and code conform to each other, i.e., they can be systematically and sufficiently mapped (ideally without information loss).

The MoCoModel module implements IModelState and the Mediator may offer it to the MoCoCode module.

ICodeState. The ICodeState interface provides functionality for extracting information on the state of MoCoCode. Hence, the elements under inspection are part of the program's abstract syntax representation (e.g., in Java: fields and class structure). The exact *inspection capabilities* that can be provided depend on the used programming language (e.g., reflection) and possibly on the execution environment (e.g., code instrumentation as used for tracing, debugging and profiling).

Additionally, the ICodeState interface provides functionality for editing selected elements of MoCoCode. In practice, often the same elements that can be inspected may be also subject to change. There is a predefined, generic way of realizing this interface – backed by guidelines – to ensure that activities that need to adjust and change code elements are handled identically across all MoCos. The exact *modification capabilities* that can be provided depend on the used programming language and possibly on the execution environment.

There is a predefined way of creating this interface, which is additionally backed by *development guidelines*. Only small and non-intrusive changes to code in the MoCoCode module are necessary to realize ICodeState.

The MoCoCode module implements ICodeState and the Mediator may offer it to the MoCoModel module.

IInterpret. The IInterpret interface provides functionality to execute parts of a model. A model interpreter is always developed for a certain meta-model. In this thesis, we assume that the models to be interpreted can be executed by traversing the model's underlying data structure.

As a MoCo can be also created without MoCoCode, the MoCo-Model must be capable of interpreting contained models itself. In the worst case, return values received from interpreting the model may need to be converted first, before they can be used in code. The Mediator may be useful to delegate modeled behavior to the PFunction port in an adequate format, or PFunction must filter the data itself. In this research, we abstract from such realization-specific issues and assume that the described data conversion step is not required.

The IInterpret interface supports the development of MoCos that consist of code, but rely on model interpretation for a subset of their functionality. That way, identified parts of the component in need for flexibility at runtime can be covered by models[6] which are easier to

---

[6]It is actually a challenge to identify the right spots in code that may need adaptation, as sketched by [1] as well as by us in the context of evolution towards DSPLs [38].

adapt. The MoCoCode may require IInterpret to redirect control flow at certain spots[7] in its code to model interpreters. Then, models can be edited on-the-fly (either manually or autonomously) and changes take effect the next time the model is interpreted.

The MoCoModel module implements IInterpret and the Mediator may offer it to the MoCoCode module.

IAction. The IAction interface provides handles to arbitrary (atomic) actions that are realized in MoCoCode. Especially in cases where the MoCoCode is built to be a library of services, models can be used to orchestrate these – for instance in the form of flow-charts where each node links to an implemented action that can be invoked via IAction. In a migration context, existing code may need to be prepared to offer such clearly defined interfaces.

The MoCoCode module implements IAction and the Mediator may offer it to the MoCoModel module that may need to invoke some of the programmed actions, e.g. during model interpretation.

4.2.3 Variability View

So far, a high-level decomposition of the MoCo Template was introduced. It shall be *tailored* to the needs of specific application contexts. Therefore, the MoCo Template itself requires the clear definition of the dependencies between all of its constituent concepts. This variability needs to be made explicit, e.g., in terms of a feature model. Then, a subset of the available concepts of the MoCo Template can be selected to form a *starter configuration*. This configuration is then implemented and extended as required for the specific application domain.

In this section, we elaborate on this aspect by presenting a *variability view* on the MoCo Template.

First, we document the base variability in Definition 4.2 using a textual representation. Intuitively, each part of the MoCo Template

---

[7]We refer to these spots as *interpretation points*.

(port, interface, or module) is organized into a tree-structure and a *variability type*[8] is assigned to each of them. This structure mimics a feature model as proposed by the FODA approach [82]. We gave an example of the visual representation of features in Section 2.3.2.

Definition 4.2: MoCo Template Base Variability

[MAN] MoCoTemplate
    [OPT] PFunction
    [OPT] PManage
    [OR] MoCoCode
        [OPT] ICodeState
        [OPT] IAction
        [MAN] ProgramElement
        [OPT] PreparedProgramElement
    [OR] Mediator
        [OPT] IModelState
        [OPT] IInterpret
        [OPT] ICodeState
        [OPT] IAction
        [OPT] DataSynchronizationAdapter
        [OPT] CodeInvocationAdapter
        [OPT] ModelInvocationAdapter
    [OR] MoCoModel
        [OPT] IModelState
        [OPT] IInterpret
        [MAN] Schema
        [OPT] SchemaExtension
        [MAN] Model
        [OPT] ModelHistory
        [MAN] ModelManager
        [OPT] ModelInterpreter

---

[8]"MAN" = mandatory, "OPT" = optional, "OR" = inclusive or, "XOR" = exclusive or

Then, additional *constraints* are given in Definition 4.3.[9]

Definition 4.3: MoCo Template Constraints

A Mediator is needed if there is a MoCoCode and a MoCoModel module.
MoCoModel $\land$ MoCoCode $\Rightarrow$ Mediator

The IAction interface requires a prepared program.
MoCoCode.IAction $\Rightarrow$ PreparedProgramElement

The ICodeState interface requires a prepared program.
MoCoCode.ICodeState $\Rightarrow$ PreparedProgramElement

The IInterpret interface requires a model interpreter.
MoCoModel.IInterpret $\Rightarrow$ ModelInterpreter

The IModelState interface recommends a model history.
MoCoModel.IModelState $\Rightarrow_*$ ModelHistory

The DataSynchronizationAdapter is recommended to realize reflection.
MoCoModel.IModelState $\land$ MoCoCode.ICodeState $\Rightarrow_*$
DataSynchronizationAdapter

The DataSynchronizationAdapter requires the Mediator to provide
additional interfaces.
DataSynchronizationAdapter $\Rightarrow$ Mediator.ICodeState $\land$
Mediator.IModelState

The Mediator's interfaces code-related require the respective MoCoCode
interfaces and the CodeInvocationAdapter.
(Mediator.IAction $\Rightarrow$ MoCoCode.IAction $\land$ CodeInvocationAdapter) $\land$
(Mediator.ICodeState $\Rightarrow$ MoCoCode.ICodeState $\land$
CodeInvocationAdapter)

The Mediator's interfaces model-related require the respective MoCoModel
interfaces and the ModelInvocationAdapter.

---

[9]The "$\Rightarrow$" represents the *logical implication* to be read as "requires" (i.e., a hard
constraint) and "$\Rightarrow_*$" represents a *proposed relationship* (i.e., a soft constraint)
to be read as "recommends".

Definition 4.3: MoCo Template Constraints (cont'd)

(Mediator.IModelState ⇒ MoCoModel.IModelState ∧
ModelInvocationAdapter) ∧ (Mediator.IInterpret ⇒
MoCoModel.IInterpret ∧ ModelInvocationAdapter)

The CodeInvocationAdapter requires at least one of the MoCoCode
interfaces.
CodeInvocationAdapter ⇒ (MoCoCode.ICodeState ∨ MoCoCode.IAction)

The ModelInvocationAdapter requires at least one of the MoCoModel
interfaces.
ModelInvocationAdapter ⇒ (MoCoModel.IModelState ∨
MoCoModel.IInterpret)

If a Mediator exists and a MoCoCode interface exists, it shall be provided by
the Mediator, too.
(MoCoCode.ICodeState ∧ Mediator ⇒ Mediator.ICodeState) ∧
(MoCoCode.IAction ∧ Mediator ⇒ Mediator.IAction)

If a Mediator exists and a MoCoModel interface exists, it shall be provided
by the Mediator, too.
(MoCoModel.IModelState ∧ Mediator ⇒ Mediator.IModelState) ∧
(MoCoModel.IInterpret ∧ Mediator ⇒ Mediator.IInterpret)

On the basis of the documented variability of the MoCo Template, different variants can be derived. To support software engineers who need to instantiate the MoCo Template, a set of *starter configurations*[10] is provided subsequently. They were already introduced in Section 4.2.2. In Table 4.1, the setup for each starter configuration is described. Each of them satisfies different requirements and is specifically suited for a certain field of application as discussed subsequently.

---

[10]The term *starter configuration* denotes a partial configuration, i.e., some variability has been resolved but some choices are still left open.

Table 4.1: MoCo Template Starter Configurations ("X" = included, "-" = excluded, "?" = open choice)

Concept Identifier	Code Only	Primarily Code	Balanced	Primarily Model	Model Only
MoCoTemplate	X	X	X	X	X
PFunction	?	?	?	?	?
PManage	?	?	?	?	?
MoCoCode	X	X	X	X	-
ICodeState	?	X	X	?	-
IAction	?	?	X	X	-
ProgramElement	X	X	X	X	-
PreparedProgramElement	?	X	X	X	-
Mediator	?	X	X	X	?
IModelState	-	X	X	?	?
IInterpret	-	X	X	?	?
ICodeState	?	X	X	X	-
IAction	?	?	X	?	-
DataSynchronizationAdapter	-	?	X	?	-
CodeInvocationAdapter	?	X	X	X	-
ModelInvocationAdapter	-	X	X	?	?
MoCoModel	-	X	X	X	X
IModelState	-	X	X	?	?
IInterpret	-	X	X	?	?
Schema	-	X	X	X	X
SchemaExtension	-	?	?	?	?
Model	-	X	X	X	X
ModelHistory	-	?	?	?	?
ModelManager	-	X	X	X	X
ModelInterpreter	-	X	X	?	?

(C1) Code Only. The *Code Only* starter configuration is the most simple one presented here. It excludes all parts of the MoCo Template that are related to models, so no Mediator is needed. If management functionality is to be provided, it must be realized purely in code. The two ports of the MoCo are not mandatory in any of the starter configurations. Still, it is recommended to introduce the Mediator, if it can be foreseen that a model shall be added later.

Conceptually, any existing software component can be mapped to the *Code Only* starter configuration. If the legacy component requires or exposes interfaces, they can be grouped at the PFunction port.

In case that existing components shall be incorporated into a MoCo-based software system, *Code Only* is a good starting point.

(C2) Primarily Code. The *Primarily Code* starter configuration is probably the most common setup. The MoCoCode is still the primary module which means that most functionality is implemented in a programming language like Java without any immediate connection to models. This code base's behavior is extended at certain points by an executable behavioral model managed by the MoCoModel and data is propagated from MoCoCode to MoCoModel. The IInterpret, ICodeState and IModelState interfaces enable these capabilities.

The managed model fulfills a role very similar to that of code written in a simpler scripting language that is invoked from a host application. Regarding management capabilities, this setup leaves the choice open.

Whenever existing components shall be enriched with models, *Primarily Code* is a good starting point.

(C3) Balanced. The *Balanced* starter configuration is a hybrid setup that combines *Primarily Code* and *Primarily Model*. It is the most complete starter configuration, but also the most complex one.

The MoCoCode is extended by executable models managed by MoCoModel that, in return, may be also linked to functionality existent in MoCoCode. Additionally, data can be synchronized from the model to the code, too, via IModelState, ICodeState and the DataSynchronizationAdapter.

We expect that such – evidently more complex – structures will evolve naturally if designers do not explicitly plan restrictions, i.e., enforce either pure *Primarily Code* or *Primarily Model* configurations.

Whenever more complex MoCos need to be developed with a nearly equal share of responsibility between models and code, then *Balanced* is a good starting point.

(C4) Primarily Model. The *Primarily Model* starter configuration is the conceptual counterpart of *Primarily Code*. The main flow is defined by MoCoModel but it also uses some functionality implemented in MoCoCode which – in this case – is used similar to a library offering reusable actions defined in MoCoCode.

When more flexibility is required and the development process supports more comprehensive and detailed (behavioral) modeling, then *Primarily Model* is a good starting point.

(C5) Model Only. The *Model Only* starter configuration is the most extreme setup presented here, when comparing it to the way software is currently being developed. It excludes MoCoCode explicitly, meaning that MoCoModel contains all the functionality for executing the model by itself.[11] Full model management capabilities can be leveraged whenever needed.

Optionally, modeled functionality can be provided via the PFunction port. Users of the MoCo cannot distinguish between offered functionality that is realized by pure models or – traditionally – by means of code only.

When the purest form of using models for software development and at runtime is desired, *Model Only* is a good starting point.

---

[11] In practice, parts of the MoCoModel module will be still realized using code, but packing these parts into a cohesive unit around the actual model(s) (e.g., in the form of *schema extensions*) highlights the shift in focus from pure code to the use of runtime models.

4.3 MoCo Execution Environment

The *MoCo Execution Environment* (see Definition 4.4) describes the required capabilities of a system for executing MoCos.

Definition 4.4: MoCo Execution Environment

The *MoCo Execution Environment* is a specification of the required functionality of a technical environment for executing instances of the MoCo Template.

Subsequently, the buildup and intended capabilities of this environment are introduced. First, *additional design considerations* are described in which we narrow down the solution space for a possible realization once more. This is followed by the description of an *execution environment architecture* which is split into a structural and a behavioral view.

4.3.1 Additional Design Considerations

We assume that there is a known, existing execution environment for the programming language chosen to be used in MoCos. In this research this basis is the JVM. The major challenge that gives rise to the requirement for extending this execution environment is that the components to be handled can consist of not only code but also of models. Intuitively, there must be an *instruction set* that can not only handle code, but can also handle model-related activities. Examples are the (i) *loading*, (ii) *initialization* and (iii) *execution* of models.

For the programming language Java, the JVM supports exactly such a set of instructions[12], where each single instruction consists of an *opcode* specifying the operation to be performed. Optionally, it is followed by operands with values to be operated upon. In the case of

---

[12]http://docs.oracle.com/javase/specs/jvms/se7/html/jvms-6.html (accessed July 6th, 2014)

the JVM, it operates on *class files* encoded in the binary format for Java code.

This bytecode is an intermediate file format and (for the most part) abstracts away from the actual programming language's syntax. Hence, there are other programming languages that (re)use the JVM as their execution environment, so the JVM can be seen as "just another processor" with its own instruction set. Among the list of JVM languages[13] are: Ada, Basic, COBOL, C, Lua, Prolog, Ruby and Scheme.

Regarding the various supported languages, we may argue that modeling languages could be probably also compiled for execution on the JVM. Hence, the very same bytecode – originally developed for Java – would be the intermediate format. Conceptually, such an approach would encode the semantics of a modeling language by mapping it to the semantics of a known programming language. This is the basis for code generation.

In this thesis, we like to execute models via model interpreters to maintain flexibility at runtime and to skip code generation or any other preparation of the original model data structure before execution.

From these initial thoughts on model and code execution, it already becomes obvious that many different ways for designing a MoCo Execution Environment are possible. As a basis for the design of the *MoCo Execution Environment* to be described here, we considered the following set of options:

(a) An existing raw input format for an execution environment (e.g., Java bytecode) is extended to represent models and the original execution machine is adjusted to support the format extensions.

(b) A process is specified that guides the systematic transformation of models to code representation (e.g., to Java) without any extensions of the target programming language.

---

[13]http://en.wikipedia.org/wiki/List_of_JVM_languages (accessed July 6th, 2014)

(c) An additional execution machine is developed for models only and it cooperates with an existing execution machine for code.

(d) A completely new MoCo Execution Environment is developed that is targeted at executing both the code and the models of any MoCo efficiently and potentially in parallel.

(e) An existing execution environment for code is used without modifications. The focus is to support additionally needed key functionality – especially for encoding models and their semantics – in the form of APIs.

In summary, we decided against the development of a totally new MoCo Execution Environment from scratch and selected alternative (e). The main reason for this choice is that the MoCo-based approach shall support existing technologies. Thus, it is not feasible to introduce a new execution machine. Still, we are aware of the possibility that, for certain application areas and requirements, it may be a better solution (e.g., in terms of execution performance) to introduce an extended or completely new form of execution environment with its own file input format and instruction set. Related research is out of the scope of this thesis, though.

In this thesis, we assume that all code is developed in Java. Hence, the JVM is a major part of the solution. We have already motivated the use of *model interpreters* to encode the semantics of a modeling language and to facilitate flexible change of software behavior at runtime.

$$EE_{moco} := EM_{cLang} + \{Interpeter_{mLang_1}, ..., Interpeter_{mLang_N}\}$$
$$(4.1)$$

In a simplified form, we can say that our intention behind the design of an execution environment EE_{moco} is to choose an existing execution machine EM for a given base programming language $cLang$ and to extend it with a set of interpreters where each one covers one specific modeling language $mLang_i$ ($i >= 1 \land i <= N$), i.e., each interpreter targets a specified meta-model. This is schematically described by Equation 4.1, where the + operator stands for *integration* and "{ }" denotes a *set*. This formula clearly states that no new MoCo Execution Environment is created from scratch. In fact, the existing EM_{cLang} serves as an executor for each $Interpreter_{mLang_i}$, too. Conceptually though, we can say that the resulting execution environment plays the role of an *abstract execution machine*, but without being present as a single physical entity.

In a concrete scenario, where Java is set (as in the rest of this thesis) and *UML activity* models as well as *event-condition-action rule* models are used, the formula would be expressed as in Equation 4.2.

$$EE_{moco} := EM_{java} + \{Interpeter_{activity}, Interpeter_{eca}\} \qquad (4.2)$$

A couple of questions arise immediately from this representation. Mainly, the integration of an existing execution machine with a set of model interpreters must be discussed. A systematic and extendable approach is required where not only a set of model interpreters is integrated once, but additional interpreters can be added and removed on demand. Additionally, it remains an open question if the model interpreters can actually cooperate and, if yes, when and how shall this be realized?

A proposal is given in the subsequent section which focuses on the design of the *execution environment architecture* for MoCos.

4.3.2 Execution Environment Architecture

The *integration* of an existing execution machine (such as the chosen JVM) with a set of interpreters must be done systematically. There must be an *execution environment architecture*, to guide its implementation. This blueprint shall be applicable in many different component-based software development scenarios.

In this section, we describe the design of such an execution environment in terms of a *structural view* and a *behavioral view*.

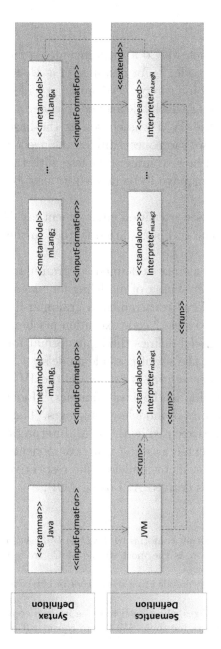

Figure 4.8: High-Level View of the MoCo Execution Environment Architecture

Structural View

Except for the *Code Only* setup, each MoCo always includes some minimum amount of infrastructure code.[14] For instance, if a *Model Only* configuration is used, the model interpreter needs to be provided for executing models. This interpreter will be developed in code.

At this point, we assume that the JVM was chosen as the base execution machine for code. Hence, we can concentrate on the needed mechanisms to execute models and how to integrate these with the JVM. We consider each modeling language to be defined at least by (i) its *syntax* and (ii) its *semantics*.

A high-level overview of the proposed execution environment architecture is sketched in Figure 4.8. The core ideas are described in the following.

- The programming languages' *syntax* is defined by grammars. meta-models define the abstract syntax of modeling languages, optionally together with additional constraints. A grammar defines the input format[15] for the single[16] code execution machine: the JVM. Likewise, a meta-model defines the input format for model interpreters and, hence, the set of possible models.
- The programming language's *semantics* is defined by the JVM that can execute code conforming to the Java grammar. Model interpreters encode the semantics of modeling languages. They are also written in Java and are executed by the JVM. Interpretation algorithms can be implemented as *stand-alone* components, or they can be *weaved* into the meta-model of the respective modeling language, i.e., into its derived API using AOP.

---

[14]By definition, an existing "legacy" component conforms to the *Code Only* setup of the MoCo Template and can be seen as the most simple MoCo from a structural perspective.

[15]This is simplified, as source code is usually compiled to machine code or bytecode, prior to execution.

[16]Mixing in multiple programming languages where each requires its own code execution machine is certainly an interesting topic. We like to consider it as future work, though.

As the designers of modeling languages are free in their choice of syntax, their meta-models may not be necessarily isolated as suggested by Figure 4.8, but indeed, there may be at least conceptual relationships between them. That is, a given modeling language, e.g., $mLang_1$, may be a subset of $mLang_2$ or may share a subset of its meta-model elements. In the context of the UML, one may want to specify the body of a method in a class diagram in terms of an activity diagram, for example, or an action inside of an activity diagram may be linked to a method of a class.

The intended *integration of modeling languages*, which gives rise to such relationships on the abstract syntax level, must be carefully considered. A simple "connection" of meta-model elements on the syntactical level is not sufficient, as the meaning needs to be defined, too. While the syntactical integration of meta-models can be considered a challenge, the semantic integration seems to be even more difficult because the meaning of all possible/desired combinations of interaction between elements of the languages to be integrated needs to be precisely defined. For now, we assume that this is manually specified.

Based on the work on GRAF [3] and early experimental implementations, we established a set of *design rules* (DRs) for engineering model interpreters for the context of MoCos. These are described subsequently.

(DR1) *There is at least one model interpreter for each meta-model that describes executable models:* There can be models that are used as data-containers (e.g., representing requirements statements) and these models do not describe executable behavior. Hence, not every modeling language necessarily needs a model interpreter. In contrast, each behavioral model shall have at least one model interpreter. If desired, multiple implementations can be provided for the same modeling language, of course.

While different variants of a model interpreter may provide the exact same functionality (e.g., with different performance properties), the separate encoding of semantics in a stand-alone interpreter eases the definition of different model semantics for the same modeling language. For instance, one interpreter may execute the modeled behavior, while a second one visualizes the model.

(DR2) *A model interpreter shall be executed in the same technical environment as the code:* Being software components themselves, stand-alone model interpreters can be developed in any language that is capable of interacting with the *host language*, in this case: Java. A minimum amount of interaction is required, because parts of the program shall invoke modeled behavior and vice versa. The overhead of communication effort between model and code (e.g., for type conversion or behavior calls) shall be kept to a minimum.

Even though it may seem feasible to develop the model interpreters in a "more efficient" lower-level language, communication with the other code parts of the MoCo– especially the MoCoCode module – may require more effort, then. Thus, all model interpreters shall be developed in the same base programming language.

(DR3) *A model interpreter can be written to fully encode the semantics of a modeling language:* One direction for developing the single model interpreters is to treat them as black-boxes that are isolated from the rest of the code and especially independent of any specific MoCoCode module that may exist in concrete MoCo instances.

Such a *stand-alone* model interpreter that is part of the MoCo infrastructure and not part of a single component definition can be replaced if an alternative realization is needed. In a single-threaded context, the same model interpreter instance can be possibly reused to execute multiple models belonging to different MoCos.

(DR4) *A model interpreter can use "semantic snippets" that are physically stored with the meta-model:* Another direction for developing the single model interpreters is to represent semantics in the form of actions that are attached to the individual meta-model elements. Such a collection of attached actions can be expressed as a *schema extension*. In this approach, the model interpreter is woven into the meta-model, i.e., into its (generated) API, so each model can execute itself.

(DR5) *An embedded model interpreter can reuse existing programmed actions of a specific MoCo:* An additional direction for developing the single model interpreters is to implement a part of the semantics by reusing code available in a specific MoCo.

More specifically, the model interpreter is still a part of the MoCoModel module, but it uses actions from the MoCoCode. That way, *tight coupling* of the specific MoCo and its model interpreter is achieved. As a result though, reusability is limited unless the model interpreter is exposed via the PFunction port of the owning MoCo.

Behavioral View

In this section, we give a *behavioral view* of the execution environment. The intention is to illustrate the major possible and necessary execution paths from a high-level perspective. The role of the JVM, model interpreters as well as their input models and related components (e.g., MoCos that use the interpreters) are clarified.

As we conceptually think of the whole execution environment as an *abstract execution machine* consisting of the JVM and a set of model interpreters, it seems natural to illustrate its behavior via a statechart as depicted in Figure 4.9.

Subsequently, we describe each state in detail. Note that no detailed states are described and that especially error handling is omitted here, as well. In addition, we focus just on MoCos in a single-threaded scenario. In a more complex system, MoCos will be mixed with

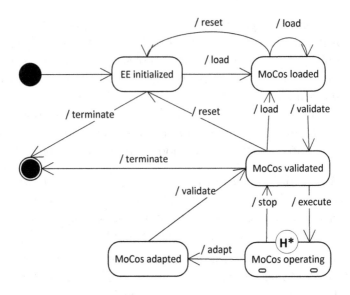

Figure 4.9: High-Level View of the MoCo Execution Environment's
States

existing components that they need to be handled according to the
life-cycle as defined by their component model.

- *EE initialized.* We assume that the execution environment is
  available and instantiated, so execution starts in the **EE initialized** state. It is possible to terminate execution already here.
  The /terminate action can be triggered from within the execution environment or by administrators. In the more common
  case, the loading of MoCos is triggered by the /load action when
  a software system is launched.

- *MoCos loaded:* A set of MoCos is prepared in memory and each
  is accessible by the execution environment when the **MoCos
  loaded** state is reached. Further MoCos can be loaded which
  is expressed by the /load action. Still, there may be issues,

especially regarding the dependencies between MoCos. Once the /validate action is triggered, this state is left.

• *MoCos validated:* Additional (consistency) checks must be carried out to make sure that the composition of loaded MoCos is valid. When this has been done via the /validate action, the MoCos validated state is reached.

In cases where composition of MoCos is statically defined, related checks can be performed offline, i.e., when packaging software prior to distribution. Even now, further MoCos can be loaded. In such a case, the /load action is triggered and the new composition needs to be checked for validity.

Validity can be defined in terms of correct interface usage but also in terms of additional constraints and invariant. These topics are not covered in this thesis and shall be considered in future work.

• *MoCos operating:* At this point, the execution environment is ready to invoke behavior encoded by the MoCos. The /execute action achieves the transition to the MoCos operating state, where the execution environment does its main job: running the (business) logic developed in a mixture of models and code.

Details of this execution are hidden here and only hinted at by the fact that MoCos operating is a *composite state*. This is illustrated in Figure 4.9 by the two additional small circles within the state symbol.

The exact invocation and interplay between the different constituents of the execution environment (e.g., the JVM and – optionally – a set of model interpreters) depends on the chosen configuration of the MoCo Template. Moreover, technical details such as the way in which model interpreters are developed (e.g., stand-alone or weaved) need to be considered. We will discuss some of these details as a part of the reference implementation in Chapter 5 and for the feasibility studies in Chapter 6.

Execution can be interrupted via the /stop action. If desired, execution can be resumed, which is modeled via the *deep history* (H∗) annotation of the MoCos operating composite state. In this case, each MoCo shall be able to recover its own state.

- *MoCos adapted:* During operation, it is possible to make changes to parts of the running software. The /adapt action symbolizes changes that can be made to code (e.g., setting new variable values), but especially to models contained in MoCos (e.g., changing the order of actions in a UML activity model). MoCos need to be validated before they can resume execution.

Besides the explicit documentation of single transitions presented so far, a path of transitions in Figure 4.9 can express more complex logic. For example, besides adaptation via model transformations, it may be needed to replace a component or to load another needed one on demand. Assuming that we are in the operating MoCos state, the following *sequence of actions* enables the "updating" of a component configuration: /stop, /load, /validate, /execute.

4.4 MoCo Service Library

The *MoCo Service Library* (see Definition 4.5) presented here describes a set of operations to support the development of software using MoCos for various use cases.

Definition 4.5: MoCo Service Library

The *MoCo Service Library* is a specification of recommended services to support the development and evolution of MoCo-based software.

Subsequently, we give a specification that needs to be implemented and extended for specific application domains and selected technologies. In this section, a *service* is a logically coherent group of operations related to a specific concern for handling MoCos.

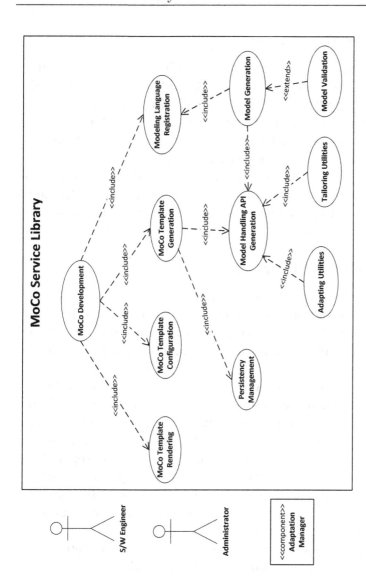

Figure 4.10: Essential Use Cases of the MoCo Service Library

4.4.1 Service Descriptions

A set of services and their dependencies is illustrated in Figure 4.10 in the form of a UML use case diagram. It shall act as a starting point for a more comprehensive library. Each service is described by (i) a *name* that hints at the functionality of the service, (ii) a *description of the capabilities* provided and (iii) a set of *inputs and outputs.*

At this point, no implementation details are given because any realization of this specification depends on a technological basis. The three stakeholders *S/W Engineer*, *Administrator* and *Adaptation Manager* are exemplarily mentioned as service consumers for illustration purposes.

MoCo Template Rendering Service

In order to support the development with MoCos, tool support is required, e.g., in the form of an IDE that can handle the components according to the MoCo concept, independently from the selected component technology. Hence, it is required to visualize the MoCo Template.

Moreover, existing components that have been developed according to the MoCo Template shall be viewable, too. This is realized by the *MoCo Template rendering service.* Only the conceptual elements are shown and the underlying technological details are hidden – this can be achieved based on a systematic mapping of the concepts of the MoCo Template to the elements of the existing component technology.

As components are rather coarse-grained, it seems feasible to visualize them and their dependencies for human inspection, communication, documentation, administration and more.

- *Inputs:* A model representation of the MoCo Template.
- *Outputs:* A rendered image or interactive view.

MoCo Template Configuration Service

For creating components that conform to the specification of the MoCo Template, it is desirable to have a tool that supports the *configuration* of the template. During this process, the software engineer can select the parts of the template that are needed and may exclude the rest. Dependencies that exist logically – e.g., between different modules – are resolved automatically.

The *MoCo Template configuration service* is especially intended to be used when setting up new components. Additionally, the very same mechanisms shall be applicable for reconfiguring existing MoCos.

Based on the properly selected elements of the template, it needs to be "materialized", i.e., each element needs to be created by using the selected target component technology. Obviously, the chosen programming language, modeling technology, component technology and the execution environment have an impact on related implementation activities.

- *Inputs:* A model representation of the MoCo Template.
- *Outputs:* A tailored model representation of the MoCo Template configuration.

MoCo Template Generation Service

The *MoCo Template generation service* allows the generation of a concrete MoCo using a specified component technology. That is, for instance, an OSGi bundle that fulfills certain additional conventions for naming and folder structures.

- *Inputs:* A MoCo Template configuration.
- *Outputs:* A concrete component-technology-specific project.

Persistency Management Service

Saving the state of a component and storing it on disk or in some other permanent storage is a common feature of component technology such as JavaBeans. Additionally, programming languages often provide persistency APIs; in the concrete case of Java there are methods for serializing (saving) and deserializing (loading) objects.

In the case of MoCos, the same functionality shall be used but with the additional requirement that each operation shall also take the potentially encapsulated runtime model(s) into account. This needs to be transparent, i.e., hidden, to the software engineers, though. The model-specific functionality is accessible for experts if required. All of this functionality is covered by the *persistency management service*.

- *Inputs:* Handles to MoCos (artifacts or runtime objects). Language-specific file-writing API.
- *Outputs:* Loaded or saved MoCos.

Administration Service

Observing the software's state and behavior is a common task for server administrators as well as software engineers who debug systems to find bugs. Additionally, SAS is observed by administrators as well as by software – the adaptation managers – to adjust the system in response to sensed changes, e.g., in the operating environment.

Finally, software needs to be observed, even when it has not yet been deployed. For example, a list of existing features and their implementation (most likely in the form of components) needs to be accessible in a systematic manner, e.g., for inspection by software engineers and architects.

The *administration service* is intended to provide these capabilities in the context of MID, where it is an essential constituent of the MoCo Execution Environment to provide information about the system's (potentially past) states.

- *Inputs:* Handles to MoCos (artifacts or runtime objects).
- *Outputs:* Views on MoCos and manipulated MoCos.

Adapting Utility Service

For manipulating the state or behavior of a MoCo at runtime, a set of operations is offered that can be used independently from the modeling languages used within each MoCo. This *adapting utility service* provides a set of (higher-level) operations for preparing and instrumenting (existing) code as needed to establish the interfaces for communication with the Mediator module. Additionally, operations for manipulating MoCos at runtime are provided. The technical basis consists of the schema-specific APIs for model manipulation, the programming language's specific meta-programming API and the MoCo-specific functionality offered via its PManage port.

- *Inputs:* Handles to MoCo runtime objects.
- *Outputs:* Instrumented and modified MoCo runtime objects.

Tailoring Utility Service

In contrast to adapting, tailoring is performed offline and usually on the level of artifacts and not on non-persistent objects in memory.[17] Hence, the *tailoring utility service* provides a set of (higher-level) operations for manipulating the persistent artifact-representation of MoCos. Especially CRUD operations on all elements of the MoCo Template are desirable.

- *Inputs:* Handles to MoCos artifacts.
- *Outputs:* Modified MoCo artifacts (copies).

Model Generation Service

In cases where code is the primary artifact in a component but models shall be used to extend its functionality, it is often desirable to extract some information that is already available in code and to represent it at the model-level such that this data can be queried, transformed and maybe even interpreted. The *model generation service* provides functionality to derive a model from annotated source code. This can be seen as a utility service for realizing some form of *reflection*.[18]

- *Inputs:* Annotated source code and a meta-model.
- *Outputs:* An initial model instance.

---

[17]From a technological point of view, the methods needed to make changes to a file are different than object manipulation: e.g., a file is parsed and can be then edited and saved; a running program needs to be instrumented or accessed via an API.

[18]We followed this approach in GRAF [3] for the special case of deriving activity diagrams from existing methods in code.

Modeling Language Registration Service

When models become first class entities, it is necessary to be able to query the available modeling languages, receive information about their properties, capabilities and intended use cases. The *modeling language registration service* offers exactly such meta-data on accessible modeling languages in a centralized fashion. This registry can be used during development, e.g., from within an IDE, but it can be also used at runtime by administrators or adaptation managers.

- *Inputs:* Meta-models, modeling language names and identifiers.
- *Outputs:* Modeling language meta-data.

Model Handling API Generation Service

For realizing the interplay between models and code it is required to *bridge* [145] the involved technological spaces in some form. A traditional way is to offer an API that can handle models. It can be generated in a similar way for a given meta-model, which is the core functionality of the *model handling API generator service*. This service can be integrated into the development environment and the derivation activity for obtaining the needed API for each meta-model is fully automated.

- *Inputs:* A meta-model.
- *Outputs:* A model handling API.

Model Validation Service

Given that models in MID become an equal partner of code in realizing functionality in software, their correctness becomes even more critical. Models need to be checked for conformance to their meta-models and optionally available constraints, e.g., encoded as logical expressions, need to be evaluated whenever a model has changed.

This requirement is not "new" by any means. All model-driven approaches require at least the syntactic correctness of their models at the time these are used. Nevertheless, when using models at runtime, the checking needs to happen on demand, because models change over time. In addition to testing executable models, all connected code elements (such as those fragments encoding actions in an activity model) may need to be inspected, as well.

The *model validation service* covers fundamental operations for checking the conformance of models to their meta-models as a starting point for more complex validation processes. Performance w.r.t. execution time is a major requirement.

- *Inputs:* A meta-model and at least one model.
- *Outputs:* True or false and a list of warnings and errors associated to meta-model elements.

4.5 Summary

In this chapter, we designed the MoCo concept comprising: (i) a *MoCo template*, (ii) a *MoCo execution environment* and (iii) a *MoCo service library*. The last two items form the MoCo Infrastructure.

This design does can be achieved in different ways using available base technology. The motivation is to allow the realization of MoCo-based software using any modern component model. The only prerequisites are that the technology of choice supports the capabilities for (i) *component definition* (encapsulation), (ii) *interface definition* (ideally: required and provided) and (iii) *encapsulation* of behavior and data. Except for the *Code Only* setup of a MoCo, a technological space for model creation and manipulation is needed, too.

In terms of execution behavior, we focused on the description of an excerpt of scenarios that cover the different types of model interpreters. Various ways for encoding semantics of a (modeling) language have been proposed in related work. Here, we encode the semantics of models in terms of algorithms that find paths through the model structure, triggering the invocation of operations on the way. Hence, the semantics of models in MoCos is assumed to be *aligned* with the modeling language's syntax.

Finally, we proposed an initial set of services to support the development of MoCo-based software systems.

Part III

Proof of Concept

5 Reference Implementation

In this chapter, a *reference implementation* of the MoCo concept is introduced. The description is subdivided into (i) experiences made with *experimental prototyping* w.r.t. using existing Java component technology and (ii) the realization of a *MoCo Core API* that supports engineering software components according to the MoCo Template as well as a first implementation of some of the proposed utility services.

The goal of this chapter is to describe *one* possible implementation of the component realization concept for a defined set of technologies. It is assumed that the reader is familiar with the Java programming language, its common APIs and libraries. Furthermore, basics of the used component models need to be known. Particular technical details are given or are referenced where relevant. The interested reader may check the latest official documentation for each single technology.

The remainder of this chapter is structured as follows. First, the results of *exploratory prototyping* with existing component technologies is described. That followed, the *MoCo Core API* (a Java API that supports the MoCo concept) is introduced along the process of building an example MoCo. This chapter ends with a *summary*.

5.1 Explorative Prototyping

The main contribution of this thesis is a *realization concept* for model-integrating software components. In order to get a realistic feeling for its practicability, a first implementation shall be realized. This requires to choose a base component technology. We start off by exploring a couple of popular ones for the Java programming language. These are namely: (i) *JavaBeans* [64], (ii) *Enterprise JavaBeans (EJB) [139]*, (iii) *OSGi* [134].

Ideally, the MoCo Template presented in Chapter 4 shall be realizable in any existing component technology. The intention here is to exemplarily inspect the properties of existing approaches for developing components in Java to gain confidence that the MoCo Template is independent of nuances of implementation, e.g., related to middleware libraries, application servers and technology-specific conventions.

Subsequently, each component technology is described in terms of a brief introduction, followed by a realization description and a list of observations made during early prototyping. We discuss *lessons learned* at the end of this section in a distilled form. They will influence the design and development of the MoCo Core API that is described thereafter in Section 5.2.

Disclaimer

The author is not an industry-level expert in the following technologies. There may be better ways to implement components in each technology, depending on the concrete version of the component technology, as well as depending on vendor-specific features, e.g., those of the execution environment such as application servers. The goal is to illustrate the systematic mapping of concepts of the MoCo Template to actual implementation elements.

5.1.1 Developing MoCos Using JavaBeans

JavaBeans – or *beans* for short – are Java classes that follow certain rules in the form of naming conventions for fields and methods as well as for the set of interfaces that need to be implemented by each class. An example is the Serializable[1] marker interface. Communication between JavaBeans is realized via event objects that are sent between an observed JavaBean and a set of listening JavaBeans.

---

[1]http://docs.oracle.com/javase/7/docs/api/java/io/Serializable.html (accessed July 9th, 2014)

Table 5.1: Mapping of MoCo Elements to JavaBeans Technology

MoCo Element	EJB Realization
MoCo	Each MoCo is a bean.
Module	Each module is a bean.
Part	Each part is represented by a simple Java class (not necessarily a bean).
Port	Each port is a simple Java interface that is implemented by the MoCo bean.
Interface	Each interface between modules is realized by events and event listeners. Providers keep a list of listeners which receive event objects through predefined methods.

Realization Description

JavaBeans were initially designed to be composed with visual *builder tools* with only minor – or even no – programming required. As the most widely known user of this component technology is Swing (an API for building graphical user interfaces), existing builder tools like the one provided as a part of the NetBeans IDE[2] are aimed at the creation of graphical user interfaces. Components that do not have a visual appearance can be still edited via property editors but there is no visual representation for the actual bean and its dependencies to other components.

The nature of this component technology led to an initial mapping of all base concepts from the MoCo Template to concrete JavaBeans elements as described in Table 5.1. It must be noted that this is not the only possible solution.

The realization of a MoCo seems straight forward using plain Java-Beans as suggested by the presented mapping rules. Each MoCo is a JavaBean and it is packed and distributed in the form of a JAR file,

---

[2]`https://netbeans.org/` (accessed July 6th, 2014)

together with its further constituents. The bean acts like a *facade* [60] that controls access to the MoCoCode, Mediator and MoCoModel modules, which are also JavaBeans. The MoCo bean stores private references to them and it is responsible for their instantiation and destruction.

The parts within modules can be either JavaBeans or simple Java classes that do not match the requirements of a component in the chosen component technology. The assumption is that any software component technology for Java can make use of simple Java classes in some way. This allows to build a widely reusable MoCo Core API that is (mostly) independent of a target component technology and its conventions.

The PFunction and the PManage ports are realized as plain Java interfaces. Therefore, only provided interfaces can be represented explicitly. The two interfaces are then implemented by the MoCo bean. Users of a MoCo shall not use this MoCo bean type directly. Instead, its interface types shall be used to point to a MoCo. This convention is not a technical necessity but it achieves the clean separation of contract and implementation.

The connections between a MoCo's modules can be realized via events and event listeners. That way, the composition approach for connecting modules within the MoCo matches the way of how communication between JavaBeans is intended to work in general. Such a design allows the use of builder tools to orchestrate the internals of a MoCo, as well. Nevertheless, this is more complicated than direct access using Java references. In practice, one may decide to hard-wire the modules for performance reasons, especially in cases where loose coupling between a MoCo's modules is less relevant.

Observations

During our first attempts to map the MoCo Template to JavaBeans technology, a couple of observations were made. We list them with a brief description. Some of these points are more general and do also

apply to classic application scenarios of the component technology
where no MoCos are used.

- *Interface realization with JavaBeans and events can be tedious:*
  JavaBeans communication is based on the concepts of event
  listeners and event objects. This requires the initial creation
  of appropriate listener interfaces, their implementation by the
  actual bean classes as well as the creation of adequate event
  types to hold the data to be transferred. Especially during
  initial programming steps, this seems tedious and may take
  some time to understand. Events need to be used for the
  external interfaces of the MoCo so it can be connected seamlessly
  with existing beans. Additionally, using the same mechanisms
  for communication *within* the MoCo, i.e., between the three
  modules, requires extra effort to conform to JavaBeans design
  rules.

- *The required persistency of JavaBeans does not come for free:*
  JavaBeans need to implement the Serializable interface or must
  provide serialization and deserialization in a custom way using
  the Externalizable[3] interface. For simple classes with primitive
  properties, the marker interface is sufficient. For the case of
  MoCos, this can become more complex when using models
  because they need to be "serializable", too. Usually, this should
  not be a problem, though, as modeling technologies provide
  mechanisms for persisting models.

- *Realization of ports as individual beans is not feasible:* An intu-
  itive approach to realize the ports of a MoCo using JavaBeans is
  to implement one bean for each port and to store them as read-
  only properties of the actual MoCo bean. From a programmer's
  perspective, the solution is fine, because access to each port and
  its provided services can be gained easily and their separation
  is done clearly, e.g., moco.getFuntionPort().someService().

---

[3]http://docs.oracle.com/javase/7/docs/api/java/io/Externalizable.
html (accessed July 9th, 2014)

The downside of this approach becomes clear, once the bean shall be used in a builder tool, for instance as provided by the NetBeans IDE. The provided "connection mode" – where developers can select a bean as an event source and a second one as a target – does only support the generation of JavaBeans boilerplate code for accessing methods of properties. Only the property representing the port can be accessed in the wizard, but none of its methods. Hence, the plugging mechanism of an IDE like NetBeans cannot be used without having to adjust the IDE.

JavaBeans technology was proposed in the late 90s (version 1.0 of the specification was published by SUN in 1996) so it is "pretty old" from a computer science perspective. During our first steps using the NetBeans IDE and its JavaBeans wizards, it became obvious that the choice of component technology has a significant impact on which parts of the MoCo concept can be easily implemented and which not. This is a trivial finding, but it should certainly not be ignored as it can have an impact on applicability.

5.1.2 Developing MoCos Using Enterprise JavaBeans

Enterprise JavaBeans are server-sided components that are developed in Java and are part of the broader Java EE technology for developing complex, distributed, secure and often web-based enterprise applications.

The EJB specification is currently available in version 3.2 [139]. Especially revision 3.0 [35] simplified the EJB architecture as its predecessors were complex, e.g., most configuration steps required the tedious creation of XML files. Most of the EJB setup can be now done via Java annotations and dependencies are injected, e.g., at deployment time. EJBs hold business logic (back ends) while other parts of Java EE are aimed at developing user interfaces (front ends).

Table 5.2: Mapping of MoCo Elements to EJB Technology

MoCo Element	EJB Realization
MoCo	Each MoCo is a session bean.
Module	Each module is a session bean.
Part	Each part is represented by a simple Java class, not necessarily a session bean.
Port	Each port is a remote EJB business interface that is implemented by MoCo.
Interface	Each interface between modules is realized as a remote business interface of the session bean and usage is implemented via EJB dependency injection.

Realization Description

Similar to beans in JavaBeans, collections of enterprise beans – especially session beans – are stored in JAR files when using Enterprise JavaBeans to develop software components. Since EJB technology was developed for use in distributed systems, it must be decided whether the component shall be accessible remotely (i.e., from other JVMs or applications) or just locally (i.e., from within the same application context).

As this component technology is by far more complex than simple JavaBeans, there are many different ways for realizing the MoCo concept. One possible mapping of the conceptual elements to the concrete Enterprise JavaBeans elements is described in Table 5.2.

The actual component is deployed as a JAR file and contains the MoCo session bean representing the MoCo to component users as a black-box. The session bean acts like a *facade* [60] for accessing the encapsulated modules. Session beans can be stateful, stateless or singleton depending on needed properties.

The MoCo Template is independent of these technology-specific concepts and software engineers need to chose the appropriate EJB annotation for their session bean on a case-by-case basis. Users of a MoCo communicate with the implementation only indirectly, i.e., via a *proxy* [60] that is automatically created and managed by the application server.

The MoCo modules are also session beans that are deployed within the same JAR file and may be hidden from external users by using the @Local annotation.

Assuming a pure EJB application context, all parts can be also session beans but most likely they will be plain classes that can be reused within any Java-based component technology. In that case, parts can be provided by other JARs files (libraries) and will be imported by the using MoCo.

The ports are represented by remote EJB business interfaces, i.e., Java interfaces that carry the @Remote annotation. Users need to get an instance of the MoCo session bean and can then cast the object to one of the port types. Prior to EJB 3.x, only one business interface was allowed for each session bean. When using such older EJB versions, the two conceptual ports of a MoCo need to be represented by a *single* business interface where the methods follow a naming convention to distinguish them, e.g., via "func" and "man" prefixes.

Each module session bean implements a set of *business interfaces*. A business interface is a standard Java interface and there is one per conceptual interface. These business interfaces shall be mostly local, i.e., the Java interfaces carry the @Local annotation, to increase performance for access within a MoCo. In practice, there may be reasons to mix in some @Remote business interfaces, as well. Please refer to the EJB specification [35] and web resources for best practices and further technical details.

Valid references to implementations of the module of each MoCo are set at deployment time via EJB's dependency injection mechanism. Technical details, like choosing between Remote Method Invocation (RMI) or direct access via a reference, are mostly hidden from software engineers. Depending on the used application server and setup of the packaged enterprise beans, simple Java references may be created instead of RMI calls to avoid the overhead of serialization and deserialization of transmitted data passed "by value".

In summary, access to modules always looks and feels identical to using a plain Java reference. Due to such details – and these are only scratching the surface of the complex Java EE world – we feel that it is difficult to define the single "right" solution for encoding MoCos. This is a natural side-effect of component models that are flexible and offer a multitude of choices for achieving the same goal.

Observations

During our first attempts to map the MoCo Template to Enterprise JavaBeans and the GlassFish[4] application server, a couple of observations were made. We list them with a brief description. Some statements may vary depending on the chosen application server implementation and the EJB version.

- *Java EE supports many tuning and configuration parameters that are mostly independent of the MoCo concept:* Building an enterprise application today means to construct a distributed, multi-tier system.

  Java EE is a full platform for developing such systems and enterprise beans are only a small part of it. Still, one can notice the complexity of the architecture in the number of possible ways of packing enterprise beans, as well as for configuring them. The application server adds further complexity.

  Even though these details are absolutely relevant when building a reusable component that fits perfectly into a specific enterprise architecture landscape, the introduced MoCo concept does not depend on them – which is positive from a theoretical point of view. Practically speaking though, this freedom of choice leaves much room for interpretation. We believe that *development*

---

[4]`https://glassfish.java.net/` (accessed July 9th, 2014)

guidelines need to be established to complement the MoCo concept, in the long run.

- *Basic component management functionality is already supported by the application server:* In contrast to more simple component technology such as the introduced JavaBeans, all session beans in Enterprise JavaBeans have a *managed life-cycle* with a set of predefined states. The application server is responsible for ensuring a proper life-cycle walkthrough. Moreover, developer can use hooks to place custom code (annotated methods) to be executed before or after state transitions.

  In addition to the deployment of new components and the removal or updating of existing ones during operation, enterprise beans can be also accessed via a control panel that is usually realized in the form of a web-interface for administrators. This user interface may need to be extended to support fine-grained and automated adaptation as well as support for model-specific operations and those offered by the PFunction port of MoCos.

- *Annotations and container services ease component development significantly:* From version 1.0 to the recent 3.x revisions, enterprise beans have become steadily more complex under the hood, but at the same time, simpler to use in common application scenarios. The most obvious example is the removal of specific framework interfaces to be implemented and the additional XML configuration files. Mostly, enterprise beans are instrumented at deployment time, i.e., dependencies are injected and the container hides most of the boilerplate code. Apparently, developers still need to understand a lot of the "magic", especially for debugging.

Enterprise JavaBeans were designed for a wide range of business applications which usually share a *multi-tier architecture*. The Java EE platform and enterprise beans support a multitude of functionality to ease the engineering of such complex distributed systems, including the simplification of database-access via @Entitiy beans.

Realizing MoCos in Java EE via enterprise beans can be done in many ways. Essentially though, the component technology offers the means for encapsulation, for realizing interfaces and for inter-component communication in general. Other capabilities shall be provided by a *MoCo Core API* which supports building the three possible modules of a MoCo.

5.1.3 Developing MoCos Using OSGi

OSGi is the specification of a *dynamic component model* for the Java programming language. Initially started in 1998 and intended for the home automation market, OSGi has become a mature basis for developing any kind of software in Java. Especially the open-source community has adopted OSGi; a good example is the Eclipse IDE.

The OSGi Alliance claims that *"the OSGi programming model realizes the promise of component-based systems"* [136]. It is noteworthy that there are two specifications: (i) *OSGi Core* [134] and (ii) *OSGi Enterprise* [135].

There are various implementations of these two specifications. While Equinox[5] provides a reference implementation of *OSGi Core*, *OSGi Enterprise* is implemented by a mixture of OSGi-internal implementations and parts of open-source projects. It seems that only members of the OSGi Alliance are granted access to packaged reference implementations of the enterprise specification. Therefore, if not stated differently, we refer to *OSGi Core* in the following.

The OSGi framework is structured into layers, whereof the "module layer" is the most critical one in our application context. It enforces the OSGi modularity concepts by *restricting the global type visibility* of Java. OSGi defines its own concepts for modularity centered around *bundles* that import and export packages and, hence, the contained types. In its purest form, OSGi controls visibility at the granularity-level of packages.

Additionally, there is the notion of a *service* that allows more fine-grained control of what functionality exactly to be required or

---

[5]`http://www.eclipse.org/equinox/` (accessed July 6th, 2014)

exposed by a bundle. By splitting the *service definition* from its
actual implementation (a.k.a. *service provider*) components do only
depend on the consumed interface and not on a specific package or
even bundle version. Services are stored in (and are retrieved from) an
OSGi-specific *service registry* that manages the set of service providers.

In summary, "plain" OSGi bundles are JAR files that have a managed life cycle and their dependencies are managed on the package
level. Such bundles can be thought of as libraries of code. OSGi
services are also deployed as bundles but their dependencies are based
on concrete interfaces represented by Java interface types. Such bundles can be thought of as more encapsulated components with clearly
defined sets of required and provided interfaces.

Realization Description

Similar to the case of EJBs, representing a MoCo in OSGi can be done
in various ways. One possible mapping of the conceptual elements to
the concrete OSGi elements is given in Table 5.3.

We recommend to encode the complete MoCo as an OSGi service
to make provided and required interfaces explicit. In order to split
the service definition from its implementation, two bundles are needed
per MoCo: one to store the service definition – an encoding of the
PFunction and PManage ports – as a set of Java interfaces and
one to store their actual implementation. In practice, this split is
not mandatory, though. A service can be registered under several
interfaces.

Because OSGi does not support composite bundles at the time of
writing this thesis[6], we decided to map modules to packages within
the service provider. The main reason is to keep the number of

---

[6]There was an early draft of how to support *composite bundles* [133] but they
are no longer part of the OSGi specification. According to bug 345790 in the
Equinox project's issue tracker (https://bugs.eclipse.org/bugs/show_bug.
cgi?id=345790 – accessed July 9th, 2014), an implementation was available
in Equinox 3.5 but this "provisional API" was rejected by the OSGi Alliance.
Framework hooks shall be used to control bundle visibility, instead.

Table 5.3: Mapping of MoCo Elements to OSGi Technology

MoCo Element	OSGi Realization
MoCo	Each MoCo is an OSGi service.
Module	Each module is a package in the OSGi service provider bundle.
Part	Each part is a type or a reference to an OSGi service.
Port	Each port is represented by a package in an OSGi service definition bundle.
Interface	Each interface is realized as a plain Java interface.

bundles for a MoCo small and to keep the internal structure of a MoCo comprehensible.

Parts are Java classes or references to types that may even reside in other bundles, e.g., in non-MoCo components. It may be feasible to reference external services, too.

Similar to Enterprise JavaBeans, it is possible that one service provider implements several services. The ports of a MoCo can be represented by either different packages within a single service definition bundle, or by a single bundle for each port. The service provider bundle implements the interfaces stored in these service definition bundles. To reduce structural complexity, we propose to have a single bundle for service definition and to use packages within this bundle for organizing sets of port interfaces.

In OSGi, all kinds of interfaces are encoded as Java interfaces. Especially each service definition is represented by a plain Java interface.

Observations

During our first attempts to map the MoCo Template to OSGi based on Equinox, a couple of observations were made. We list them with a brief description subsequently.

- *Physical unit representation is not unique:* Simple bundles manage type visibility on the level of packages and that they offer sets of types to be instantiated and used by others [134].

  Services support more control over dependencies in terms of service interfaces that are provided or required by a service. Technically speaking, a service is a plain old Java object that is declared and instantiated within a bundle. The service is registered with the *OSGi service registry* that can be queried for *service providers* implementing a certain *service definition*. Details such as a version number or even custom service properties can be added to the request, too.

  Hence, a service seems the right way to implement MoCos and its constituents such as modules and parts. It is possible to realize multiple services in one bundle, so it would be still possible to map each module to one service and to keep the complexity in terms of the number of bundles at a minimum. Still, by registering a module as a service, it will become available to other bundles via the OSGi service registry by default. According to our solution concept though, modules are placed inside of a MoCo and shall not be accessible directly. Hence, we make use of packages to represent modules that can be easily hidden.

  Depending on the concrete area of application, a different setup may be feasible, though. For instance, if modules shall be reusable services, there are ways to implement *service hooks* that control their the visibility, but this requires a deeper understanding of the OSGi framework and involves additional development effort.

- *Hooks and management agents can support the extension of an OSGi framework to MoCos:* The OSGi specification foresees *hooks* as an extension mechanism for the framework. For example, there are hooks that can be used to add custom code when a bundle is installed, gets activated or generally changes its state. The visibility of services can be influenced manually using similar hooks to simulate composite bundles, as well.

  At this point, we assume that using these *framework extensions*, it will be possible to add functionality such as the loading of models to existing OSGi bundles for a more convenient handling of MoCos. Moreover, *management agents* such as the Equinox console can be extended with custom commands and we envision that certain MoCo utility services can be realized as such.

The OSGi specification defines a modularity concept for Java that is based on cutting global type visibility and on controlling the visibility of types by its own runtime environment. This environment supports the dynamic installing, starting, stopping and updating of bundles as well as the management of multiple bundle versions and their dependencies. A service registry supports the publishing of Java objects as services that can be retrieved utilizing service definitions in the form of Java interfaces (in fact, all class types are accepted).

Due to its dynamic nature, OSGi has become the basis for modern Java enterprise servers, but this technology can be also used standalone and in other application domains like embedded systems. Various implementations of the standard can be used for different application scenarios such as enterprise software or embedded systems.

As the goal of here is to illustrate the feasibility of the MoCo approach to building software using runtime models for flexible systems, we believe that it is reasonable to use and extend the already mature and well-established OSGi bundles and their runtime environment.

5.1.4 Lessons Learned

Up to now, we discussed possible ways to use existing component technologies for realizing the MoCo Template. In the following, we summarize some of our observations in a more generalized form of *lessons learned*. Even though some of them seem more than obvious, we like to document them here explicitly. The following list is not ordered.

L1) *Limitations are already dictated by the chosen component model and technology:* Only a small set of capabilities is required to realize the structure of a MoCo. Especially the externally visible structure, e.g., the two ports and the actual component, is mostly simple to achieve because each component technology defines a way for interface declaration and definition.

Regarding the internal structure, different approaches may be followed, depending on the non-functional properties to be achieved. For example, one may use the same component structure to encapsulate modules and parts, too, but this approach is not always technically possible and also adds too much complexity for a single MoCo. In cases where reuse of these modules is not required and additional overhead is associated with the realization of the internal interfaces for communication between the modules, a more simple (but not necessarily hard-coded) approach is recommended.

Regarding non-functional properties like variability and adaptivity, the chosen component technology can have a deep impact. Obviously, it is a major advantage if code can be reloaded and updated at runtime (e.g., as possible with OSGi) or if there is already a container technology that manages the life-cycle of components and supports their inspection via a web-interface (e.g., as possible with EJB). While some mechanisms for managing variability and adaptivity are partially supported, they need to be extended with additional utility services for the easy handling of MoCos and their associated models.

L2) *Communication approach between modules must be chosen carefully:* Since each chosen component technology defines a precise way of expressing interfaces, it seems obvious to follow the same patterns for realizing the modules and parts, too. The expected effect would be that all units are wired in the same way, independent of their granularity or position in the component containment hierarchy. Reuse is facilitated and the software is developed in a uniform way.

However, we have experienced that, as long as no true additive/-composite component concept is supported by the component technology, this approach is not feasible. Workarounds lead to overly complex solutions. Therefore, direct connections are established using plain Java references where possible and only the outer "shell" of a MoCo is represented in a component technology conforming way.

L3) *Component management cannot be done via a port only:* The MoCo Template proposes PManage, a port for exposing all kinds of management facilities for maintaining the component. Assuming that the component model of choice is slightly more mature than JavaBeans, an execution environment is usually defined that manages components throughout their lifecycle. It seems reasonable that low-level management functionality that is technology-depending shall be accessed via mechanisms specific to the chosen component model and technology.

All application-specific management tasks shall be accessible via PManage. These may even include the checking of additional constraints or utility services. MoCo designers may still find a clean way to offer technology-specific management functionality through a management port, of course.

L4) *Models at runtime can (partially) compensate for a lack of dynamism in a component model:* Some component models are more flexible than others w.r.t. their support for changes during deployment and at runtime. While OSGi, for instance, explicitly allows and supports dynamic change, other component models such as JavaBeans are static. Depending on the component model of choice, architects and component designers may like to place different subsets of the MoCo's functionality in either the MoCoCode or in the MoCoModel module.

If the bounds of functional units at which adapting or tailoring is required can be aligned with reasonably coarse-grained code elements – namely classes – and the component model supports the reloading or updating of them at runtime, then such functionality may be kept in MoCoCode. Otherwise, if the component model is rather static, then variable or adaptable functionality shall be realized within MoCoModel.

Existing modern component technology can facilitate the development of MoCos, but even older approaches seem feasible if parts of the application logic is suited to be represented by executable models. Depending on the concrete implementation and available tools, performance and ease of development will be two key decision factors.

L5) *The MoCo Core API shall be realized as simple as possible:* One may argue that, to unleash the full potential of each concrete component technology, a custom implementation of the MoCo Template for each technology is suited best. Obviously, an implementation of the MoCo concept for one specific component technology can leverage all of its specific capabilities.

Such a solution will be hard to reuse in the context of another component model, though, due to its dependencies to libraries, a certain runtime environment, assumptions and conventions. Thus, we propose to split the implementation the MoCo concept into (i) a reusable MoCo Core API and (ii) an optional and tight integration with an existing component technology.

L6) *The MoCo Template shall communicate an idea rather than an inviolable structure:* Having experienced the different possible ways for expressing the concepts of the MoCo Template – even for just three existing component models – it is obvious that the specification of the template must leave some room for creative application. Obviously, a specification of the complete MoCo concept needs to be as precise as possible. Still, there must remain room for different implementation approaches.

Software architects shall read the MoCo concept as a description of a structure and capabilities to be achieved. It is enhanced with guidelines on the most essential structural decisions which are expressed by means of a template. The idea of handling models and code equally within a modular system of software units is the essential goal to be achieved.

Summing up, it seems that existing component technology in Java can be used to represent the structure of MoCos as it does only require basic capabilities such as encapsulation and clean interfaces. The exact encoding depends on the capabilities and conventions for the selected component technology. Here, we select OSGi.

In terms of realizing MoCos as reusable black-boxes with clearly defined interfaces, we did not observe severe limitations, which is only logical because the required capabilities are central to any existing component models. When it comes to the two non-functional properties we investigate in this thesis, i.e., variability and adaptivity, differences become more obvious.

Especially the needed tailoring steps such as adding or removing elements from components during the early build phases are not explicitly part of the inspected component specifications. Only minor changes such as the setting of attributes or the initial configuration via constructor operations are usually discussed. Even in cases where code generation is performed from a more abstract component base description, tailoring steps are rarely discussed (except for works on SPLs).

Regarding adaptivity and the needed adapting steps, the picture is slightly different. Especially modern dynamic component models like OSGi support the loading of new components at runtime and existing ones can be updated. These mechanisms are rather coarse-grained, though. When changing only a small part of the internals, the whole component needs to be replaced. Adaptation is limited to the bounds of components. This suits many application scenarios in practice, though.

To ensure that the MoCo concept is a practical and enhancing addition to existing component-based approaches, variability and adaptivity (within MoCos) are in the focus of this component realization concept.

5.2 MoCo Core API

In this section, we describe the *MoCo Core API* by using it to build a sample project step-by-step. The MoCo Core API is an API we developed in Java that supports creating MoCos with OSGi technology according to the MoCo Template as introduced in Chapter 4.

At the time of writing this thesis, the MoCo Execution Environment consists of the JVM and a set of application-specific model interpreters. Currently, the MoCo Service Library is only partially covered by the MoCo Core API, JGraLab and by application-specific functionality. Elegant tool support and a complete and generic implementation of all services is subject to future work.

The running example is a component called HelloWorldPrinter that prints the familiar "Hello World!" string to the console and supports some basic management operations, as well. It is not our intention to show a realistic component but to demonstrate how to use some of the commonly used features offered by the MoCo Core API. The sample component is illustrated in Figure 5.1 in the concrete syntax of UML component diagrams.

HelloWorldPrinter has a PFunction and a PManage port; each with a single interface. Remember, that there may be an arbitrary number of interfaces at each port, though. PFunction provides the IPrint interface for printing a welcome message. Furthermore, PManage provides the ITextAccess interface for accessing the carried model. It allows counting the number of stored sentences (this is a *model*

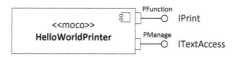

Figure 5.1: Simple HelloWorldPrinter MoCo

query) and provides a method for adapting the welcome message from "Hello World!" to "Good Morning World!" (this is a *model transformation*). In the following, we describe the essential steps of developing this sample component using models and code.

First, the project structure for the MoCo is described. Then, each interface of the MoCo is defined. Based on these interfaces, the mediator is implemented. Afterwards, the interfaces are implemented using code and a model. The MoCo is prepared for use by adding code for registering the MoCo with the OSGi service registry. Then, invoking the provided interface methods from another OSGi bundle is demonstrated and the printed output is shown. Finally, the steps for realizing internal interfaces (between MoCoCode and MoCoModel) are described, too.

> **Attention**
>
> Code listings shown in the following are usually excerpts. To keep the listings small, boilerplate parts are skipped (e.g., package imports, repetitive steps and JavaDoc).

5.2.1 Setting up the Project Structure

Here, a MoCo is represented by an *OSGi bundle*, i.e., by a "plug-in project" in Eclipse terminology. The target execution environment is Equinox. The *project structure* is depicted in Figure 5.2. At the time of writing this thesis, the project needs to be created manually. In the future, an Eclipse wizard that triggers a project generation tool will be provided.

```
▲ 🖳 HelloWorldPrinter [implementation/HelloWorldPrinter]
   ▷ 🗁 JRE System Library [JavaSE-1.7]
   ▷ 🗁 Plug-in Dependencies
   ▲ 🗁 src
      ▲ 🏢 de.uni_koblenz.ist.manesh.phd.samples.hello_world_printer
         ▷ 🏢 glue
         ▷ 🏢 moco_code
         ▷ 🏢 moco_model
         ▷ 🏢 ports
         ▷ 🗋 Activator.java 1940 manesh
   ▷ 🗁 modelGen
   ▷ 🗁 .settings
   ▷ 🗁 META-INF
   ▷ 🗁 resources
      📄 .classpath 1727 manesh
      📄 .project 1722 manesh
      📄 build.properties 1727 manesh
```

Figure 5.2: OSGi Project Structure of the HelloWorldPrinter MoCo in
Eclipse

The META-INF folder and the build.properties file are specific to
OSGi and include details such as the imported and exported Java
packages as well as information for exporting the bundle project as a
JAR file. The rest of the project structure is not specific to OSGi.

Especially the package structure in the src folder chosen here is
a *convention* proposed by us. It comprises (i) the moco_code
package for code, (ii) the moco_model package for models, (iii) the
glue package for the mediator and (iv) the ports package for storing
interfaces related to the function and management ports.

The second source folder, named modelGen, is only added here to
separate utility code from the actual component logic. It contains
Java code for generating a model. This model is stored as a TGraph
file (.tg) in the resources folder.

5.2.2 Defining the MoCo's Interfaces

The interfaces of a MoCo are represented as pure Java interfaces,
no additional constraints exist and no assumptions are made. The
two interfaces of the sample component (IPrint and ITextAccess) are

placed in the ports.function and ports.manage sub-packages of the
MoCo, respectively. Both are introduced subsequently.

```
1  package de.uni_koblenz.ist.manesh.phd.samples.hello_world_printer.ports.
       function;
2
3  public interface IPrint {
4      void printWelcome();
5  }
```

Listing 5.1: IPrint Interface at PFunction

Listing 5.1 shows the IPrint interface file. In line 1, the package's
fully qualified name reveals that it is a *function* type of interface, i.e.,
it belongs to the conceptual PFunction port. The printWelcome()
method shall print a welcome string to the available console.

```
1  package de.uni_koblenz.ist.manesh.phd.samples.hello_world_printer.ports.
       manage;
2
3  public interface ITextAccess {
4      public int countSentences();
5      public void changeToGoodMorning();
6  }
```

Listing 5.2: ITextAccess Interface at PManage

Listing 5.2 shows the ITextAccess interface file. In line 1, the package's fully qualified name reveals that it is a *manage* type of interface,
i.e., it belongs to the conceptual PManage port. The countSen-
tences() method shall return the total number of (welcome) sentences
stored in the component. The changeToGoodMorning() method shall
change the welcome string to be printed to the available console. In
this example, the default message is "Hello World!" and the changed
message is "Good Morning World!".

Note that the definition of the MoCo's interfaces does not reveal *how*
they are implemented internally, i.e., the MoCoCode and MoCoModel
share of the HelloWorldPrinter is invisible to its users. This ensures,
that the component can be invoked from existing Java code.

5.2.3 Deriving a Default Mediator

The mediator delegates incoming calls from the ports to either the code
or model part that implements the invoked method (e.g., printWel-
come()). A mediator knows a set of *method providers* and dispatches
incoming calls to a matching one for execution. Internally, this is
realized with a hash map in the Mediator base class. The structure
of a mediator is well-defined and it depends on the set of interfaces
of the MoCo. The mediator code for our sample component, the
HelloWorldPrinter, is listed in Listing 5.3.

```
1   package de.uni_koblenz.ist.manesh.phd.samples.hello_world_printer.glue;
2
3   // Skipping imports...
4
5   public class HelloWorldPrinterMediator extends Mediator implements
        IPrint, ITextAccess {
6       @Override
7       public void printWelcome() {
8           invokeAndCatch("printHello");
9       }
10
11      @Override
12      public int countSentences() {
13          return invokeAndCatch("countSentences");
14      }
15
16      @Override
17      public void changeToGoodMorning() {
18          invokeAndCatch("changeToGoodMorning");
19      }
20  }
```

Listing 5.3: HelloWorldPrinterMediator Code

As the fully qualified package name reveals, the HelloWorldPrinter-
Mediator is placed in the glue package of the MoCo. By convention,
this is the package for mediator code. The name of the class can be
freely chosen and it must extend the abstract Mediator class provided
by the MoCo Core API. Because a mediator acts as a *facade* [60]
to the internal realization of the MoCo's provided interfaces, it implements all interfaces made available in the components *.ports.*

packages. In this example, these are the IPrint and ITextAccess interfaces. All methods of these interfaces need to be implemented. These are (i) printWelcome(), (ii) countSentences() and (iii) changeToGoodMorning().

We recommend that a mediator shall not directly implement the functionality, but it shall delegate incoming calls to a concrete implementation available in MoCoModel or MoCoCode. A call to the method invokeAndCatch(String methodName, Object... args) – inherited from the base Mediator – does the job of finding an appropriate implementation available in the MoCo and invoking it.

The implemented *resolution strategy* requires at least the method-Name, i.e., the name of the exposed method at one of the MoCo's port interfaces. The list of args, i.e., parameters of the method to invoke, needs to be only provided if the method has a parameter list. invokeAndCatch() catches exceptions, too. Due to this simple structure, a default mediator code can be fully generated. There are some *limitations* with the current approach, though.

First, if two interfaces define the very same method (w.r.t. its signature, excluding the return type) they cannot be distinguished. From a purely technical perspective, this is a common Java limitation. From a designer's point of view, interface methods with the same name but different behavior need to be implemented by different classes. In the scope of this thesis, we assume that a single mediator suffices, but leave it open to the user of the MoCo Core API to implement multiple mediators.

Second, a string-based solution, as followed by the current MoCo Core API (resolving methods by name), has its weaknesses: spelling mistakes or refactorings of names may quickly result in erroneous code. Code generation and an extended IDE can support developers, though. Exploring different approaches is subject to future work.

5.2.4 Implementing the Provided Interfaces

At this point, the project structure of the component was created, its interfaces were defined and a mediator was implemented as a facade to dispatch incoming calls to actual implementations. In the MoCo Core API, these implementations are represented by an abstract base type, the MoCoObject. There two are different, concrete derived types: the MoCoModelObject (to represent parts of the MoCoModel) and the MoCoCodeObject (to represent parts of the MoCoCode). Such *method providers* are registered with a Mediator via its addMoCoObject(MoCoObject obj) method.

Each MoCoObject can expose methods to be available for the mediator they are registered with. This is accomplished by annotating a Java method using the @Export annotation. @Export has a set of *optional attributes*:

- category: This enumeration-typed attribute sets the conceptual interface type (see MoCo Template). The set of available types is defined by an enumeration (UNKNOWN, ACTION, CODE_STATE, MODEL_STATE, INTERPRET). Currently, this attribute can be queried, but it is not actively used by the MoCo Core API. Defaults to UNKNOWN.
- priority: This integer-typed attribute supports resolving conflicts between redundant implementations of port methods based on priority. Defaults to 0.
- portMethodName: This string-typed attribute can be set in case that the annotated method's name does not match the name of the port's interface method. Defaults to "" (the empty string).

In the following, we describe the common way of using the MoCoObject types by implementing the provided methods of the HelloWorldPrinter's interfaces.

printWelcome() as MoCoCode

We start by realizing functionality in code. A default implementation for printing the "Hello World!" message to the console is realized by the PrintMethodProvider shown in Listing 5.4. It does not use any model, the PrintMethodProvider is of type MoCoCodeObject and the class is placed in the moco_code package of the component.

```
1  package de.uni_koblenz.ist.manesh.phd.samples.hello_world_printer.
       moco_code;
2
3  public class PrintMethodProvider extends MoCoCodeObject implements
       IPrint {
4    @Override
5    @Export(category = MethodCategory.ACTION)
6    public void printWelcome() {
7      System.out.println("Hello World!");
8    }
9  }
```

Listing 5.4: PrintMethodProvider Code

In line 3 of Listing 5.4, we can see that PrintMethodProvider implements the IPrint interface in the usual Java fashion. The @Export annotation in line 5 marks the printWelcome() method so it will be known by the mediator. We set the optional category attribute to mark the method as an ACTION type. In line 7, the method directly prints the welcome message to the standard console.[7] To illustrate how to provide *variations* of behavior, a second implementation of the printing method is shown in Listing 5.5.

```
1  package de.uni_koblenz.ist.manesh.phd.samples.hello_world_printer.
       moco_code;
2
3  public class PrintMethodProvider2 extends MoCoCodeObject {
4    @Export(category = MethodCategory.ACTION, priority = 10)
5    public void printHello() {
6      System.out.println("Hello World 2!");
7    }
8  }
```

Listing 5.5: PrintMethodProvider2 Code

There are two things to notice here. First, the PrintMethodProvider2 does not implement IPrint explicitly in line 3. Technically, the @Export annotation and an identical signature is all a mediator requires. Even though there are obvious advantages of using an interface type *explicitly* (i.e., using Java's **implements** keyword), there

---

[7]In a legacy MoCo, a MoCoObject would act as a (small) proxy to existing code.

are cases in which it makes sense to remove this dependency at the type level. For instance, if the implementation of a single interface is spread across MoCoCode and MoCoModel, explicit typing would require to implement stubs of the otherwise "empty" methods. An example for such *partial interface implementation* is given in the MoCoModel examples shown later in this section. Java does not support this built-in.

Second, the provided printHello() method is annotated with priority = 10, thus *redefining* the first implementation provided by the PrintMethodProvider with default priority shown in Listing 5.4. At runtime, the Mediator base class resolves conflicts by invoking the method with the highest priority. The priority mechanism can be also used by tools during development time, e.g., to express configurations of method variations.

To illustrate the use of the third optional attribute of @Export, Listing 5.6 shows the PrintMethodProvider3 realizing another variation of the print method. This time, the name of the method is different than declared in IPrint. The print() method is still registered with the Mediator as an implementation of the printHello() method, as the portMethodName = "printHello" in line 4 states. The MoCo Core API logs a warning whenever such a "redefinition" happens. As this method provider comes with the high priority = 12, it will be the invoked behavior among the three available variations, so far.

```
1  package de.uni_koblenz.ist.manesh.phd.samples.hello_world_printer.
       moco_code;
2
3  public class PrintMethodProvider3 extends MoCoCodeObject {
4      @Export(category = MethodCategory.ACTION, priority = 12,
           portMethodName = "printHello")
5      public void print() {
6          System.out.println("Hello World 3!");
7      }
8  }
```

Listing 5.6: PrintMethodProvider3 Code

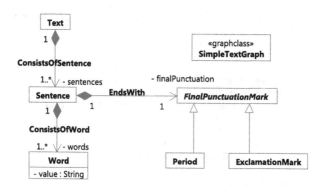

Figure 5.3: A Simple Meta-Model for Text (in grUML)

printWelcome() as MoCoModel

Three variations of the printWelcome() method implementation were described up to now. All of them are implemented as MoCoCode. Here, we provide a fourth variation that uses a model. The setup consists of (i) a simple *meta-model* for describing text (abstract syntax), (ii) a *model interpreter* that traverses models conforming to the meta-model and prints modeled sentences (semantics) and (iii) a *model manager* that defines how to access a persisted model[8].

The *meta-model* called SimpleTextMetaModel is illustrated in Figure 5.3 using grUML syntax. Usually, one would describe text using a *grammar* because it is better suited for expressing the structure of textual languages. In a meta-model, the order of words is not expressed clearly, for example.[9] Still, we use a meta-model here for illustration purposes.

According to the meta-model, text consists of one or more sentences. Each sentence consists of one or more words, where the value attribute stores the word as a string. A sentence ends with either a period or an exclamation mark.

---

[8]In the concrete realization, there is a *model generator* class that creates a text model (an instance of the SimpleTextMetaModel meta-model).

[9]Using TGraphs for implementation, model elements (vertices, edges) *are* ordered.

```
1  package de.uni_koblenz.ist.manesh.phd.samples.hello_world_printer.
       moco_model;
2
3  // Skipping imports...
4
5  public class SimpleTextModelInterpreter extends
6         AbstractModelInterpreter<SimpleTextGraph> {
7      @Export(category = MethodCategory.INTERPRET, priority = 20,
           portMethodName = "printHello")
8      public void interpret() {
9          log.info("Started interpreting...");
10         final SimpleTextGraph g = getModel();
11         for (final Text t : g.getTextVertices()) {
12             printText(t);
13         }
14         log.info("Fini!");
15     }
16
17     private void printText(Text t) {
18         for (final Sentence s : t.get_sentences()) {
19             int wordCount = s.getDegree(ConsistsOfWord.EC,
20                                 EdgeDirection.OUT);
21             for (final Word w : s.get_words()) {
22                 System.out.print(w.get_value());
23                 // Leave no blank between last word and punctuation.
24                 if (wordCount > 1) {
25                     System.out.print(" ");
26                     wordCount--;
27                 }
28             }
29             printPunctuation(s.get_finalPunctuation());
30         }
31     }
32
33     private void printPunctuation(FinalPunctuationMark punctuation) {
34         if (punctuation instanceof Period) {
35             System.out.print(". ");
36         } else if (punctuation instanceof ExclamationMark) {
37             System.out.print("! ");
38         }
39     }
40 }
```

Listing 5.7: SimpleTextModelInterpreter Code

The *model interpreter* for this example is sketched in Listing 5.7.
The SimpleTextModelInterpreter class extends the AbstractModelInterpreter provided by the MoCo Core API, which provides a means

for handling a reference to a model of a certain type (here: Simple-TextGraph as defined by the *graph class* in the grUML meta-model). This base class is a MoCoModelObject that can act as a *method provider* for a mediator.

The model interpreter is placed in the moco_model package and uses the Java API that was generated from the meta-model. The involved steps for generating the meta-model-specific API in JGraLab are described in Section 2.3.3. We describe the code of the model interpreter here step by step to give readers a more concrete impression of the steps involved in providing an executable MoCoModel.

The interpret() method shown in line 9 is marked with @Export so it is exposed to the mediator. It is an INTERPRET method and the priority = 20 attribute ensures that this variation will be the preferred one over the other three methods implemented in MoCoCode. The portMethodName = "printHello" is required to establish the mapping to the interface method of IPrint that shall be redefined.

The rest of the implementation is pure Java using types from the generated meta-model API. Starting in line 18, printText(Text t) iterates over the set of sentences and words, printing their value to the console. At the end of a sentence, printPunctuation(FinalPunctuationMark punctuation) is invoked, as shown in line 29, to handle printing of the period or exclamation mark to the standard console.

Now that the meta-model and an interpreter exists, it is required to tell the MoCo Core API where to load the model for this MoCo from. Here, we assume that a serialized model is located in the MoCo. In case that only a single model is used within the MoCo, the current solution is to derive from the abstract AbstractModelManager class as shown in Listing 5.8.[10]

This SimpleTextModelManager class is placed in the moco_model package and extends the AbstractModelManager. The only method to be implemented is createDefaultModelConnection(). Here, the

---

[10]In future versions of the MoCo Core API, a default model manager may no longer be required when a default location for model files is assumes. Still a model manager can be extended to perform conformance checks on models (e.g., after a transformation) or to check access rights and more.

TGModelSerializer utility class is used to return the required Model-
Connection from a file as shown in line 14. The location of the model
is hard-coded to "/resources/HelloWorldModel.tg" in this example.

```
1   package de.uni_koblenz.ist.manesh.phd.samples.hello_world_printer.
       moco_model;
2
3   // Skipping imports...
4
5   public class SimpleTextModelManager extends AbstractModelManager {
6       @Override
7       protected ModelConnection createDefaultModelConnection() throws
           IOException {
8           final TGModelSerializer ser = new TGModelSerializer();
9           return ser.deserialize(getModelInputStream(), null,
10              SimpleTextMetaModel.class.getClassLoader());
11      }
12
13      private InputStream getModelInputStream() throws IOException {
14          return getClass().getResourceAsStream("/resources/HelloWorldModel.
           tg");
15      }
16  }
```

Listing 5.8: SimpleTextModelManager Code

countSentences() as MoCoModel

The countSentences() method is one of two methods offered at the
ITextAccess interface located in the *.ports.manage package of the
MoCo. Its task is to *query* the contained model and to count the
number of sentences stored in it. To demonstrate the mentioned
partial interface implementation capability of the MoCo Core API, we
split the implementation of the ITextAccess interface into two classes.

The realization of the countSentences() method is provided by the
ModelReadAccessor class located in the moco_model package as
described in Listing 5.9.

This ModelReadAccessor is a class that implements read-only access to the model. Hence, it contributes partially to the implementation of the ITextAccess interface. This can be seen in line 5, where
the @PartiallyImplements annotation is used to mark the class. The

ModelReadAccessor is a MoCoModelObject as it needs direct access
to a model.

```
1   package de.uni_koblenz.ist.manesh.phd.samples.hello_world_printer.
        moco_model;
2
3   // Skipping imports...
4
5   @PartiallyImplements(interfaces = { ITextAccess.class })
6   public class ModelReadAccessor extends MoCoModelObject {
7       @Export(category = MethodCategory.MODEL_STATE)
8       public int countSentences() {
9           // Hidden: get model reference, call countSentencesWithAPI() and
            countSentencesWithGReQL() and log their return values.
10      }
11
12      private int countSentencesWithAPI(SimpleTextGraph g) {
13          int count = 0;
14          for (final Sentence s : g.getSentenceVertices()) {
15              count++;
16          }
17          return count;
18      }
19
20      private int countSentencesWithGReQL(SimpleTextGraph g) {
21          final GreqlQuery q = GreqlQuery.createQuery("count(V{Sentence})");
22          final int count = (int) q.evaluate(g);
23          return count;
24      }
25  }
```

Listing 5.9: ModelReadAccessor Code

The countSentences() method is properly exported using the @Ex-
port annotation. This is shown in line 7. As this method operates
on the model, the category is set to MODEL_STATE as a hint for
managing the component.

The internals of the method are hidden here, as no special task is accomplished. Simply put, countSentences() retrieves a valid reference
to the model and invokes countSentencesWithAPI() and countSen-
tencesWithGReQL(). Each time, the result is logged, too.

countSentencesWithAPI(), starting in line 12, uses the *generated
API* to get all sentences stored in the model. Then, the local count

variable is incremented in a loop. The result is returned. There is nothing special about this pure Java implementation.

In contrary, countSentencesWithGReQL(), starting in line 20, uses a *GReQL expression* [52] to query the number of all sentences in the model. In line 21, the query object is built. "count(V{Sentence})" is the full query. count() returns the number of elements in a given collection. V{Sentence} returns the set of all *vertex elements* in the model that are of type Sentence. Remember, this type was defined in the meta-model depicted in Figure 5.3. The result of the query's evaluation is returned as an integer.

changeToGoodMorning() as MoCoModel

The changeToGoodMorning() method is the second of two methods offered at the ITextAccess interface located in the *.ports.manage package of the MoCo. Its task is to *transform* the contained model so it represents the sentence "Good Morning World!". This message can be printed by invoking the developed model interpreter again after the transformation finished.

Implementing interfaces at the conceptual PManage port is identical to implementing interfaces of the conceptual PFunction port. Users of the MoCo Core API can follow the same steps. Here, the method is provided by a Java class that implements all functionality that modifies the model. This class, the ModelWriteAccessor, is shown in Listing 5.10.

The ModelWriteAccessor is a MoCoModelObject. As it does not implement all of the methods of ITextAccess, a hint is placed in the form of the @PartiallyImplements(interfaces = ITextAccess.class) annotation shown in line 5. This annotation is optional but is intended to be used by an IDE to support developers with static checking. For example, a tool could check if the exported methods really belong to one of the listed interfaces.

In line 8, the exported method is annotated as MODEL_STATE. The method changeToGoodMorning() starts by retrieving a reference to the model as illustrated in line 13.

```
1   package de.uni_koblenz.ist.manesh.phd.samples.hello_world_printer.
        moco_model;
2
3   // Skipping imports...
4
5   @PartiallyImplements(interfaces = { ITextAccess.class })
6   public class ModelWriteAccessor extends MoCoModelObject {
7      @Export(category = MethodCategory.MODEL_STATE)
8      public void changeToGoodMorning() {
9         log.info("Transforming the 'Hello World!' model...");
10
11        final SimpleTextGraph g;
12        try {
13           g = (SimpleTextGraph) getModelManager().
           getDefaultModelConnection().getRawModel();
14        } catch (final Exception e) {
15           throw new RuntimeException("Could not load the SimpleTextGraph",
           e);
16        }
17
18        final Word good = g.createWord();
19        good.set_value("Good");
20
21        final Word morning = g.createWord();
22        morning.set_value("Morning");
23
24        // The "Hello World!" sentence.
25        final Sentence s = g.getFirstSentence();
26
27        // Find "Hello" and "World".
28        Word hello = null;
29        Word world = null;
30        final Iterator<Word> iter = s.get_words().iterator();
31
32        while (iter.hasNext()) {
33           final Word w = iter.next();
34           if (w.get_value().equals("Hello")) {
35              hello = w;
36           } else if (w.get_value().equals("World")) {
37              world = w;
38           } else {
39              throw new IllegalStateException(
40                  "Detected illegal input model containing Word: "
41                      + w.get_value());
42           }
43        }
44
45        if (hello != null && world != null) {
46           // Delete hello.
```

```
47        g.deleteVertex(hello);
48
49        // Add "Good Morning World".
50        // First and only Edge points to "World" Word.
51        final Edge eWorld = s.getFirstConsistsOfWordIncidence();
52
53        // Add the created words in order.
54        final Edge eGood = s.add_words(good);
55        final Edge eMorning = s.add_words(morning);
56
57        // Ensure the right order.
58        eWorld.putIncidenceAfter(eMorning);
59
60        // Exclamation mark is kept from old model.
61      } else {
62        throw new RuntimeException(
63                "Did not detect 'Hello' and/or 'World' Word. Check input
        model!");
64      }
65
66        log.info("Fini!");
67    }
68  }
```

Listing 5.10: ModelWriteAccessor Code

In case that the model was made available successfully, API methods generated by JGraLab are used to find the words "Hello" and "World" in lines 28-37. Then, in line 47, we delete the word with value "Hello" first. The new words ("Good", "Morning") are added and to the model in lines 51-55. Additional code in line 58 ensures the right order of words by sorting the incidences of the sentence such that the word "Morning" follows "World". The exclamation mark available in the old model is reused as it was not removed from the model, before.

The listed transformation, written in Java, can be also implemented by using a transformation language such as GReTL [54]. For rather simple manipulations (as required in this example), we experienced that using the generated API from the meta-model is sufficient.

5.2.5 Registering the Implemented Functionality as OSGi Services

By now, all parts of the MoCo are ready to be used. As we decided to use OSGi technology, the MoCo is an OSGi bundle. Such bundles contain packages with code that can be exported for use by other Java code (usually also OSGi bundles) that import these packages. In the scope of this thesis, we prefer to use the more advanced *OSGi services*[11].

Technically speaking, such a service can be defined either by a Java class or by a Java interface. The common way is to use an interface type, though. It is also recommended to split the *service declaration* from the *service definition* (implementation) so the implementation can be swapped at runtime. In our small example, we did not follow this guideline to simplify the example. Each bundle may use and/or register a number of services with a *service registry* that is managed by the OSGi runtime environment. Similar to bundles, services can be started and stopped at any time.

There are two ways of realizing such services: *programmatically* (i.e., using pure Java) or *declaratively* (i.e., using XML files). Although the latter one requires (almost) no programming, it introduces additional dependencies to specific plug-ins that may not be available in the same way in different OSGi runtime environments. Additionally, more *magic* is happening in the background. Thus, we decided to provide the example in the form of the programmatic implementation. Subsequently, we describe the related steps to finish the implementation of our small sample MoCo.

The Activator class shown in Listing 5.11 is specific to OSGi. It acts as an *entry point* to the bundle and always implements the BundleActivator interface specified by OSGi. In the context of MoCos, we use the Activator (i) to provide service objects and (ii) to retrieve service objects. In this example, the MoCo only provides implementations and does not require any service references.

---

[11]An excellent tutorial on OSGi services can be found online: http://www.vogella.com/tutorials/OSGiServices/article.html (accessed April 30th, 2014).

```
1   package de.uni_koblenz.ist.manesh.phd.samples.hello_world_printer;
2
3   // Skipping imports...
4
5   public class Activator implements BundleActivator {
6       private HelloWorldPrinterMediator printerMediator;
7       private ServiceRegistration<IPrint> printServiceRegistrationRef;
8       private ServiceRegistration<ITextAccess> accessServiceRegistrationRef;
9
10      @Override
11      public void start(BundleContext bundleContext) throws Exception {
12          // Initialize the mediator.
13          printerMediator = HelloWorldPrinterMediator.getBuilder().create();
14
15          // Register IPrint and ITextAccess services.
16          printServiceRegistrationRef = bundleContext.registerService(IPrint.
            class, printerMediator, null);
17          accessServiceRegistrationRef = bundleContext.registerService(
            ITextAccess.class, printerMediator, null);
18      }
19
20      @Override
21      public void stop(BundleContext bundleContext) throws Exception {
22          printServiceRegistrationRef.unregister();
23          accessServiceRegistrationRef.unregister();
24      }
25  }
```

Listing 5.11: Bundle Activator Code of HelloWorldPrinter

In the current implementation, each MoCo is represented by an instance of its mediator which is initialized by the Activator. The HelloWorldPrinterMediator reference is declared in line 6. Additionally, the MoCo manages references to the provided interface implementations registered with OSGi in the form of ServiceRegistration references shown in lines 7 and 8 point. These three references are initialized, when the bundle is started, i.e., when the start() method is invoked. The service objects are unregister when the bundle is stopped, i.e., when stop() is invoked.

First, the mediator is initialized and instantiated. This is done in line 13, using the getBuilder() utility method. Internally, a Mediator-Builder object is constructed. This is a *helper class* provided by the

MoCo Core API. It instantiates a set of available MoCoObject classes and also sets the available ModelManager. Currently, this method needs to be provided by the developer. We skipped it in Listing 5.3 and provide the code here in Listing 5.12.[12]

```
1    public static MediatorBuilder getBuilder() {
2        return new MediatorBuilder(HelloWorldPrinterMediator.class)
3            .addMoCoObjectTypes(PrintMethodProvider.class,
4                PrintMethodProvider2.class, PrintMethodProvider3.class,
5                SimpleTextModelInterpreter.class,
6                ModelReadAccessor.class, ModelWriteAccessor.class)
7            .setModelManager(SimpleTextModelManager.class);
8    }
```

Listing 5.12: MediatorBuilder Code in HelloWorldPrinterMediator

Now, the mediator has been created. Remember, that it plays the role of a proxy that realizes the provided interfaces. Here, we have two interfaces: core functionality is represented by IPrint and management functionality is represented by ITextAccess. In lines 16 and 17 of Listing 5.11, the freshly created mediator object is added to the OSGi registry twice: once as a provider of the IPrint interface and once for the ITextAccess interface.

registerService is an OSGi method that takes three parameters: (i) the *class type* under whose name the service can be located, (ii) the actual *service object* and (iii) optional *property values* for the service (not used here).

To clean up properly, each registered service reference is removed from the registry when the bundle is stopped. This is done in lines 22 and 23 of Listing 5.11 by calling unregister() on the service registration references.

---

[12]Note, how *method chaining* is supported by the designed MoCo Core API: addMoCoObjectTypes() returns a MediatorBuilder again such that setModelManager() can be invoked directly. Only the developed MoCoObject classes are passed, as well as the SimpleTextModelManager class.

5.2.6 Using the MoCo

The HelloWorldPrinter MoCo is ready to be used. Here, we show how to use it from another OSGi bundle. The name of the using component is HelloWorldPrinterUser. Basically, it is an OSGi project with an Activator class as shown in Listing 5.13.

```java
 1  package de.uni_koblenz.ist.manesh.phd.samples.hello_world_printer_user;
 2
 3  // Skipping imports...
 4
 5  public class Activator implements BundleActivator {
 6      private IPrint printerService;
 7      private ITextAccess accessTextService;
 8
 9      @Override
10      public void start(BundleContext bundleContext) throws Exception {
11          final ServiceReference<IPrint> printLoaderServiceRef =
            bundleContext
12              .getServiceReference(IPrint.class);
13          printerService = bundleContext.getService(printLoaderServiceRef);
14
15          final ServiceReference<ITextAccess> accessTextLoaderServiceRef =
            bundleContext
16              .getServiceReference(ITextAccess.class);
17          accessTextService = bundleContext.getService(
            accessTextLoaderServiceRef);
18
19          // Invoke the print method (''Hello World!'').
20          printerService.printWelcome();
21
22          // Invoke the count method (API + GReQL).
23          accessTextService.countSentences();
24
25          // Invoke the model transformation.
26          accessTextService.changeToGoodMorning();
27
28          // Invoke the print method (now: ''Good Morning World!'').
29          printerService.printWelcome();
30      }
31  }
```

Listing 5.13: Bundle Activator Code of HelloWorldPrinterUser

The goal of the HelloWorldPrinterUser is to invoke all of the available methods of the HelloWorldPrinter MoCo. Therefore, it needs to obtain a valid service reference to each of the two interfaces.[13]

The dependency to the MoCo is realized by declaring two references, one for each interface type as shown in lines 6 and 7. The start() method is invoked each time the HelloWorldPrinterUser bundle is started.[14] Then, a ServiceReference for each interface type is requested. This is done by using the automatically initialized bundle's context handle, **bundleContext**, for calling **getServiceReference()**. Based on this reference, **getService()** returns the actual service object of type IPrint in line 13 and of type ITextAccess in line 17, respectively.

From line 20 on, the welcome message is printed to the console, the number of sentences is requested, the model is transformed and the welcome message is printed again.

```
1   osgi>
2   Warning: printHello() redefined by object of class
        SimpleTextModelInterpreter
3   Warning: printHello() redefined by object of class PrintMethodProvider3
4   INFO SimpleTextModelInterpreter.interpret: Started interpreting...
5   Hello World!
6   INFO SimpleTextModelInterpreter.interpret: Fini!
7   INFO ModelReadAccessor.countSentences: Result counted via API: 1
8   INFO ModelReadAccessor.countSentences: Result counted via GReQL: 1
9   INFO ModelReadAccessor.countSentences: Returning 1
10  INFO ModelWriteAccessor.changeToGoodMorning: Transforming the 'Hello
        World!' model...
11  INFO ModelWriteAccessor.changeToGoodMorning: Fini!
12  INFO SimpleTextModelInterpreter.interpret: Started interpreting...
13  Good Morning World!
14  INFO SimpleTextModelInterpreter.interpret: Fini!
```

Listing 5.14: Console Output After Running HelloWorldPrinterUser

---

[13]Technically, the retrieved service object is, in both cases, an instance of the HelloWorldPrinterMediator. A single reference could be retrieved and then cast. This is not good practice, because the implementing service object may change.

[14]The chosen OSGi runtime ensures that bundles are loaded and started in the proper order.

Assuming that the priorities of the exported methods in all available MoCoObject classes is set to the values presented earlier, then the MoCoModel is used to output the welcome message by means of model interpretation as shown in Listing 5.7. The output is listed in Listing 5.14 for completeness.

5.2.7 Implementing Internal Interfaces

In the example shown so far, the focus was set on how to realize exposed interfaces of a MoCo in either MoCoCode or MoCoModel. The mediator has the additional capability of controlling internal communication between these two parts of a MoCo. This was described earlier when we introduced the MoCo Template. Subsequently, the HelloWorldPrinter is extended to show how to realize internal interfaces with the current MoCo Core API version.

Assume, the MoCo shall be extended: each time its text model is queried for its state, an email shall be sent to a predefined receiver with the number of sentences contained in the model. The functionality for sending an email is an *action* that is offered by MoCoCode.

To implement this, it is required to (i) declaring the internal interface for printing, (ii) implement this interface as a MoCoCodeObject class, (iii) register this method provider with the mediator and (iv) invoke this MoCoCode interface from the ModelReadAccessor.

Declaring the IEmail Interface

IEmail is a simple interface for sending an email as shown in Listing 5.15. This interface is internal to MoCoCode and it is not exposed by the OSGi bundle, i.e., the package is not exported.

```
1  package de.uni_koblenz.ist.manesh.phd.samples.hello_world_printer.
     moco_code;
2
3  public interface IEmail {
4      boolean sendMail(String sender, String receiver, String message);
5  }
```

Listing 5.15: IEmail Interface Code

The file is placed in the `moco_code` package as shown in line 1. In line 4, the single method named `sendMail` is declared. A `sender` (email address), `receiver` (email address) and an arbitrary string are the required input parameters for this simple example. Obviously, one would introduce an `Email` type in a more sophisticated program.

Implementing IEmail as a MoCoCodeObject

`EmailMethodProvider` implements `IEmail` as a stub that simulates sending an email by simply printing data (sender, receiver, message) to the console. The code is given in Listing 5.16.

```
1   package de.uni_koblenz.ist.manesh.phd.samples.hello_world_printer.
        moco_code;
2
3   // Skipping imports...
4
5   public class EmailMethodProvider extends MoCoCodeObject implements
        IEmail {
6       @Override
7       @Export(category = MethodCategory.ACTION)
8       public boolean sendMail(String sender, String receiver, String
            message) {
9           if (sender == null || sender.trim().isEmpty() || receiver == null
                || receiver.trim().isEmpty() || message == null) {
10              log.info("Failed to send email.");
11              return false;
12          } else {
13              log.info("Sending Email...");
14              System.out.println("From: " + sender);
15              System.out.println("To: " + receiver);
16              System.out.println("Message: " + message);
17              log.info("Fini!");
18              return true;
19          }
20      }
21  }
```

Listing 5.16: EmailMethodProvider Code

The `EmailMethodProvider` class is placed in the `moco_code` package as shown in line 1. Line 3 reveals that it is a `MoCoCodeObject` and that it implements `IEmail`. More importantly, the `sendMail` method is annotated with `@Export` so it can be invoked by the MoCo's mediator.

The category is of type ACTION to make the relationship to the MoCo Template explicit and to provide this meta-data for potentially following management operations to be executed on the MoCo.

The actual email sending activity is simulated here. In lines 14-16, the passed data is simply printed to the standard output, i.e., to the console. The method returns false if at least one parameter was faulty, otherwise true.

Registering the EmailMethodProvider with the Mediator

To be able to invoke the MoCoCode behavior somewhere from Mo-CoModel (in a way that the mediator controls it), the mediator needs to be aware of it. We let the HelloWorldPrinterMediator implement the IEmail interface. In Listing 5.17, the extended mediator code is shown. Previous code from Listing 5.3 is hidden where possible to highlight only additions.

```
1  package de.uni_koblenz.ist.manesh.phd.samples.hello_world_printer.glue;
2
3  // Skipping imports...
4
5  public class HelloWorldPrinterMediator extends Mediator implements
       IPrint, ITextAccess, IEmail {
6      @Override
7      public boolean sendMail(String sender, String receiver, String
           message) {
8          return invokeAndCatch("sendMail", sender, receiver, message);
9      }
10
11     // Skipping additional methods...
12  }
```

Listing 5.17: Extended HelloWorldPrinterMediator Code

In line 7, the sendMail method is defined and it simply invokes the familiar protected invokeAndCatch utility method of the Mediator base class. The very same mechanism was used earlier to dispatch incoming requests from an external interface. Technically though, only IPrint and ITextAccess are visible to users of the MoCo. IEmail as well as the HelloWorldPrinterMediator are both hidden types.[15]

Note that a default mediator can be still generated. The only addition is that the internal interface types need to be made available to the code generator tool. Such a tool does not need to distinguish between internal or external (port) interfaces. An identical generation procedure can be followed for both cases.

Invoking the EmailMethodProvider from MoCoModel

To illustrate invoking coded functionality for sending an email, we assume that the number of sentences queried shall be sent to a predefined email every time the ModelReadAccessor's countSentences method is called. The extended code is shown in Listing 5.18.

```
1   package de.uni_koblenz.ist.manesh.phd.samples.hello_world_printer.
        moco_model;
2
3   // Skipping imports...
4
5   @PartiallyImplements(interfaces = { ITextAccess.class })
6   public class ModelReadAccessor extends MoCoModelObject {
7       @Export(category = MethodCategory.MODEL_STATE)
8       public int countSentences() {
9           // Hidden: Invoke the two private variations for model querying.
10
11          // Demonstrate the use of MoCoCode.
12          final String sender, receiver;
13          sender = receiver = "manesh@uni-koblenz.de";
14          final String message = "Model query counted " + greqlCount + "
                sentences in model.";
15          getMediatorAs(IEmail.class).sendMail(sender, receiver, message);
16
17          // Return counted number of sentences.
18      }
19
20      // Skipping additional methods...
21  }
```

Listing 5.18: Extended ModelReadAccessor Code

---

[15] A user of the MoCo could still (attempt to) invoke the **sendMail** method, e.g., using reflection. This is not a *secure* implementation.

In lines 12-14, the parameters for sending an email are prepared. Then, in line 15, the email is sent by using an implementation of the IEmail interface.

A convenience method, getMediatorAs, can be called within each MoCoObject. This method encapsulates the detection of an appropriate implementation of this interface in the form of a method provider – this is either a MoCoModelObject or a MoCoCodeObject. Thus, the current MoCo Core API provides a *generic mechanism* for realizing arbitrary kinds of interfaces between MoCoCode and MoCoModel. The specifically mentioned internal interfaces as part of the MoCo Template are realized in this way.

5.2.8 Final Architectural Structure

To summarize and to conclude this section on the use of the MoCo Core API, the *final architectural structure* of the created software is described. In Figure 5.4, the architecture is illustrated. Most parts were introduced in detail before. The goal of this section is to provide a detailed picture of all the developed pieces.

First, let us briefly describe each element of the presented example MoCo:

- *HelloWorldPrinter:* A MoCo that prints a welcome message and offers one interface for functionality and one for its management. This is the main component developed in this example. It offers two interfaces (IPrint, ITextAccess) that are implemented internally using code and a model.

  The HelloWorldPrintMediator acts as a facade for all classes that are subtypes of MoCoCodeObject or MoCoModelObject. These register themselves with the mediator which can choose how to delegate incoming requests.

  There are different variations of the IPrint interface implementations. As described before, these are: PrintMethodProvider, PrintMethodProvider2, PrintMethodProvider3 and SimpleTextModelInterpreter.

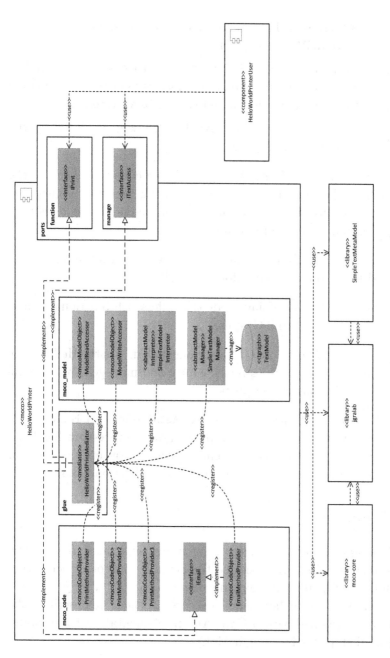

Figure 5.4: Final Structure of the HelloWorldPrinter MoCo

ITextAccess is realized partially by two classes (ModelReadAccessor, ModelWriteAccessor).

Internally, there is the IEmail interface that is implemented to offer email sending functionality which is used to send an email each time the model is queried (ModelReadAccessor).

The raw model data, the TextModel, is encapsulated by the SimpleTextModelManager.

- *SimpleTextMetaModel:* A library of Java code that contains the API of the meta-model for representing text that consists of sentences, words and final punctuation marks. The code is fully generated using a jgralab tool.

- *moco-core:* A library of Java code that provides the base types and tools to realize the MoCo Template.

- *jgralab:* A library of Java code that offers rich functionality and tools to work with TGraphs.

- *HelloWorldPrinterUser:* A component that uses the HelloWorld-Printer and triggers its functionality and management capabilities for demonstration purposes.

The HelloWorldPrinter, SimpleTextMetaModel and HelloWorld-PrinterUser were created as a simple example. moco-core has been developed to support the component realization concept proposed in this thesis. Details on jgralab can be found in Section 2.3.3.

5.3 Summary

In this chapter, we introduced a *reference implementation* of the MoCo concept. First, we described the possible ways of implementing the MoCo Template with existing component technology, namely JavaBeans, Enterprise JavaBeans and OSGi. Then, we described the use of the developed MoCo Core API implementation by stepping through all steps for building a MoCo.

For each of them the explored component technology (i) a *realization description* was given that includes a mapping of the conceptual MoCo elements to the respective component technology and (ii) a list of *observations* made during prototyping. The lessons learned were summarized, in the end. Obviously, the choice of a component technology has a direct impact on how the MoCo Template can be implemented and a dynamic component model can support the MoCo idea even better. Still, MoCos developed with static component technologies can especially support achieving adaptation using models.

We were able to define reasonable mappings for all three component technologies. In doing so, we noticed that there is no "single right way" of mapping the MoCo concept. In fact, it seems to be more relevant to agree on a mapping at the beginning of development and to use this as an implementation pattern throughout a project. During the feasibility studies described in the next chapter, we will use the mapping defined earlier for OSGi.

Based on the explorative prototyping phase, we described the use of the developed MoCo Core API step by step by implementing a *"Hello World" example*. A detailed technical introduction and detailed source code examples were given. This example covered all aspects of developing a MoCo, i.e., (i) setting up the project structure, (ii) defining the component's interfaces, (iii) deriving a default mediator, (iv) implementing the provided interfaces, (v) registering the implemented functionality with OSGi and (vi) using the component.

Finally, more advanced details, such as implementing the internal interfaces of a MoCo explicitly as well as a visual description of the developed sample component, were described.

6 Feasibility Studies

In this chapter, we present the setup and results of two *feasibility studies* that we carried out in two different application domains: (i) developing an *insurance sales app* (ISA) for the Android mobile operating system and (ii) developing a software simulation of a *dynamic access control product line* (DAC-PL).

The intention behind these sample applications is to provide a common basis for exploration and illustration of fundamental concepts and issues related to building modular software with MoCos.

The remainder of this chapter is structured as follows. First, the *goals of the studies* are listed. That followed, both studies are described. A *discussion* of the studies' goals and results, including threats to validity is given. This chapter ends with a *summary*.

6.1 Goals of the Studies

We are aware of the fact that these feasibility studies could have been carried out along two axes, i.e., with different component technologies and with multiple modeling languages. Here, we decided to focus on the use of different modeling languages. The topic of using different component technologies for realizing MoCos was sketched in Section 5.1.

The primary *goals* to be achieved with these feasibility studies were:
- to explore the feasibility of building software with MoCos (*practicality*),
- to gain realistic hands-on experience with the development workflow and design of MoCos (*implementation*) and
- to experience how to embed different (executable) modeling languages in MoCos (*genericity*).

Subsequently, each study is described in terms of the needed domain-specific knowledge, use cases or user workflows as well as the chosen software architecture using MoCos. Finally, threats to validity are discussed, as well.

6.2 Study 1: Insurance Sales App

In order to study the feasibility of the introduced MoCo Template and its reference implementation, we developed a fictional[1] scenario of an insurance company that equips its field staff with an assistive *Insurance Sales App*[2] (ISA) for the Android mobile platform. We found this context to be suitable for the study, because it requires a flexible software solution. In the insurance domain, parts of the application logic such as the fee computations depend on frequently changing laws and other impact factors so the software needs to be *permanently evolved.*

Moreover, different user roles (e.g., car or home insurance specialist) require *different variants* of ISA. These variants need to be provided whenever a user with a different role starts using a new device. Since sales staff cannot rely on a fast internet connection to be available everywhere, all data needed must be stored on the mobile device.

Finally, parts of the fee calculations may even depend on geo-locations. A smart sales application needs to *adapt itself* automatically to support its users before a meeting with a (potential) customer.

We chose the Android mobile platform due to the availability of sensor modules that can be used to influence the state of the application in addition to user input. The rather limited amount of resources (compared to a desktop environment) was another influence factor for choosing a mobile platform to experiment with MoCos in such an environment.

---

[1] Although fictional, our selected scenarios are based on background information collected in interviews with a German insurance company.

[2] The term "app" is commonly used to describe a *mobile application*, i.e., software for a smart phone or tablet.

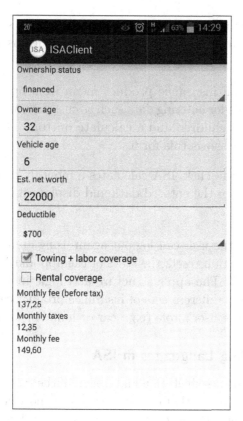

Figure 6.1: Screenshot of the ISA Android Application's Insurance Product Form

6.2.1 User Workflow

The typical *workflow* of an ISA user consists of the following steps:

1. The user starts ISA and is presented with a simple log-in screen, that is more of a user role picker consisting of two buttons for car and home insurance specialists respectively.

2. After picking a role, ISA shows a menu with a selection of three different insurance product calculation forms for the chosen domain.

3. Clicking an insurance product menu item opens a form with input fields for entering data such as customer age, yearly income, amount of children and a calculate button. The screenshot in Figure 6.1 shows this form.

4. Upon button click, ISA calculates a monthly insurance product fee based on the entered data and displays it at the bottom of the form.

At any time, the user can log out again using an application menu entry. That function resets the state of the app and the log-in screen shows up again. The app's structure and logic includes variability, i.e., ISA provides different sets of insurance product calculation forms depending on the user's role (e.g., car or home insurance specialist).

6.2.2 Modeling Languages in ISA

During requirements elicitation and design of the system, we identified the parts of the system that contain variability and will be (most likely) subject to change. Based on the interviews with domain experts, we knew that the insurance fee formulas will need to change frequently and they will change depending on the location of a customer. Changes are rather *fine-grained*, i.e., at the level of formulas and within MoCos.

The different insurance products and the dependency to the role of the sales person is another source of variability. Changing a role means to change the available business logic as well as its depending fraction of the user interface. This is rather *coarse-grained* variability, i.e., at the system level, between MoCos that can be changed or replaced.

We decided to incorporate three modeling languages into the design and implementation of ISA. Each is represented by its own meta-model as follows:

- *ComputationMetaModel:* The *ComputationMetaModel* represents insurance fee computation formulas based on (simple) arithmetics. Naturally, we use a textual concrete syntax for models of this kind. The associated meta-model is shown in Figure 6.2.

- *GUIMetaModel:* The *GUIMetaModel* represents graphical user interfaces in a technology-independent way. We use a simplified visual concrete syntax for models of this kind to represent layout and position information. The associated meta-model is shown in Figure 6.2.

- *FeatureMetaModel:* The *FeatureMetaModel* encodes variability [82] in the form of an "and-or tree" structure with additional relationships and links to implementing OSGi bundles. We use a visual concrete syntax for models of this kind. The associated meta-model is shown in Figure 6.4.

Instances, i.e., models that conform to these meta-models, are initially developed in parallel to the code as a part of the components and are also used by ISA at runtime.

Subsequently, we focus especially on the use of these models in the MoCos built for ISA. The concrete architecture of ISA is introduced thereafter.

Insurance Fee Computation Models

In our insurance company scenario, updates should be cheap to roll out to client devices. Assuming bad Internet network coverage and additional roaming fees, Internet data traffic must be kept down to a minimum. The use of OSGi as the component technology facilitates updating individual bundles, so it is not necessary to update the whole app every time a change is required.

However, assuming that the *computational instructions* of an insurance product module are encoded as an *executable model*, it is possible to roll out (compact) delta updates in the form of model

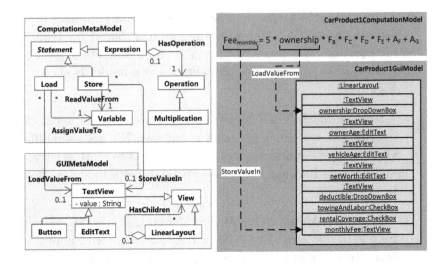

Figure 6.2: Excerpt of the Computation and GUI Meta-Models With the Conforming Compound Product Model

transformations that update the component's business logic without replacing it. That way, changes to the fee computation formulas can be systematically encoded in a repeatable format.

GUI View Hierarchy as a Reflective Model

The Android SDK provides an elaborate system for creating arbitrary *view hierarchies*[3] and *layouts* using an XML notation. A layout description is part of an Android app's resource files and is converted into a binary representation at compile time. Each resource is assigned a uniquely generated identifier number that is used to reference and load (layout) resources at runtime.

Despite the technical advantages that come with the existing Android layout mechanisms, we decided to re-create a custom layout description that is interpreted at runtime. This has the advantage that

---

[3]In Android, user interfaces are created by combining *views* such as buttons and check-boxes.

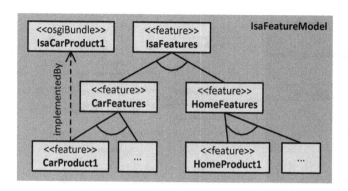

Figure 6.3: Visual Representation of ISA Features

a platform-independent model of the user interface can be rendered for ISA on Android, but it may be used on another platform, as well. For that reason we designed a simplified GUI modeling language.

This design decision also opened doors to further model-related advantages. For instance, links between individual view elements of a GUI model to variables of a computation model can be created if associations were foreseen at the meta-model-level. That way, no further code needs to be developed by hand for reading input values from the GUI elements whenever an insurance fee needs to be computed. Instead, the computation model interpreter can access these values directly by following links of a variable in the formula to the associated GUI input element.

Likewise, it is also not necessary to read back the computation result from the interpreter into Android text display view elements. The state of the native Android GUI is synchronized with the GUI model via an event system, which saves some tedious manual programming work that may be error-prone.

Feature Configuration Model

A feature model is used to describe different configuration possibilities of ISA based on the chosen user role. That model contains links from

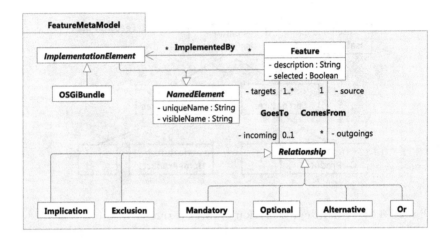

Figure 6.4: Feature Meta-Model Excluding Constraints

insurance calculation features to OSGi bundles. Feature models are typically design time artifacts used to express and communicate high level requirements for various feature configurations of a product, but they can be very helpful at runtime, as well.

In Figure 6.3, an example feature model is depicted that distinguishes between car and home insurance features. It conforms to the meta-model illustrated in Figure 6.4. It allows for flexible reconfiguration of ISA based on a feature selection and transformations on the *feature configuration model*[4] of ISA which is managed by the IsaConfig at runtime.

Besides orchestrating and configuring the flow and internal structure of the application, a feature configuration can also be validated against the constraints as defined by the feature meta-model.

Upon feature selection, the state of the model is validated and, then, the overall app configuration changes are propagated to the rest of ISA. As a result, the main menu is refreshed, for example, in case the current user role changed. The feature model interpreter ensures

---

[4]Here, a feature configuration is a feature model [82] with a valid feature selection.

that the actual OSGi bundles that implement a feature are started or stopped according to the selection state of the associated feature in the feature configuration model.

6.2.3 ISA Architecture

ISA has been implemented in a completely component-based manner based on a combination of traditional Java libraries, existing Android components and MoCos. The developed *architecture* is illustrated with a UML component diagram in Figure 6.5.

Components can *provide* and *use* interfaces. Since we are using the IBM RSA tool, a provided interface is illustrated as a "ball" with a direct connection to the realizing component. Usage of these interfaces is illustrated by dashed lines with an open arrow head. Stereotypes are used to mark simple components («component»), conventional Android components («app») and MoCos («moco»). Port interfaces of MoCos are marked with the «pFunction» or the «pManage» stereotype, respectively.

The IsaMetaModelApi component provides an API for creating and editing the models. This model-specific API is fully generated by JGraLab tools based on a meta-model diagram designed with the IBM Rational Software Architect.[5] There is a single meta-model that consists of sub-meta-models, where each describes one specific modeling language. This *integrated meta-model* enables associations between elements of the different meta-models. An excerpt is illustrated in Figure 6.2.

The host Android app (not illustrated) starts the IsaSession MoCo which uses the ICreateFormUi interface to display the role picker. ICreateFormUi is realized by the IsaUserInterface MoCo which receives a GUI model as input. GUI models are encapsulated by product-specific MoCos such as IsaCarProduct1. IsaUserInterface traverses the received GUI model and builds a corresponding Android view hierarchy that is immediately visible. The native view hierarchy is kept in sync with the GUI model, i.e., this is a reflective approach.

---

[5]The foundations of using TGraphs were introduced in Section 2.3.3.

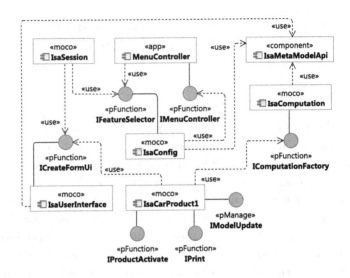

Figure 6.5: Logical View of the ISA Architecture With one Active Insurance Product

Upon user role selection, IsaSession selects the corresponding role feature through IFeatureSelector. This interface allows access to the feature configuration model MoCo.

As an extension of the feature configuration model, some features are linked to component identifiers. The relationship between features (problem space) and the available software components that contribute to their realization (solution space) is clearly documented. This knowledge is not only used during development of ISA, but also at runtime. Therefore, ISA can be seen as a *Dynamic Software Product Line* (DSPL) [63].

IsaConfig contains a model interpreter that can execute feature configurations. Two cases are distinguished when this feature configuration changes:

- If the selected user role was changed, then IsaConfig updates the application's main menu by using the IMenuController interface to display a list of available insurance products for the selected role. The MenuController implements this functionality.

- Otherwise, if an insurance product feature has been selected, IsaConfig determines the corresponding OSGi bundle that implements the product feature and activates it.[6] Deactivation of features and, hence, the stopping of associated OSGi bundles, is done analogously.

In this specific example, IsaCarProduct1 is activated which includes business logic for a specific car insurance product. A detailed description of this example MoCo is given in the following.

Example MoCo: IsaCarProduct1

The implementation structure of IsaCarProduct1 is exemplarily described here. It is depicted in Figure 6.6.

Ports. In the logical architecture shown in Figure 6.5, IsaCarProduct1 uses the ICreateFormUi provided by IsaSession and IComputationFactory provided by IsaComputation. In this specific Java-based implementation, the use of interfaces is realized by passing references to an activate() method offered by IProductActivate. This interface belongs to the MoCo's function port.

IReport is another functionality-related interface that enables the printing of details about this specific product's insurance fee.

This particular MoCo supports dynamic updates of its contained GUI and computation model via the IUpdateModel interface at the manage port. It facilitates the fine-grained manipulation of this particular insurance product. For instance, it is possible to update the insurance formula and the associated GUI by using a model transformation that can be passed to IUpdateModel.

Mediator. In this example, the ProductMediator simply receives calls to the MoCo's ports and delegates them to the registered internal

---

[6]The details of OSGi bundle handling via Apache Felix are not visualized in Figure 6.5.

MoCoObject instances that are located either in the MoCoModel or in the MoCoCode module.

MoCoCode. The EmailReportGenerator can generate an email with details on the selected insurance product offer, for the current user, based on data stored in the ProductModel. Since each registered MoCoObject can access the mediator of a MoCo, the EmailReportGenerator can use the ProductMediator to obtain access to the model's state via the ProductModelManager.

MoCoModel. The ProductActivator implements activate(). This method is offered by the IProductActivate interface. References to two model interpreters are passed to this initialization procedure: a computation model interpreter (realized in IsaComputation) and a GUI model interpreter (realized in IsaUserInterface). The ProductActivator prepares the ProductComputation and ProductUi with these model interpreters.

This MoCo carries the ProductModel, which consists of two parts: CarProduct1ComputationModel[7] and CarProduct1GuiModel as illustrated in Figure 6.2. Internally, both parts are represented by a single TGraph. This is possible, because both sub-models conform to the same *integrated meta-model*. There are links between GUI elements and computation variables in order to read user input from input fields (loadInto) or to output a computed result to a text view (storeIn). These links are used by the two model interpreters.

The embedded ProductModelManager controls access to the ProductModel. Moreover, it enables the systematic updating of the product's business logic and corresponding GUI representation via the IModelUpdate interface.

---

[7] Fee calculations are simplified and not based on any real-world insurance product.

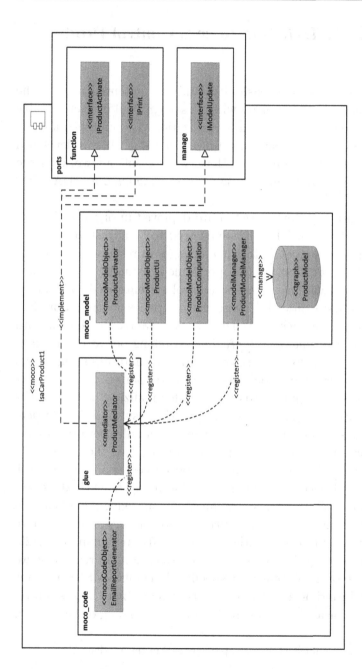

Figure 6.6: Implementation View of the IsaCarProduct1 MoCo

6.3 Study 2: Dynamic Access Control Product Line

In this section, a second feasibility study is presented around the theme of *dynamic access control* where a system shall protect valuable physical and software assets in an organization. We published a study around the same idea in the context of DSPLs [45].[8] It was developed with our GRAF [3] technology. Here, we present our work on the construction of a *Dynamic Access Control Product Line* (DAC-PL) with MoCos.

Access Control Systems (ACSs) are deployed in organizations to protect critical assets. These systems need to be adjustable to cope with different contextual factors like changes in resources or requirements. Still, adaptation is often performed manually. In addition, different product variants of access control systems need to be developed together systematically. These characteristics demand a product line engineering approach for enhanced *reuse*. Moreover, to cope with uncertainty at runtime, *adaptivity*, i.e., switching between variations in a cyber-physical domain (re-configuration) and adjusting access policies (behavior adaptation), needs to be supported.

No matter what approach is followed for realizing *access control* (role-based, attribute-based, etc.) in practice, especially in physical access control systems, managing changes is normally performed manually. Changes to access control policies are required though, e.g., to consider new employees, visitors with special needs, or varying business processes. Hence, Dynamic Access Control Systems (DACSs) are needed that can adjust themselves quickly to suit emerging situations.

Generally, we noticed that *adaptive security* and *self-protection* have not been widely addressed in the adaptive software community [120] and the access control domain is not an exception. Particularly, we are not aware of a solution that specifically combines SPL technology [116] and runtime adaptation in this domain. Since access control systems can be available in different variants depending on the needed

---

[8]Some of the text published in our paper is reused in this section.

security features, following the SPL approach seems natural, though. Furthermore, once a DACS was deployed, it needs to stay continuously and actively in place. Therefore, it is desirable to develop security systems that adapt themselves during operation.

6.3.1 System Use Cases

The relevant *system use cases* and some of the associated stakeholders are illustrated by the UML use case diagram shown in Figure 6.7. Software engineers are excluded as this role is associated with mostly all of the use cases. The intention of this section is to communicate the requirements for the DACS from a high-level perspective.

The most critical function of the system is to *control user access to rooms.* Everybody who enters, leaves and moves inside of the protected building – including the organization's staff – is assigned a set of roles. These roles are associated with *access rules.* An administrator can *define access rules* and this is especially done once when the system is installed and maintained but also when some unforeseen event happens that forces a manual change of these rules.

Besides, there is a set of foreseen events that may occur[9] either at development time or at some point after deployment. These events need to be treated systematically. Usually, this involves additional conditions and a set of actions to be carried out to cope with the emerging stress situation. Hence, administrators can *define adaptation rules* separately from the core logic of the DACS and in a predefined way, e.g., in the form of ECA-rules.

For example, the system can *change access rules dynamically when a Very Important Person (VIP) visits.* This use case is a special case of a more abstract use case to *change access rules autonomously.* In fact, this function is at the heart of the DACS and distinguishes it from static ACSs. In order to adapt the access rules on-the-fly, it requires to *sense the VIP location.* Only managers are allowed to access the

---

[9]We assume that it is foreseen that something *may* happen, but the time of its occurrence is unknown as well as certain details such as the specific system state at that time.

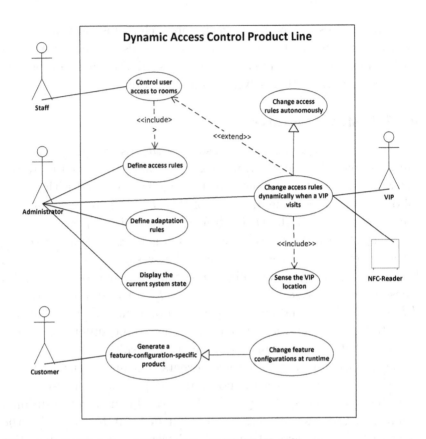

Figure 6.7: High-Level View of the DAC-PL Use Cases

same room the VIP is currently in. Additionally, administrators can *display the current system state* to monitor the software as it operates.

Moreover, the product can be delivered and deployed in various configurations, i.e., we assume that the DACS is developed as an SPL. These configurations are based on features and are usually defined in cooperation with a customer of the ACS.

Based on a valid selection of features, it is possible to *generate a feature-configuration-specific product* (tailoring). Similarly to the autonomous change of access rules, the fundamental features of the software can be changed as well, i.e., it is possible to *change feature configurations at runtime* (adapting) to cope with emerging situations such as the unexpected visit of a VIP.

Description of the User Interface

A screenshot of a running instance of the product line, developed with a combination of MoCos and regular OSGi bundles, is given in Figure 6.8.[10] The illustrated running system is started in the *premium* configuration, i.e., all available features of the DACS simulation are enabled. The simulation is built around different windows that are responsible for certain tasks. A high-level description is given subsequently:

- *Dynamic Access Control System - Simulation:* This window provides a visual representation of the current state of (i) the *environment*, i.e., the rooms in a top-down view, (ii) the *assets* to be protected, i.e., the rooms and persons (shown as circles), (iii) the available *sensors*, i.e., camera sensors placed in the corners of rooms as well as card readers placed at the doors (both shown as rectangles) and (iv) the *effectors*, i.e., the doors (shown as rectangles with rounded edges) that are placed in the real world. In our case, this is the rendering of simulated data as we do not use hardware sensors in real rooms. The software could take inputs from real sensors, though.

- *Event Generator:* This window is required to drive the simulation and would not be part of a real DACS. It allows the definition of events using a DSL with a simple textual concrete syntax. That way, a simulation run can be repeated by providing the exact same sequence of events. For example, events may be the detection of a user by a camera sensor and the request for access by a person via a card reader sensor.

---

[10]Note that the labels (R1, R1D1S, ...) and arrows in the top-down-view of rooms are added for illustration purposes and are not part of the actual model.

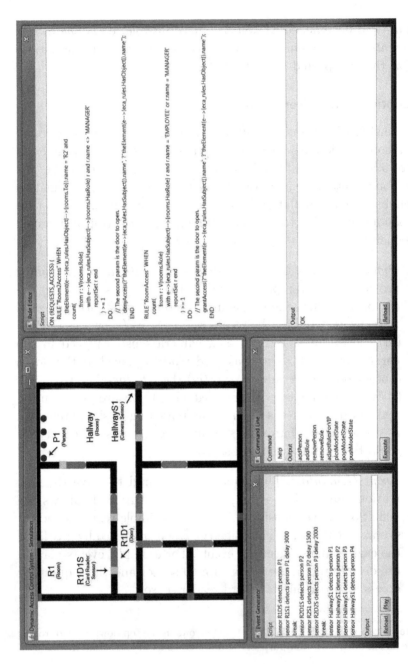

Figure 6.8: Screenshot of the DAC-PL Simulation With Rendered Person, Room and ECA Rule Models

- *Command Line:* This window is a small command panel that allows administrators to interact with the DACS in a command-line fashion. Here, persons and roles may be registered with the system and removed again. Additionally, access rules can be adapted and the state of the models in the system can be saved and restored again at any time. That way, any changes made, e.g., in consequence to the simulated events or user interaction via the command line interface can be rolled back.

- *Rule Editor:* This window provides a view on the set of rules encoded in the system. Primarily, these are access rules that determine the conditions under which a certain role may enter a room or not. These rules are developed as ECA-rules represented in a textual concrete syntax. Since all kinds of events may be received, not only access control can be realized, but also adaptation of the system by triggering a model transformation in the action part of a rule.

The whole simulation relies heavily on the use of models. This topic is covered, next.

6.3.2 Modeling Languages in DAC-PL

During requirements elicitation and design of the DAC-PL, we identified the parts of the system that contain variability as well as those that may be subject to change at runtime.

Access control systems tend to be pretty complex, depending on the available kinds of sensors, effectors and the kinds of assets to be protected. This variability gives rise to an SPL approach where variability is explicitly modeled. Moreover, the access rules need to be specifically adaptable, i.e., manually and by adaptation managers that may be enriched with application-specific adaptation rules. For administrators, information about the assets to be protected need to be made explicit, as well.

We decided to incorporate four modeling languages into the design and implementation of the DAC-PL simulation. Each is represented by its own meta-model as follows:

- *PersonMetaModel:* The *PersonMetaModel* represents persons that are assigned one or more roles. These persons and roles have unique names. We use a simplified visual concrete syntax for models of this kind. The associated meta-model is shown in Figure 6.10.

- *RoomMetaModel:* The *RoomMetaModel* represents the physical structure of the rooms in an organization's building; typically this is an office. Rooms and doors can be protected by sensors such as cameras and card readers. We use a simplified visual concrete syntax for models of this kind. The associated meta-model is shown in Figure 6.10.

- *EcaRuleMetaModel:* The *EcRuleMetaModel* represents rules that are associated with an event type and actions that can be executed whenever a condition holds. This modeling language is the basis for encoding access rules as well as adaptation rules. Naturally, we use a textual concrete syntax for models of this kind. The associated meta-model is shown in Figure 6.11.

- *FeatureMetaModel:* The *FeatureMetaModel* encodes variability in available sensors and effectors of the DAC-PL and is technologically equivalent to the meta-model introduced in Section 6.2.2 for ISA. In contrast, we use a table-like concrete syntax for models of this kind here. The associated meta-model is shown in Figure 6.4.

Instances, i.e., models that conform to these meta-models, are initially developed in parallel to the code as a part of the components and are also used by DAC-PL at runtime.

Subsequently, we focus especially on the use of these models in the MoCos that comprise the DAC-PL simulation. The concrete

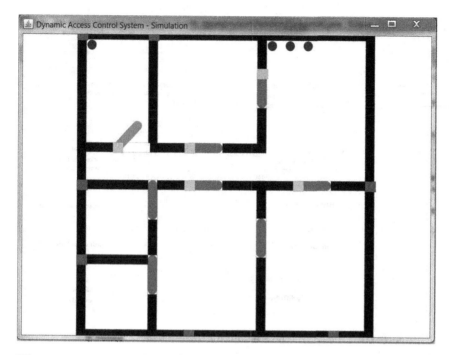

Figure 6.9: Visual Representation of Persons, Rooms and Sensors

architecture is introduced thereafter in terms of components and connectors .

Person Model

In the access control setting, information about persons needs to be available. These persons may work in the organization or may just visit it. Among these persons, different roles can be identified. Examples are employee, manager, guest and VIP. Initially, before system deployment, a base model can be created that covers all known employees and their roles. This model needs to be maintained to reflect organizational changes over time as well as temporary visitors. This data can be edited via the provided command line tool.

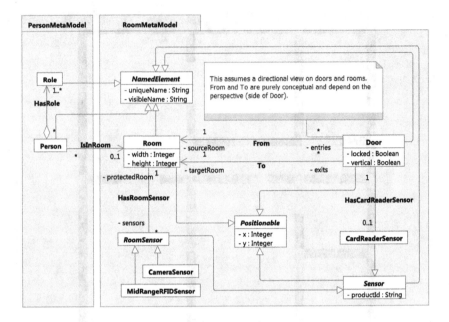

Figure 6.10: Excerpt of the Person and Room Meta-Models

In a typical software development project, such information is surely stored in a (relational) database. Although this would be possible in our case, too, we decided to represent person-related information in a model, more concretely: by a TGraph. This has the advantage that all models in MoCos can be treated equally, i.e., the same model query and transformation languages can be used throughout the whole DAC-PL study.

In addition, person data is not only used for access control but it is also associated to information captured by other models. For instance, persons can be located in rooms. Therefore, keeping all models in the same technological space[11] was a natural decision.

---

[11] Relational databases can be seen as another technological space in which models can be expressed.

Room Model

The central topic of the DACS is to protect rooms from being entered by unauthorized persons. The planning of what rooms to protect, which sensors to use and how many doors are available can be supported by a floor plan. This is an easy to understand top-down view on the organization's building structure that can be used for communication among all stakeholders that are responsible for planning, introducing and managing a DACS.

Motivated by this obvious way of communicating about access control to different rooms, we decided to use the same model at runtime, as well. That way, a familiar view can be reused and the state of doors (open, closed) and protecting sensors such as card readers can be visualized for administrators. Moreover, the position of persons may be rendered into this view if such data is available, e.g., from advanced camera sensors. This is an example for merging information from different but linked models.

Access and and Adaptation Rule Models

Assuming that the fictional organization has a varying number of important and less important visitors as well as staff that may work in different office locations, it is impossibly to manually keep track of all access rules. An example for an access rule is given in Listing 6.1.

Let us describe the concrete syntax briefly as this is an example where we integrate an existing language (GReQL [55]) into the newly designed ECA-rule modeling language. Rules can react to certain events.

The ON keyword is used to define a block in which a set of rules can be defined that may react to the event type. Lines 2, 9 and 13 reveal the basic structure of such a rule. Following the RULE keyword, a rule name is defined. Then, following the WHEN keyword, a condition is specified which needs to be true for the rule to execute its action part as defined after the DO keyword. The rule ends with the END keyword. Conditions are specified in GReQL, which is a model query language for TGraphs.

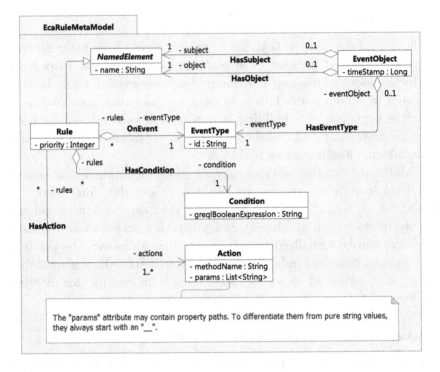

Figure 6.11: Excerpt of the ECA Rule Meta-Model

In this particular study, the event object of a rule can be always accessed as the **e** variable. Without going into the specific details of the query language, the condition checks if the subject associated with the event object has the role of EMPLOYEE or MANAGER. This is done in lines 3 to 8. A person may have different roles, so the result set is checked to be >= 1 in line 8. The query is formulated based on the meta-model for ECA-rules defined in Figure 6.11.

The action part of this rule invokes a Java method called **grantAccess**. It is part of a base API for writing access rules. In this specific case, the two required parameters (a person and a door identifier) are also extracted from the model, again using GReQL. The ? keyword

tells the interpreter that no pure string but a query expression is
passed that needs to be evaluated.

```
1   ON (REQUESTS_ACCESS) {
2       RULE "RoomAccess" WHEN
3           count(
4               from r : V{rooms.Role}
5               with e-->{eca_rules.HasSubject}-->{rooms.HasRole} r and
6                   r.name = 'EMPLOYEE' or r.name = 'MANAGER'
7               reportSet r end
8           ) >= 1
9       DO
10          // The second param is the door to open.
11          grantAccess(?"theElement(e-->{eca_rules.HasSubject}).name",
12              ?"theElement(e-->{eca_rules.HasObject}).name");
13      END
14  }
```

Listing 6.1: An Access Rule as an ECA-Rule Model in Concrete
Syntax

Some access rules need to be changed over time, in case that other
(physical) sensors are installed or the DACS configuration is modified.
For instance, in a *standard configuration*, the DACS does not support
person detection. This feature as well as the required camera sensors
need to be bought extra as they belong to a *premium configuration*.

Therefore, access rules can be changed manually via a console and
using a textual syntax, but there are also adaptation rules that can
react to changes and modify the installed DACS. Since the access
rules as well as the adaptation rules are both represented by models
internally, adaptation rules can also transform the access rules. Indeed,
adaptation rules may adapt themselves, too.

Except for the different actions, access rules and adaptation rules
are both based on the *EcaRuleMetaModel*. Actions can be arbitrary
Java methods available in a MoCo. For access control, they may grant
or deny access. Analogously, for adaptation, the generated meta-
model-specific API can be used to develop model transformations.

Feature Configuration Model

Given the various numbers of sensors that can support different levels of accuracy (e.g., short and mid-range sensors, camera sensors), different variations of a DACS can be derived from the DAC-PL. To make variability explicit, a feature model is established during design and development of the product line. The developing organization can provide default configurations such as a standard and premium DACS. A table representation of the feature configurations is given in Table 6.1.

If desired, customers can choose from the set of features themselves and their feature selection can be validated at the model-level. The associated components[12] (classical software components, libraries and MoCos) are selected accordingly.

Besides this design and development support, the deployed DACS carries its feature configuration in a MoCo, i.e., the feature configuration model remains active at runtime. This model is a high-level representation of the system's capabilities, described using access control terminology. Because this problem space view is linked to the implementing software components, i.e., to the solution space elements, architectural reconfiguration can be achieved, too. More specifically, adaptation rules can query (condition) and modify (action) the feature configuration model as the DACS operates.

Of course, autonomous reconfiguration is limited by the actually available software and hardware. In case that a certain change is sensed frequently, generic adaptation rules may propose to upgrade the system. Another application for this is the case in which a premium DACS is available and a VIP visits. Only then, the available camera sensors (see Table 6.1) are enabled to realize person tracking. Once the VIP left the building (this can be sensed by a camera at the entrance and is confirmed by security staff), the cameras are disabled again as a result of interpreting the most recent feature configuration model.

---

[12]The underlying meta-model for feature models, presented in Figure 6.4, contains an **ImplementedBy** association.

Table 6.1: Table Representation of two DAC-PL Feature Configurations ("X" = included, "-" = excluded, "?" = open choice)

Feature Identifier	Standard	Premium
[MAN] DacsFeatures	X	X
[MAN] AccessRuleType	X	X
[XOR] Fixed	X	-
[XOR] Adaptable	-	X
[MAN] UserIdentification	X	X
[OR] CardReader	X	X
[OR] Camera	-	X

6.3.3 DAC-PL Architecture

The DAC-PL has been implemented in a completely component-based manner based on a combination of traditional Java libraries, OSGi bundles and MoCos. The developed *architecture* is illustrated with a UML component diagram in Figure 6.12.

Components can *provide* and *use* interfaces. Since we are using the IBM RSA tool, a provided interface is illustrated as a "ball" with a direct connection to the realizing component. Usage of these interfaces is illustrated by dashed lines with an open arrow head. Stereotypes are used to mark simple components («component») and MoCos («moco»). Port interfaces of MoCos are marked with the «pFunction» or the «pManage» stereotype.

The DacCameraDriver and the DacCardReaderDriver are both MoCos developed in a "code only" setup. They provide the software drivers for the camera as well as the card reader (hardware) sensors.

Event Handling

Sensor events are published to and received from the DacEventBus via the IEventPublish and IEventSubscribe interfaces. This component is a simple OSGi bundle that acts as a communication bus between all components. On this bus, especially simulated sensor events are sent. Real hardware could publish events to this bus, too.

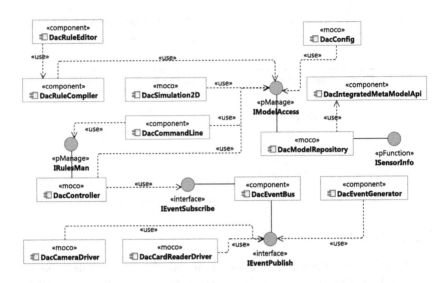

Figure 6.12: Logical View of the DAC-PL Architecture

The DacEventGenerator OSGi bundle generates a stream of sensor events that can be described in a simple textual language[13] shown in the event generator window in Figure 6.8. Additionally, this component provides a GUI written in SWT for typing in event descriptions as well as for visualizing the state of execution by highlighting the currently active event generation statement being sent to the DacEventBus.

Access and Adaptation Rule Handling

The DacController is a MoCo in a "balanced" setup that can interpret access rules as well as adaptation rules. It also includes a base action API to be used in the action part of ECA-rules (e.g., print, access, deny...). Moreover, it also includes management functionality to be

---

[13]In contrast to the other languages developed in the study, this language was developed ad-hoc in code based on simple string splitting without an explicit meta-model.

executed from the command line window for editing rules, for example, via the IRulesMan interface.

This MoCo listens to the DacEventBus and, besides enforcing access control rules, it acts as a simple adaptation manager, too. In this solution, access rules and adaptation rules are treated equally, i.e., the *analyze* and *planning* phases of the traditional MAPE-K loop are simplified by a priority-based solution for choosing the next rule to be executed. In order to support the querying of recent events in a similar way to all other models, incoming events are propagated to the DacModelRepository via IModelAccess. The EcaRulesMetaModel supports the representation of these reified event objects.

The DacRuleEditor is a simple OSGi bundle that provides an editor window for typing in access rules and adaptation rules. This textual representation is compiled to an ASG representation (conforming to the *EcaRuleMetaModel*) and any valid model can be rendered as text in the DacRuleEditor. This is especially useful whenever the rules model changes: the DacRuleEditor can update its view on request.

Derivation of the ASG for rules is performed by the DacRuleCompiler. It is developed as an OSGi bundle that creates a TGraph from the textual concrete syntax representation of ECA-rules. The resulting model is merged into the *integrated model* that is provided/encapsulated by the DacModelRepository. It is merged, because there needs to be a direct linking of the event objects to the source/target. These may be doors, persons or sensors, for instance.

Central Model Repository

This DacModelRepository is a MoCo in a "model only" setup that stores models of the PersonMetaModel, RoomMetaModel, EcaRuleMetaModel and FeatureMetaModel as one integrated base model. This MoCo provides ISensorInfo, a function interface for accessing sensor-specific information without the need for querying the model explicitly. Raw model access is controlled via the IModelAccess management interface.

All models here conform to a single integrated meta-model that comprises all used meta-models. This enables the direct association of modeling languages which is ideal for administrators that need a global view on the system. Queries and transformations can be executed on selected parts of the resulting *compound model*. DacIntegratedMetaModelApi contains the generated Java API in an OSGi bundle. The code is derived based on the meta-models represented as UML class diagrams as depicted in Figure 6.10, Figure 6.11 and Figure 6.4. This code is generated by JGraLab and it is used as a library.

Human Administration Support

To support system administration, the DacCommandLine OSGi bundle provides a simple command line interface developed in SWT. A list of pre-defined commands can be executed here and software developers can extend this list, of course. Amongst others, there are commands for adapting the access rules to support the visit of a VIP. In this case, only managers may be with a VIP in the same room, so the rules model is updated to reflect this and person tracking may be enabled, too. All of this can be done by transforming models at runtime in this architecture.

In terms of visualization and administration support, the DacSimulation2D MoCo in its "model only" setup can interpret the room model and visualize contained rooms, doors, sensors and persons (if position data is available). The GUI is created in Swing, and AWT is used for 2D rendering during model interpretation.

Feature-Based Runtime Reconfiguration

Finally, DacConfig is a MoCo in a "model only" setup that can interpret feature configuration models. While traversing the model, the interpreter follows the links between features and associated components (here: always an OSGi bundle, may be a MoCo) that are also represented in the model. From a high-level perspective, two kinds of actions are performed by the model interpreter:

- If a feature is selected as part of the feature configuration, then the linked components are started. If an implementation of the required component is not available, it needs to be downloaded or provided by an administrator.
- Otherwise, if a feature is not part of the configuration, then the model interpreter attempts find and stop any running instances.

6.4 Discussion

In this section, we *discuss* some of the findings of the conducted studies. The basis for this discussion are the created artifacts as well as the experiences made during the design and development of the two feasibility studies with MoCos.[14]

6.4.1 Revisiting the Studies' Goals and Results

We introduced three goals for the feasibility studies in Section 6.1. In the following, we discuss the obtained related results for each goal. The outcomes of both studies are presented in a condensed form.

On Feasibility of Building Software With MoCos

This goal is related to studying the *practicality* of the MoCo approach.

Based on the experienced gained from developing the two non-trivial systems (ISA and DAC-PL), we are convinced that integrating models and code in the broader context of component technology is feasible. All capabilities of components remain intact, while the internal realization of the encapsulated application logic and data can be represented by models or code. At the high-level of system design, software architecture can be described as usual using existing

---

[14]The discussion section is partially based on text from one of the author's publications [42].

component diagrams such as those shown for ISA in Figure 6.5 and DAC-PL in Figure 6.12.

Component developers have the opportunity to embed their own *DSMLs*. Assuming that software is already being developed in a model-driven manner, existing design-time models can be reused (e.g., feature models, architecture models). Additionally, depending on the expected need for adaptation at runtime, new modeling languages can be developed to be integrated with components. We designed the modeling languages in parallel to planning the software architecture, which allowed us to clearly relate MoCos to the languages they shall use.

Choosing the fraction of a MoCo to be represented by a model is a *creative task* that requires experience and slightly different skills than conventional software development. The initially sketched pure kinds of MoCos from the spectrum of MoCos seem to be helpful to communicate the idea but during development, it was hard to make a choice for the right MoCo starter configuration. Components were developed iteratively.

On the Development Workflow and Design of Software With MoCos

This goal is related to studying the *implementation* of the MoCo approach.

When realizing the reference implementation, and during the development of the Android application, the (selective) use of models had exactly the impact that is usually associated with models. That is, since MoCos embed models for the flexible parts, these were – in our case – also the critical domain-dependent constituents of the software system. By designing the meta-models for each individual modeling language, we were forced to explicitly introduce and label concepts and their relationships (even across meta-models). Thereby, we automatically tended to use terms and concepts defined in the models when designing and discussing the implementation of MoCos.

In addition, a similar effect as in MDA can be observed. That is, while models include the domain-specific knowledge (e.g., the basic GUI elements), a model interpreter encodes the technology-specific knowledge (e.g., about Android GUIs). Due to this decoupling of domain knowledge and realization technology, when migrating a "model-only" MoCo to another platform, only model interpreters need to be replaced and the modeled application logic can be fully reused. Of course, additional effort is required if the component technology and the programming language are also changed.

Regarding the implementation of the MoCo Template, there is no strict mapping from the concepts to a concrete realization. In our reference implementation, we developed the `Mediator` base class in such a way that it can act as a registry for different `MoCoObject` instances, i.e., objects of type `MoCoCodeObject` and `MoCoModelObject`. If these types implement an interface, the mediator can be asked for an implementation of this interface and it determines a matching implementation. While this achieves the flexibility to make changes to the internal wiring between the code and model fraction of the MoCo, the direct mapping of the realization to the MoCo Template is less visible when inspecting the source code.

In the MoCo Core API, the internal interface types from the MoCo Template are represented as annotations for marking single methods as `IModelState`, `ICodeState`, `IInterpret` or `IAction`, respectively. Another implementation of the MoCo concept may differ from this implementation and may provide concrete Java interfaces for each of the conceptual interfaces.

On Embedding Different (Executable) Modeling Languages in MoCos

This goal is related to studying the *genericity* of the MoCo approach.

It is relatively easy to embed different kinds of models into a MoCo. Communication between models located in different MoCos is done in the traditional way using component interfaces. Single models can co-exist side-by-side and can be referenced from multiple

MoCoModelObjects. Neither the MoCo Template, nor the presented reference implementation depend on the syntax or semantics of these models. In cases where a model consists of sub-models that conform to different modeling languages, their meta-models need to be integrated first so that queries, transformations or interpreters can operate on them.[15] In ISA, this was the case with the *ComputationMetaModel* and the *GUIMetaModel*, for example.

Regarding executable models embedded in MoCos, we experimented with two approaches: developing (i) a *stand-alone interpreter* and (ii) a *weaved interpreter*. Both achieve the same goal but the non-functional properties are different.

A stand-alone interpreter uses the generated meta-model API and it does not have to be delivered together with the meta-model. There can also easily be different model interpreters for the same meta-model.

In contrary, a weaved interpreter is – as the name suggests – weaved into the generated meta-model API (e.g., using AOP) such that the meta-model elements can execute themselves. Conceptually, this approach of storing related operations *with* a meta-model seems desirable. In practice though, this means that different interpreters will be weaved into the same meta-model API and they need to be separated using naming conventions or similar mechanisms. Moreover, different MoCos may need only a subset of the provided interpreters. If there shall be no variants of the meta-model, each MoCo will always have access to all weaved model interpreters automatically which is not desirable in most cases.

With existing technologies, we prefer the development of stand-alone model interpreters.

6.4.2 Threats to Validity

There are some *threats to validity* regarding the results of the presented work.

---

[15]In fact, the merging of meta-models originates from the limitations of existing technological modeling spaces. A concept for *meta-model inheritance* may solve some shortcomings.

First, our impression that the presented approach is feasible is based on two studies with a single component technology (i.e., OSGi) and two software developers.

Moreover, the *size of the studies* is not "industrial scale". Especially the writing of queries, transformations and model interpreters will be more challenging, the more concepts and relationships a meta-model consists of. Therefore, software engineers need a check list that supports them with making the decision on what parts to model and what parts to program. In future work, we plan to establish such guidelines for applying the MoCo concept.

Regarding statements on performance (memory, execution), we have not studied the details of our specific implementation, yet. At this point in time, we can only state that the developed projects in the two feasibility studies were usable without noticeably bad response times. Only the initiation of the ported Apache Felix OSGi runtime took around five seconds to load on our Android device[16]. Depending on the non-functional requirements of the application domain, model execution by means of interpretation may need to be optimized (e.g., for real-time embedded systems).

Advocates of a dynamic component model such as OSGi may argue that if a change to a component is required, it can be (simply) updated during runtime without using models. While this remains true, our technical solution allows the fine-grained querying, tailoring and adapting of selected parts of the MoCos' internals without fully replacing it. Fixing mistakes in insurance fee computation models in ISA or modifying access rules via an adaptation rule in DAC-PL are two examples. To the best of our knowledge, similar mechanisms for code do not exist.

Regarding the rationale for developing a component as a MoCo and choosing the portion to be modeled, one may argue that the same capabilities could have been realized without models or with another (existing) software language. Of course, the design decisions made

---

[16]We tested ISA on the European variant of Samsung's Galaxy Note III running Android 4.4.2.

in the feasibility studies are partially biased by us as the designers of the MoCo concept. We attempted to mitigate this threat by implementing the feasibility studies in tight cooperation with an external and experienced software engineer.[17]

6.5 Summary

In this chapter, we presented the design and development of two software systems that were created using a mixture of existing software components and libraries as well as a set of MoCos. Despite the initial overhead and increased complexity, development steps could be carried out faster after an initial learning curve. This could be noticed especially during the second study.

1. *ISA:* The *Insurance Sales App* (ISA) was developed to explore the practicality of developing a MoCo-based system for a mobile platform. Three modeling languages were used in this Android app (computation, GUI and feature models), all of which were used at runtime to achieve adaptability and adaptivity.

2. *DAC-PL:* The *Dynamic Access Control Product Line* (DAC-PL) was developed to explore the use of MoCos in a traditional desktop environment. Four modeling languages were used in this simulation (person, room, rules and feature models), all of which where used at runtime. In contrast to ISA, a command line tool exists to support administrators to make manual changes, too.

The results of the initially set goals of the studies related to (i) practicality, (ii) implementation and (iii) genericity were successfully met as described.

---

[17]Thomas Iguchi supported development of the MoCo Core API, ISA and DAC-PL.

Part IV

Finale

7 Conclusions and Future Work

In this chapter, the thesis is concluded. The goal is to provide a brief but adequately detailed overview on some of the essential outcomes of our research.

The remainder of this chapter is structured as follows. First, *conclusions* are drawn by discussing the research results in the context of the initially described research goals and research questions. Moreover, possible directions for *future work* are given. This chapter ends with a brief *summary* and concluding remarks.

7.1 Conclusions

The presented research advances the state of the art in software engineering by introducing the systematic combination of models and code as two constituents of a software component with equal rights. These Model-Integrating Components (MoCos) are the units of composition in a novel software development paradigm called Model-Integrating Development (MID). An initial step towards achieving this vision has been taken.

In the following, we discuss the research goals and answer the research questions introduced in Section 1.3.

RG1: Understanding the Essential Requirements for Model-Integrating Software

We introduced and discussed common design and development tasks when developing adaptable and adaptive software. These exemplary use cases were chosen based on previous experiences collected in the GRAF and COBRA projects as well as related works. As a result, the tendency towards a combination of adaptivity and variability management can be noticed throughout the dissertation. Both conducted studies can be seen as DSPLs [63, 69].

(RQ1) *Which kinds of relationships do exist between models and code?*

A set of possible relationships between models and code were presented as a part of the exemplary use cases for MoCos in Section 3.1. Additionally, we described a *spectrum of MoCos* in which components consist of different combinations of models and code in Section 4.2. Concrete usage scenarios for models are described for the MoCos of ISA and DAC-PL as a part of Chapter 6.

Moreover, we attempted to describe the relationships and to classify them, which resulted in generic descriptions such as *use, extend, restrict* and *reflect*. Some of these relationships are bidirectional and reflect the intended equal roles of each side as well as the symmetry in MoCos. We excluded these early and probably subjective ideas in this thesis, though, because the *intended meaning* of a relationship between models and code seems to be more relevant than a technical relationship (e.g., shaped by the technological modeling space). The semantics of the specific modeling language is essential for describing the actual kinds of relationships between its models and code.

In this work, we have focused on an integration between models and code using architectural techniques that abstract from the concrete relationships between models and code by treating both as modules within a MoCo.

(RQ2) *What are alternatives for designing and formalizing interfaces between models and code?*

Software architects think and design systems in terms of "components and connectors". Additionally, a practical solution is required for designing and formalizing interfaces between models and code that can be easily used by software developers. Therefore, existing component technologies need to be supported.

Naturally, this leads to interface definitions that are based on existing formalisms provided by programming languages and component technologies.

During exploratory prototyping described in Section 5.1, we experimented with different component technologies and realized MoCos in different ways. Amongst others, we tested the straightforward hard-coding of all parts of the MoCo Template. Especially this approach was static and too complex to do manually for each MoCo.

We decided to use the *mediator pattern* [60] between the MoCoCode and the MoCoModel modules of a MoCo. It enables the decoupling of both sides and, in the form in which we designed and implemented it, also enhances adaptability. Especially the MoCoModel can be used like Java code and partially[1] hides the embedded raw model(s) and operations on them.

(RQ3) *How can knowledge that is stored in models be accessed from outside of a component?*

If accessing the model data is a critical part of the MoCo's functionality (e.g., a MoCo is a data provider similar to a database), then a function interface shall be provided. If read-only access is needed, the portion of the model may be wrapped by a value object and sent to another MoCo for further processing.

Models that are obtained from a central data source can be retrieved from a "repository MoCo" and all using components only hold references to the model data. We have especially applied this approach to the design of the DAC-PL.

In cases where raw access to a model shall be granted for adaptation rules or manual changes from a command line, for example, the PFunction port of a MoCo shall provide clear interfaces for this purpose.

---

[1]Software developers of a MoCo are, of course, aware of the fact that the MoCoModel encapsulates models and they may know the meta-model to send a query from the MoCoCode to the MoCoModel via an appropriate interface.

(RQ4) *What kinds of conflicts with existing component models are there?*

At this point we have not identified severe conflicts with existing component models for realizing MoCos. Instead, we presented an exploratory implementation of the MoCo Template using OSGi. The current design is realizable with only little requirements for the component model: it assumes that clear definition of interfaces and component scope (encapsulation and information hiding) are supported. This may change with more advanced forms of the MoCo concept in future iterations, though.

(RQ5) *How to control the joint execution of models and code?*

To control the joint execution of models and code, it is required to build on the foundations provided by programming languages and component technologies. To simplify the approach, we chose to realize model execution not by a dedicated virtual machine, but by a set of model interpreters written in the same language as the code part of the MoCos. Hence, the execution of models and code follows the same principles as joint execution of objects and components. Although this simplification would technically allow the *parallel execution of model and code parts* of a MoCo, we have not yet investigated this topic.

RG2: Defining a Generic and Modular Realization Concept for Model-Integrating Software

We presented the MoCo Template in Section 4.2, a design of its execution environment in Section 4.3 as well as a set of supporting services in Section 4.4.

(RQ6) *What is a reasonable blueprint for a MoCo (e.g., regarding: structure, interfaces, connection between model and code)?*

We believe that this first iteration is already a reasonable blueprint for a MoCo and software development during the feasibility studies did support our claim. The separation into

MoCoCode and MoCoModel modules seems straightforward. The design of the communication middleware in the form of a mediator that sits in between these two is a design choice that was motivated by the need for separation of concerns but also by the flexible coupling of both sides. In earlier work on GRAF [3], we had used a system-wide, layered and hard-wired approach.

The driving idea behind the internal interfaces of a MoCo are based on our idea of a set of base operations that we collectively address as QTI (query/transform/interpret). Due to the desired symmetry between MoCoCode and MoCoModel, similar capabilities shall be available on either side. Technical limitations on the code side make realizing query and transform operations on models more difficult than on the code side, where the execution of models with interpreters is more costly in comparison to invoking code. This supports our claim about flexibility and performance regarding the spectrum of MoCos.

(RQ7) *How to achieve interaction and composition between MoCos?*

To achieve interaction and composition between MoCos in a practical way, the MoCo concept fully relies on the existence of common interface technologies as offered by programming languages and component technologies. Different MoCos can provide and require interfaces via their PFunction port. For management concerns, interfaces at their PManage port can be offered as needed.

Dynamism at the architectural level, i.e., the possibility to change component composition at runtime, depends on the chosen component technology and is not influenced by the MoCo concept. The additive composition of MoCos (composite MoCos) is out of the scope of this work.

RG3: Providing a Reference Implementation for the Realization Concept

We implemented the MoCo concept using Java, TGraphs and the OSGi component technology as provided by Equinox and Felix. This reference implementation consists of the MoCo Core API with elementary types and interfaces for realizing the MoCo Template. The MoCo Execution Environment consists of the JVM, the chosen OSGi runtime and the set of domain-specific model interpreters. Additionally, the MoCo Service Library proposes an initial set of utility operations that were implemented by the MoCo Core API, JGraLab and application-specific code.

(RQ8) *What are the necessary technological prerequisites for implementing the MoCo concept?*

Regarding the necessary technological prerequisites for implementing the MoCo concept, it can be said that the bare minimum is to provide:

- *A general purpose programming language:* Given that software has been always developed in the form of code using some sort of (high-level) programming language or (lower-level) instruction sets, a general purpose programming language is also one essential constituent of the technological basis for developing MoCos. This language is used to communicate with existing software systems, libraries and APIs as well as for the development of high-performance application logic within MoCos.
- *A technological space for modeling:* Being able to establish communicate between models and code in the same base (programming) language without further complicated bridging is a good starting point. In our solution, we assume that the Mediator is capable of talking directly to the interfaces provided by the MoCoCode module. This simplifies the internal structure of a MoCo quite a bit.

More importantly though, the chosen technological modeling space shall support querying and transforming models
based on a textual notation that can be easily passed as a
string parameter. Although not a mandatory requirement,
a compiled language will hinder the use of querying and
transforming in interactive scenarios, e.g., inspecting and
changing the system from an administration panel. In this
thesis, we relied on the textual syntax of GReQL and used
the generated Java API to develop model transformations.[2]
In addition, it must be possible to control model access
in a unified way across all MoCos. Frequently required
operations include accessing a model as a copy or via a
reference to the actual model instance. MoCos may include
a model or just a reference to the model data that is
possibly used by multiple components at once. For fine-
grained control of model states at runtime, a model history
is needed to save a state and to restore it. We implemented
a stack-based solution in DAC-PL where push and pop
commands can be sent from the command line interface.

– *A component technology:* The basis for realizing the "wrap-
ping" of MoCos is a component technology. Commonly,
this technology was developed for the chosen programming
language or is at least compatible with it. To the best of
our knowledge, there is (currently) no other choice anyways
as there is no executable component technology for models
available in practice. Code is the primary development
artifact.

In case that no deep integration with the chosen component
technology is desired, the only real requirements are (i) that
a formalism for defining interfaces between components
is provided and (ii) that components encapsulate their
internals, i.e., they hide internal details and keep them

---

[2]Transformations of TGraphs can be developed in GReTL and FunnyQT, too.
Arbitrarily complex transformations can be used with MoCos.

out of reach of its users.[3] To support the application of the MoCo Core API with existing component models, we implemented it in a way that does not depend on any specific capabilities of OSGi.

(RQ9) *How can MoCos be implemented to support design, evolution and self-adaptation of software?*

Regarding the *design* an implementation of MoCos, we conclude that it is not only sufficient to provide a MoCo Core API, but more importantly, a set of tools and extensions of the preferred IDE is required.

In its current form, the realization of the MoCo concept is actually *heavy-weight* in the sense that the user of the MoCo Core API still needs to consider some small steps; especially when setting up the MoCo the first time as well as when preparing the mediator and registering available implementations in terms of MoCoObject from MoCoModel and MoCoCode modules.

Besides these limitations that we plan to address in future work, we were able to show some opportunities of using MoCos for *evolution and self-adaptation*. Via the PFunction port, designers of MoCos can explicitly provide additional capabilities for managing the component that go beyond the business logic. Based on the provided flexibility provided by the MoCo Core API to change method implementations in the MoCoCode and the ability to modify the model(s) in the MoCoModel, human administrators as well as adaptation managers can interact with the MoCo at runtime and modify its state (within the defined scope of management capabilities).

---

[3]If not supported by the chosen component technology, encapsulation may be also achieved by disciplined programming (to some extent).

RG4: Evaluating the Approach's Potential for Success

We described how we explored the realization of two non-trivial software systems following the MoCo concept supported by the realized MoCo Core API.

(RQ10) *Does the MoCo concept abstract reasonably well from different modeling languages (genericity)?*

Regarding the genericity of our solution, our feasibility studies suggest that the MoCo concept abstracts reasonably well from different modeling languages, indeed. We fail at providing a (formal) proof, though. We assume that all models used with MoCos are described in terms of meta-models as this is the state of the art in software engineering and has its roots in database systems. For executable models, at least one model interpreter needs to be developed. This enforces the precise definition of the modeling language's execution semantics.

We started our research with a background in SAS and SPLE with a bias for modeling, software architecture design and related topics.

Based on the findings presented in this dissertation, we conclude with confidence that our initial *hypothesis*, proposed in Section 1.1, holds. Yet, we have to acknowledge that there is still plenty of research and development work required to provide a complete solution of MoCos to achieve the vision of MID. This topic is covered in the following section where directions for future work are proposed.

7.2 Future Work

Limitations of the current approach open the door for future work. Next, we provide an unsorted list of topics to motivate further research.

- *Extension of the MoCo concept for additive composition:* Although we discussed three different kinds of composition for MoCos in Section 3.1.4, the additive composition of MoCos was decided to be future work. A clean conceptual basis for the development of such composite MoCos needs to be designed and it must be investigated which existing component models can be used to realize *composite MoCos*.

- *Architectural views for MoCos:* In this work, we have described MoCos using component diagrams and textual descriptions. As a first step towards a standardization of documenting MoCos, we propose that existing architectural view models need to be extended to show the MoCo-specific information such as the "type" of the MoCo in the spectrum, its ports, modules and wiring setup with the mediator as well as the used modeling language(s). Possibly, this could be implemented in the form of a UML profile for compatibility with existing tools.

- *Deep incorporation with a component technology:* In case that a conceptually strong component model and a realizing component technology is available, one may consider a tighter integration of the MoCo concept with it. On the down-side, this results in a MoCo Core API that will depend on the capabilities of the component technology.

  Assuming that state changes in the components life-cycle can be intercepted, e.g., via hooks provided by the component technology, models could be loaded or serialized back to disk. Additionally, existing management capabilities such as command line consoles could be extended to realize an administration panel that supports all mechanisms for handling components provided by the component technology, e.g., the starting, stopping and updating of components at runtime, as well as modifications of MoCo internals.

- *Light-weight implementation:* The current reference implementation is rather heavy-weight. Self-adaptive systems are often real-time embedded systems, so it seems reasonable to provide an implementation with a low memory-footprint and more efficient wiring mechanisms for the mediator, e.g., no reflection shall be used for dynamic method calls.

- *Security concept:* We need to design and implement a (role-based) security concept for MoCos to protect the ports and provided interfaces from being misused. Especially access to the PManage port needs to be limited and controlled.

- *Focus on* variability management: The MoCo concept supports the definition of adaptable components. We already used feature models in our feasibility studies. We propose to dive deeper into the application of MoCos for engineering SPLs and DSPLs. For example, a specialized MoCo Template may always carry variability-related meta-data in the form of a model and there may be specific reusable tailoring services.

- *Extended technological modeling space:* Amongst others, querying and transforming models that are distributed across multiple MoCos has shown to be a frequently required task. Even though this breaks with encapsulation, it seems desirable to create views on these models on the fly so they can be treated like a single (integrated) model for maintenance tasks.

  Moreover, developing model interpreters needs to be done more systematically. We envision the generation of skeletons for model interpreters, e.g., based on annotations in the meta-model. Additionally, it seems desirable to support transaction-based model manipulations for situations in which concurrent manipulation of the model data is a critical requirement.

- *Tool-support:* Dealing with models and code within the same IDE and within software components gives raise to new challenges for developers. Moreover, the creation of the initial Java project structure for MoCos and the continuous configuration of mediators should be automated. Also, fine-grained capabilities offered by the MoCo Core API, such as the partial interface implementation, require additional checks within the IDE.

- *Further evaluation and benchmarking:* In addition to our pre-liminary results that hint at the feasibility of the MoCo concept, it is required to explore the potential and drawbacks of using MoCos in more detail. For example, a comparative study (most likely with two groups of master students) could be conducted to collect further practical evidence.

  In addition, the implications of using different modeling lan-guages, especially those proposed by the UML, need to be in-vestigated. Comparable numbers on performance, e.g., memory consumption and execution times, need to be collected, too.

7.3 Summary

In this chapter, we summarized the results of our journey towards model-integrating software components. Being inspired by previous work on SAS and SPLs, we designed a component realization concept and provided a first implementation using existing technologies.

In the following, we revisit the issues initially stated in the abstract.[4]

- *Achieving variability and adaptivity:* Since models are integrated parts of MoCos, runtime querying and transformation of models is supported. Thereby, self-adaptation is possible (e.g., using event-condition action rules) using the services of the techno-logical modeling space. Tailoring of components is supported by similar operations: Models in MoCos can be edited within an editor and model transformations can be applied as a part of build scripts. That way, variants of a MoCo can be derived based on a variability model, for instance, to support software product line engineering. Adapting and tailoring are based on the same operations of the modeling technological space.

- *Reducing redundancy:* At the artifact level, the MoCo concept reduces redundancy in the sense that it systematically embeds executable models into software components. For this subset of models, no code is generated. The models are directly executed

---

[4]The bullet list is taken directly from one of the author's publications [42].

by model interpreters. There is no redundancy unless it is introduced willfully.

At runtime, patterns like architectural reflection and models@runtime are based on propagating values from code objects to a reification layer. Thereby, redundancy is introduced deliberately which requires a thorough construction of the "causal connection" between models and code. This is supported by the mediator.

- *Avoiding inconsistencies between model and code:* MID builds on the ideas of MDSD. Especially, when keeping the domain-logic in models and the platform-specific technical logic in code, the core ideas of MDSD may still be used. Furthermore, the MoCoCode may be developed in a model-driven manner. In this case, the handling of consistency between the models and the code derived from them (*vertical consistency*) does also not differ from MDSD.

  Consistency between code and models inside a MoCo (*horizontal consistency*) must be handled by the development technique like in conventional consistency assurance between several code parts. But, consistency between several models inside one MoCo may potentially also be described explicitly using the technological modeling space's constraint description language.

  In principle, the models of a MoCo may be also used to generate its MoCoCode. Here, the model may either be deleted after code generation (which we call *freezing* of the model) or it may be kept (which would be another example of the deliberate use of redundancy inside the MoCo). In the latter case, the demand for consistency of model and code is an instance of horizontal consistency, since both do coexist inside one component.

We summarize that software can be constructed with MoCos and that this approach offers some interesting directions, but there are also new challenges ahead. Under the umbrella of the DFG project "MoSAiC", this research will be continued.

Appendix

Appendix

Glossary

Some of the definitions below were discussed and written together with Daniel Mies during supervision of his Diploma thesis [106].

abstract syntax

> The *abstract syntax* of a software language defines its significant concepts and the relationships among them.

adaptation

> An *adaptation* is a planned sequence of actions that makes a system suitable for a new condition.

adaptation manager

> An *adaptation manager* is a subject, e.g., a software component, that performs the process of adapting.

adaptation rule

> An *adaptation rule* is a formally specified statement that encodes a condition on a measurable change event in the context and/or the self and provides an adaptation as a reaction.

adapting

> *Adapting* is a process that operates on a software system to adjust it to varying requirements at runtime by executing adaptations.

adaptivity

> *Adaptivity* is the ability of a system to make controlled, i.e., meaningful, changes to its own states and behavior to suit changing conditions at runtime.

adaptivity management

Adaptivity management is the process of engineering software with adaptivity and controlling its evolution.

asset

An *asset* is something of some value for a company, e.g., software, hardware but also staff and its knowledge.

bean

A *bean* is a software component represented by a Java class that follows the implementation conventions given by either the JavaBeans or the Enterprise JavaBeans component model.

common object request broker architecture

The *Common Object Request Broker Architecture* (CORBA) is a specification of an object-oriented middleware for developing distributed software in heterogeneous operating environments.

compiler

A *compiler* is a computer program that translates an instance of one software language into an instance of another (possibly lower-level) software language.

component

A *component* is "a unit of composition with contractually specified interfaces and explicit context dependencies only" [129].

component model

A *component model* is a specification that defines standards and conventions for the structure and composition of components that conform to it.

component technology

A *component technology* is a concrete and utilizable implementation of a (formal) component model.

concrete syntax

The *concrete syntax* of a software language defines the looks of its instances (programs, models).

connector

A *connector* is a communication link between at least two components.

constraint

A *constraint* is a Boolean expression defined over a subset of elements of a given meta-model and it can be evaluated on models.

core asset

A *core asset* is "a reusable artifact or resource that is used in the production of more than one product in a software product line" [100].

dynamic component model

A *dynamic component model* is a component model that provides a means for managing changes to components and connectors at runtime.

dynamic software product line

A *Dynamic Software Product Line* (DSPL) is a software system that achieves adaptivity within a predefined (but not necessarily fixed) state-space by applying and evolving proven variability management techniques as proposed in the field of SPLE.

dynamic SPLE

Dynamic Software Product Line Engineering (DSPLE) is a software development approach comprising mature methods, best practices and tools for building and evolving DSPLs.

enterprise bean

An *enterprise bean* is a software component represented by a Java class that follows the implementation conventions given by the Enterprise JavaBeans component model.

Enterprise JavaBeans

Enterprise JavaBeans^{TM} is a software component model for Java that is aimed at facilitating the development of server-sided components in complex n-tier enterprise applications.

environment

An *environment* is a system that contains the surroundings or conditions in which another system operates.

Equinox

The *Equinox* framework is a Java-based software reference implementation of the OSGi Core specification.

event-condition-action rule

An *event-condition-action rule* (ECA-rule) is an expression that consists of an event, a condition and an action. The intended semantics of an ECA-rule is: "when an event occurs, check the condition and if it holds, execute the action" [47].

execution semantics

Execution semantics is the description of how a valid program or model is executed as a sequence of (computational) actions.

feature

A *feature* is a distinguishable concept of a product that is relevant for at least one stakeholder.

feature configuration

A *feature configuration* is an instance of a feature model.

feature model

A *feature model* is a model that captures stakeholder-visible variability in the problem space in terms of features (with unique identifiers) as well as their relationships.

feedback loop

A *feedback loop* is a circular path that leads from the initial collection of change information about an observed system back to its subsequent modification.

Felix

Felix is a Java-based software implementation of the OSGi Core specification under the Apache license.

freezing

Freezing is the process of transforming a subset of the models within a MoCo to code without introducing redundancy.

FunnyQT

FunnyQT is a Closure API for querying and transforming TGraph-based and EMF-based models developed by Tassilo Horn.

glue code

Glue code is code that connects different functional units without contributing any special functionality by itself.

inspection

Inspection is the planned activity of accessing information about an object to check its properties and/or logical statements related to it.

interpretation point

> An *interpretation point* is a marked spot in code where control flow is redirected to invoke a model interpreter whenever a formally defined condition is met.

interpreter

> An *interpreter* is a computer program that systematically traverses an instance of a software language and, thereby, executes specific actions.

introspection

> *Introspection* is a special case of inspection where the subject and object are identical.

java archive

> A *java archive* (JAR) is a ZIP file with the "*.jar" extension for the distribution of Java class files and further resources.

Java EE

> *Java EE* (Java Platform, Enterprise Edition) is a specification of a software architecture for transaction-based execution of distributed Java applications with a focus on web-based systems.

JavaBeans

> *JavaBeans*^{TM} is a software component model for Java that is aimed at facilitating the development of components that can be composed together into applications by end users.

JGraLab

> *JGraLab* (the Java Graph Laboratory) is a versatile Java library for developing and managing models based on TGraphs.

MAPE-K loop

MAPE-K loop is the name for a feedback loop that consists of monitoring, analyzing, planning and executing activities and is supported by at least one knowledge-base [86].

melting

Melting is the process of transforming a subset of the code within a MoCo to models without introducing redundancy.

meta-model

A *meta-model* is a formalization of allowed model elements, their relationships and optional constraints defining the abstract syntax of a modeling language.

MoCo Execution Environment

The *MoCo Execution Environment* is a specification of the required functionality of a technical environment for executing instances of the MoCo Template.

MoCo Infrastructure

The *MoCo Infrastructure* is a set of software libraries, tools and guidelines that supports the development of software systems according to the MoCo concept.

MoCo Service Library

The *MoCo Service Library* is a specification of recommended services to support the development and evolution of MoCo-based software.

MoCo Template

The *MoCo Template* is a specification of the possible constituents of concrete MoCos (instances). This template describes all concepts and possible relationships among them abstractly. It must be configured and instantiated for a specific context of use.

model

"A *model* is a purposeful description of a system which, on the one hand, permits similar observations and conclusions as the original system and, on the other hand, simplifies this reality to the problem-related aspects by abstraction." [148, Translation from German original].

model execution

Model execution is the process of traversing a model in its abstract syntax representation and thereby invoking specified actions for model elements.

model interpreter

A *model interpreter* is software that executes models based on their ASG representation. It encodes (parts of) their execution semantics.

Model-Integrating Component

A *Model-Integrating Component* (MoCo) is a non-redundant, reusable and executable combination of logically related models and code in an integrated form where both parts are stored together in one component.

model@run.time

"A *model@run.time* is a causally connected self-representation of the associated system that emphasizes the structure, behavior, or goals of the system from a problem space perspective" [14].

modeling

Modeling is the (creative) process of planning, designing, implementing and evolving models.

MoSAiC project

The *Model-integrating Self-Adaptive Components (MoSAiC) project* is a DFG-funded joint project between the University of Koblenz-Landau and the University of Paderborn.

OSGi

$OSGi^{TM}$ (formerly the abbreviation for "Open Services Gateway initiative") is the name of a hardware-independent specification of a dynamic component model for Java.

OSGi Alliance

$OSGi^{TM}Alliance$ is "a worldwide consortium of technology innovators that advances a proven and mature process to create open specifications that enable the modular assembly of software built with Java technology" [136].

OSGi bundle

An *OSGi bundle* (or simply: *bundle*) is the basic building block, i.e., a modularization unit, in the OSGi component model.

OSGi service

An *OSGi service* (or simply: *service*) is a Java object that is registered under at least one interface with the service registry specified by the OSGi component model.

port

A *port* is a structural element that marks an interaction point between a component and its environment via provided and required interfaces.

product

A *product* is the output of an engineering/manufacturing process which is usually produced for sale. A product can be a member of a product line.

product line

A *product line* is a collection of products with a common, managed, set of features, which focus on a domain specific need. It consists of a variety of core assets.

runtime model

> A *runtime model* is a model that offers "abstractions of runtime phenomena" [59].

schema

> The term *schema* is used as a synonym for meta-model in this research.

schema extension

> A *schema extension* is "everything that can be added to a base schema that is not a transformation" [126].

self

> A *self* is a system that is considered as the object of introspection. It is disjoint from its environment but can communicate with it, e.g., via a set of defined interfaces.

self-adaptive software

> *Self-adaptive software* (SAS) is software that can react to sensed changes in its operating environment (and in itself) by modifying its own state or behavior at runtime.

semantic snippet

> A *semantic snippet* is a piece of code that is associated with a (typed) meta-model element and that encodes behavior to be executed for each occurrence of an instance of the meta-model element that is on a path walked along by a model interpreter.

session bean

> A *session bean* is a special kind of enterprise bean that can be stateful or stateless and performs business operations which can be invoked by clients locally and remotely.

software language

"The term "software language" refers to artificial languages used in software development including general-purpose programming languages, domain-specific languages, modeling and meta-modeling languages, data models, and ontologies." [122].

software language engineering

"*Software Language Engineering* (SLE) is the application of systematic, disciplined, and quantifiable approaches to the development (design, implementation, testing, deployment), use, and maintenance (evolution, recovery, and retirement) of these languages." [122].

software product line

A *Software Product Line* (SPL) is a product line where each product is a software system.

software product line engineering

Software Product Line Engineering (SPLE) is a software development paradigm with organized reuse and organized variability on the basis of a common platform [15].

software system

A *software system* is a set of programs and their accompanying documentation that is helpful for their usage [50].

state

A *state* is the particular condition that a system is in at a specific point in time.

system

A *system* is a set of connected elements, i.e., entities and their attributes, which operate together and form a complex whole.

tailoring

Tailoring is a process that operates on a set of artifacts to derive the variation needed for engineering a specific product variant.

TGraph

The *TGraph* class of graphs, i.e., typed, attributed and ordered directed graphs, is a general graph class for graph-based modeling.

TGraph schema

A *TGraph schema* is a meta-model in the technological space of TGraphs.

variability

Variability is the ability to select from a set of different possibilities that cover the same concern.

variability management

Variability management is the process of engineering software with variability and controlling its evolution.

variation

A *variation* is a logically coherent asset fragment that is explicitly associated with at least one variation point.

variation model

A *variation model* is a model that captures (fine-grained) variability in the solution space in terms of variation points and variations with unique identifiers.

variation point

A *variation point* is a point in an asset at which a decision between different but logically coherent functional units can be made.

view

> A *view* is "a representation of a whole system from the perspective of a related set of concerns" [78].

viewpoint

> A *viewpoint* is "a specification of the conventions for constructing and using a view" [78].

Acronyms

AC

Autonomic Computing.

ACS

Access Control System.

AOP

Aspect-Oriented Programming.

API

Application Programming Interface.

ASG

Abstract Syntax Graph.

BPMN

Business Process Model and Notation.

CASE

Computer-Aided Software Engineering.

CBSD

Component Based Software Development.

CBSE

Component-Based Software Engineering.

CIL

Common Intermediate Language.

CLI

Common Language Infrastructure.

CMOF

Complete MOF.

COBRA

COre software development for BRAking.

COP

Component-Oriented Programming.

CORBA

Common Object Request Broker Architecture.

CRUD

Create, Read, Update and Delete.

CVL

Common Variability Model.

DACS

Dynamic Access Control System.

DFG

Deutsche Forschungsgemeinschaft.

DSL

Domain Specific Language.

DSML

Domain-Specific Modeling Language.

DSPL

Dynamic Software Product Line.

DSPLE

Dynamic Software Product Line Engineering.

ECA-rule

Event-Condition-Action rule.

EJB

Enterprise JavaBeans.

EMF

Eclipse Modeling Framework.

EMOF

Essential Meta Object Facility.

FODA

Feature-Oriented Domain Analysis.

FORM

Feature-Oriented Reuse Method.

fUML

Foundational UML.

FWR

From-With-Report.

GRAF

Graph-based Runtime Adaptation Framework.

GReQL

Graph Repository Query Language.

GReTL

Graph Repository Transformation Language.

grUML

Graph UML.

GUPRO

Generic Understanding of Programs.

IBM RSA

IBM Rational Software Architect.

IDE

Integrated Development Environment.

JAR

Java ARchive.

JVM

Java Virtual Machine.

MDA

Model-Driven Architecture.

MDSD

Model-Driven Software Development.

MID

Model Integrating Development.

MoCo

Model-Integrating Component.

MOF

Meta Object Facility.

MoSAiC

Model-integrating Self-Adaptive Components.

OCL

Object Constraint Language.

OMG

Object Management Group.

QTI

Query/Transform/Interpret.

RMI

Remote Method Invocation.

SAS

Self-Adaptive Software.

SCS

Slip Control System.

SLA

Service Level Agreement.

SLE

Software Language Engineering.

SLO

Service Level Objective.

SPL

Software Product Line.

SPLE

Software Product Line Engineering.

UML

Unified Modeling Language.

VIP

Very Important Person.

WSLA

Web Service Level Agreement.

XMI

XML Metadata Interchange.

xUML

Executable UML.

Bibliography

[1] Mehdi Amoui. *Evolving Software Systems for Self-Adaptation.* PhD thesis, University of Waterloo, 2012. http://uwspace.uwaterloo.ca/bitstream/10012/6643/1/ AmouiKalareh_Mehdi.pdf (accessed July 6th, 2014).

[2] Mehdi Amoui, Mahdi Derakhshanmanesh, Jürgen Ebert, and Ladan Tahvildari. Software Evolution Towards Model-Centric Runtime Adaptivity. In Tom Mens, Yiannis Kanellopoulos, and Andreas Winter, editors, *CSMR*, pages 89–92. IEEE Computer Society, 2011.

[3] Mehdi Amoui, Mahdi Derakhshanmanesh, Jürgen Ebert, and Ladan Tahvildari. Achieving Dynamic Adaptation via Management and Interpretation of Runtime Models. *Journal of Systems and Software*, 85(12):2720 – 2737, 2012. http://www.sciencedirect.com/science/article/ pii/S0164121212001458 (accessed July 6th, 2014).

[4] Konstantinos Angelopoulos, Vítor Estêvão Silva Souza, and João Pimentel. Requirements and Architectural Approaches to Adaptive Software Systems: A Comparative Study. In *Proceedings of the 8th International Symposium on Software Engineering for Adaptive and Self-Managing Systems*, SEAMS '13, pages 23–32, Piscataway, NJ, USA, 2013. IEEE Press.

[5] Interim Report: ANSI/X3/SPARC Study Group on Data Base Management Systems 75-02-08. *FDT - Bulletin of ACM SIGMOD*, 7(2):1–140, 1975.

[6] Ozalp Babaoglu, Márk Jelasity, Alberto Montresor, Christof Fetzer, Stefano Leonardi, Aad van Moorsel, and Maarten van Steen. *Self-star Properties in Complex Information Systems: Conceptual and Practical Foundations*, volume 3460 of *Lecture Notes in Computer Science*. Springer-Verlag New York, Inc., 2005.

[7] Cyril Ballagny, Nabil Hameurlain, and Franck Barbier. MO-CAS: A State-Based Component Model for Self-Adaptation. In *Self-Adaptive and Self-Organizing Systems, 2009. SASO '09. Third IEEE International Conference on*, pages 206–215. IEEE, September 2009.

[8] Jan Baltzer. Analysis of Platform Variability. Master's thesis, Universität Koblenz-Landau, Koblenz, Germany, 2013.

[9] Nelly Bencomo, Gordon Blair, Robert France, Freddy Muñoz, and Cédric Jeanneret. 4th International Workshop on Models@run.time. In Sudipto Ghosh, editor, *Models in Software Engineering*, volume 6002 of *Lecture Notes in Computer Science*, pages 119–123. Springer Berlin Heidelberg, 2010.

[10] Nelly Bencomo, Robert B France, Sebastian Götz, and Bernhard Rumpe. Summary of the 8th International Workshop on Models @ Run.time. In *MoDELS@Run.time*, 2013. http://ceur-ws.org/Vol-1079/summary.pdf (accessed July 6th, 2014).

[11] Nelly Bencomo, Svein Hallsteinsen, and Eduardo Santana de Almeida. A View of the Dynamic Software Product Line Landscape. *Computer*, 45(10):36–41, October 2012.

[12] Nelly Bencomo, Jaejoon Lee, and Svein Hallsteinsen. How dynamic is your Dynamic Software Product Line? In *4th International SPLC Workshop on Dynamic Software Product Line 2010*, volume Second Vol of *ACM International Conference Proceeding Series*. ACM, 2010.

[13] Jean Bézivin, Frédéric Jouault, and Patrick Valduriez. On the Need for Megamodels - Preliminary Draft. (1):1–9, 2004.

[14] Gordon Blair, Nelly Bencomo, and Robert B. France. Models@run.time. *Computer*, 42(10):22–27, 2009.

[15] Günter Böckle, Peter Knauber, Klaus Pohl, and Klaus Schmid, editors. *Software-Produktlinien: Methoden, Einführung und Praxis*. Dpunkt Verlag, 2004.

[16] Manuel Bork, Leif Geiger, Christian Schneider, and Albert Zündorf. Towards Roundtrip Engineering - A Template-Based Reverse Engineering Approach. In Ina Schieferdecker and Alan Hartman, editors, *Model Driven Architecture – Foundations and Applications*, volume 5095 of *Lecture Notes in Computer Science*, pages 33–47. Springer Berlin Heidelberg, 2008.

[17] Jan Bosch and Rafael Capilla. Dynamic Variability in Software-Intensive Embedded System Families. *Computer*, 45(10):28–35, October 2012.

[18] Marco Brambilla, Jordi Cabot, and Manuel Wimmer. *Model-Driven Software Engineering in Practice*. Morgan & Claypool, 2012. http://www.mdse-book.com/ (accessed July 6th, 2014).

[19] Frederick P. Brooks Jr. *The Mythical Man-Month: Essays on Software Engineering*. Addison-Wesley Longman Publishing Co., Inc., first edition, 1975.

[20] Frank Buschmann, Regine Meunier, Hans Rohnert, Peter Sommerlad, and Michael Stal. *Pattern-Oriented Software Architecture: a System of Patterns*. John Wiley & Sons, Inc., 1996.

[21] Javier Cámara, Pedro Correia, Rogério De Lemos, David Garlan, Pedro Gomes, Bradley Schmerl, and Rafael Ventura. Evolving an Adaptive Industrial Software System to Use Architecture-based Self-adaptation. In *Proceedings of the 8th International Symposium on Software Engineering for Adaptive and Self-Managing*

Systems, SEAMS '13, pages 13–22, Piscataway, NJ, USA, 2013.
IEEE Press.

[22] Rafael Capilla, Jan Bosch, and Kyo-Chul Kang, editors. *Systems and Software Variability Management: Concepts, Tools and Experiences.* Springer; Auflage: 2013, 2013.

[23] Stefano Ceri and Giuseppe Pelagatti. *Distributed Databases: Principles and Systems.* McGraw-Hill Inc., 1984.

[24] Lianping Chen, Muhammad Ali Babar, and Nour Ali. Variability Management in Software Product Lines: A Systematic Review. In *Proceedings of the 13th International Software Product Line Conference*, SPLC '09, pages 81–90, Pittsburgh, PA, USA, 2009. Carnegie Mellon University.

[25] Betty H.C. Cheng, Rogério Lemos, Holger Giese, Paola Inverardi, Jeff Magee, Jesper Andersson, Basil Becker, Nelly Bencomo, Yuriy Brun, Bojan Cukic, Giovanna Marzo Serugendo, Schahram Dustdar, Anthony Finkelstein, Cristina Gacek, Kurt Geihs, Vincenzo Grassi, Gabor Karsai, Holger M. Kienle, Jeff Kramer, Marin Litoiu, Sam Malek, Raffaela Mirandola, Hausi A. Müller, Sooyong Park, Mary Shaw, Matthias Tichy, Massimo Tivoli, Danny Weyns, and Jon Whittle. Software Engineering for Self-Adaptive Systems: A Research Roadmap. In Betty H.C. Cheng, Rogério Lemos, Holger Giese, Paola Inverardi, and Jeff Magee, editors, *Software Engineering for Self-Adaptive Systems*, volume 5525 of *Lecture Notes in Computer Science*, pages 1–26. Springer Berlin Heidelberg, 2009.

[26] Shang-Wen Cheng. *Rainbow: Cost-Effective Software Architecture-Based Self-Adaptation.* PhD thesis, Carnegie Mellon University, 2008.

[27] Paul Clements and Linda Northrop. *Software Product Lines: Practices and Patterns.* SEI Series in Software Engineering. Addison-Wesley Professional, 2001.

[28] Paul C. Clements, Lawrence G. Jones, John D. McGregor, and Linda M. Northrop. Getting there from here: a roadmap for software product line adoption. *Communications of the ACM*, 49(12):33–36, 2006.

[29] Michelle L. Crane and Juergen Dingel. Towards a UML Virtual Machine: Implementing an Interpreter for UML 2 Actions and Activities. In *Proceedings of the 2008 conference of the center for advanced studies on collaborative research meeting of minds - CASCON '08*, page 96, New York, New York, USA, October 2008. ACM Press.

[30] Ivica Crnkovic, Séverine Sentilles, Aneta Vulgarakis, and Michel R. V. Chaudron. A Classification Framework for Software Component Models. *IEEE Transactions on Software Engineering*, 37(5):593–615, 2011.

[31] Krzysztof Czarnecki and Ulrich W. Eisenecker. *Generative Programming: Methods, Tools, and Applications*. ACM Press/Addison-Wesley Publishing Co., New York, NY, USA, 2000.

[32] Krzysztof Czarnecki and Andrzej Wąsowski. Feature Diagrams and Logics: There and Back Again. *11th International Software Product Line Conference (SPLC 2007)*, pages 23–34, September 2007.

[33] Rogério de Lemos, Holger Giese, Hausi A. Müller, and Mary Shaw, editors. *Software Engineering for Self-Adaptive Systems II*. 2010.

[34] Rogério de Lemos, Holger Giese, Hausi A. Müller, Mary Shaw, Jesper Andersson, Marin Litoiu, Bradley Schmerl, Gabriel Tamura, Norha M. Villegas, Thomas Vogel, Danny Weyns, Luciano Baresi, Basil Becker, Nelly Bencomo, Yuriy Brun, Bojan Cukic, Ron Desmarais, Schahram Dustdar, Gregor Engels, Kurt Geihs, Karl M. Göschka, Alessandra Gorla, Vincenzo Grassi,

Paola Inverardi, Gabor Karsai, Jeff Kramer, Antónia Lopes, Jeff Magee, Sam Malek, Serge Mankovskii, Raffaela Mirandola, John Mylopoulos, Oscar Nierstrasz, Mauro PezzÃÍ, Christian Prehofer, Wilhelm Schäfer, Rick Schlichting, Dennis B. Smith, João Pedro Sousa, Ladan Tahvildari, Kenny Wong, and Jochen Wuttke. Software Engineering for Self-Adaptive Systems: A Second Research Roadmap. In Rogério de Lemos, Holger Giese, Hausi A. Müller, and Mary Shaw, editors, *Software Engineering for Self-Adaptive Systems II*, volume 7475 of *Lecture Notes in Computer Science*, pages 1–32. Springer Berlin Heidelberg, 2013.

[35] Linda DeMichiel and Michael Keith. JSR 220: Enterprise JavaBeans, Version 3.0 - EJB 3.0 Simplified API. Technical report, Sun Microsystems, Inc., Santa Clara, California, 2006. http://download.oracle.com/otndocs/jcp/ejb-3_0-fr-eval-oth-JSpec/ (accessed July 6th, 2014).

[36] Johan den Haan. Model Driven Development: Code Generation or Model Interpretation?, 2010. http://www.theenterprisearchitect.eu/blog/2010/06/28/model-driven-development-code-generation-or-model-interpretation/ (accessed July 6th, 2014).

[37] Mahdi Derakhshanmanesh. Leveraging Model-Based Techniques for Runtime Adaptivity in Software Systems. Master's thesis, Universität Koblenz-Landau, Koblenz, Germany, 2010. http://userpages.uni-koblenz.de/~litdb/dasa//thesis/getthesis/1939 (accessed July 6th, 2014).

[38] Mahdi Derakhshanmanesh. Taking a Glimpse at Reengineering Challenges in Evolution Towards Dynamic Software Product Lines. *Softwaretechnik-Trends*, 33(2), 2013.

[39] Mahdi Derakhshanmanesh, Mehdi Amoui, Greg O'Grady, Jürgen Ebert, and Ladan Tahvildari. GRAF: Graph-based Runtime Adaptation Framework. In *Proceeding of the 6th international symposium on Software engineering for adaptive and*

self-managing systems - SEAMS '11, pages 128–137, New York, NY, USA, May 2011. ACM Press.

[40] Mahdi Derakhshanmanesh, Jürgen Ebert, Mehdi Amoui, and Ladan Tahvildari. Introducing Adaptivity to Achieve Longevity for Software. In Ralf Reussner, Alexander Pretschner, and Stefan Jähnichen, editors, *Software Engineering 2011 Workshopband*, volume P-184, pages 59–70. Gesellschaft für Informatik, 2011.

[41] Mahdi Derakhshanmanesh, Jürgen Ebert, and Gregor Engels. Why Models and Code Should be Treated as Friends. *Softwaretechnik-Trends*, 34(2), 2014. Presented at MMSM – a satellite event of Modellierung 2014. http://pi.informatik.uni-siegen.de/stt/34_2/01_Fachgruppenberichte/MMSM2014/MMSM2014_Paper1.pdf (accessed January 30th, 2015).

[42] Mahdi Derakhshanmanesh, Jürgen Ebert, Thomas Iguchi, and Gregor Engels. Model-Integrating Software Components. In Juergen Dingel and Wolfram Schulte, editors, *Model Driven Engineering Languages and Systems, 17th International Conference, MODELS 2014, Valencia, Spain*, September 28 - October 3, 2014. To appear.

[43] Mahdi Derakhshanmanesh, Joachim Fox, and Jürgen Ebert. Adopting Feature-Centric Reuse of Requirements Assets: An Industrial Experience Report. In *Proceedings of the 16th International Software Product Line Conference - Volume 2*, pages 2–9, New York, NY, USA, 2012. ACM.

[44] Mahdi Derakhshanmanesh, Joachim Fox, and Jürgen Ebert. Requirements-driven incremental adoption of variability management techniques and tools: an industrial experience report. *Requirements Engineering*, 19(4):333–354, 2014.

[45] Mahdi Derakhshanmanesh, Mazeiar Salehie, and Jürgen Ebert. Towards Model-Centric Engineering of a Dynamic Access Control Product Line. In *Proceedings of the 16th International*

Software Product Line Conference - Volume 2, pages 151–155, New York, NY, USA, 2012. ACM.

[46] Elisabetta Di Nitto, Carlo Ghezzi, Andreas Metzger, Mike Papazoglou, and Klaus Pohl. A journey to highly dynamic, self-adaptive service-based applications. *Automated Software Engineering*, 15(3-4):313–341, 2008.

[47] Klaus R. Dittrich, Stella Gatziu, and Andreas Geppert. The Active Database Management System Manifesto: A Rulebase of ADBMS Features. In Timos Sellis, editor, *Rules in Database Systems*, volume 985 of *Lecture Notes in Computer Science*, pages 1–17. Springer Berlin Heidelberg, 1995.

[48] E2E Technologies. White Paper: Direct Model Execution – The key to IT productivity and improving business performance, April 2008. `http://www.omg.org/news/whitepapers/2008-05-05_E2E_White_Paper_on_Direct_Model_Execution.pdf` (accessed July 6th, 2014).

[49] Jürgen Ebert. Efficient interpretation of state charts. In Zoltán Ésik, editor, *Fundamentals of Computation Theory*, volume 710 of *Lecture Notes in Computer Science*, pages 212–221. Springer Berlin / Heidelberg, 1993.

[50] Jürgen Ebert. Grundlagen der Softwaretechnik (Lecture). Institute for Software Technology, University of Koblenz-Landau, 2011. `http://www.uni-koblenz-landau.de/koblenz/fb4/institute/IST/AGEbert/teaching/ss2011/gst` (accessed July 6th, 2014).

[51] Jürgen Ebert. Vertiefung Softwaretechnik: Domänenspezifische Sprachen (Lecture). Institute for Software Technology, University of Koblenz-Landau, 2013. `https://www.uni-koblenz-landau.de/koblenz/fb4/ist/rgebert/teaching/wise1314/vst` (accessed July 6th, 2014).

[52] Jürgen Ebert and Daniel Bildhauer. Graph Transformations and Model-driven Engineering. chapter Reverse En, pages 335–362. Springer-Verlag, Berlin, Heidelberg, 2010.

[53] Jürgen Ebert and Angelika Franzke. A Declarative Approach to Graph Based Modeling. In ErnstW. Mayr, Gunther Schmidt, and Gottfried Tinhofer, editors, *Graph-Theoretic Concepts in Computer Science*, volume 903 of *Lecture Notes in Computer Science*, pages 38–50. Springer Berlin Heidelberg, 1995.

[54] Jürgen Ebert and Tassilo Horn. GReTL: an extensible, operational, graph-based transformation language. *Software & Systems Modeling*, pages 1–21, 2012.

[55] Jürgen Ebert, Bernt Kullbach, Volker Riediger, and Andreas Winter. GUPRO - Generic Understanding of Programs An Overview. *Electronic Notes in Theoretical Computer Science*, 72(2):47–56, November 2002. http://www.sciencedirect. com/science/article/pii/S1571066105805286 (accessed July 6th, 2014).

[56] Jürgen Ebert, Volker Riediger, and Andreas Winter. Graph Technology in Reverse Engineering, The TGraph Approach. In Rainer Gimnich, Uwe Kaiser, Jochen Quante, and Andreas Winter, editors, *10th Workshop Software Reengineering (WSR 2008)*, volume 126, pages 67–81, Bonn, 2008. GI.

[57] Jürgen Ebert, Roger Süttenbach, and Ingar Uhe. Meta-CASE in Practice: a Case for KOGGE. pages 203–216. Springer, 1997.

[58] David F. Ferraiolo and D. Richard Kuhn. Role-Based Access Controls. In *Proceedings of 15th National Computer Security Conference*, pages 554 – 563, Baltimore MD, 1992. http:// csrc.nist.gov/rbac/ferraiolo-kuhn-92.pdf (accessed July 6th, 2014).

[59] Robert France and Bernhard Rumpe. Model-driven Development of Complex Software: A Research Roadmap. In *2007*

Future of Software Engineering, FOSE '07, pages 37–54, Washington, DC, USA, 2007. IEEE Computer Society.

[60] Erich Gamma, Richard Helm, Ralph Johnson, and John Vlissides. *Design Patterns: Elements of Reusable Object-Oriented Software.* Addison-Wesley Longman Publishing Co., Inc., Boston, MA, USA, 1995.

[61] David Garlan, Shang-Wen Cheng, An-Cheng Huang, Bradley Schmerl, and Peter Steenkiste. Rainbow: Architecture-based self-adaptation with reusable infrastructure. *IEEE Computer*, 37:46–54, 2004.

[62] David Garlan, Robert Monroe, and David Wile. ACME: An Architecture Description Interchange Language. In *Proceedings of the 1997 Conference of the Centre for Advanced Studies on Collaborative Research*, CASCON '97, pages 7–. IBM Press, 1997.

[63] Svein Hallsteinsen, Mike Hinchey, Sooyong Park, and Klaus Schmid. Dynamic Software Product Lines. *Computer*, 41(4):93–95, April 2008.

[64] Graham Hamilton. Sun Microsystems JavaBeans. Technical report, Sun Microsystems Inc., Mountain View, California, 1997. http://www.oracle.com/technetwork/java/javase/documentation/spec-136004.html (accessed July 6th, 2014).

[65] O. Haugen, B. Moller-Pedersen, J. Oldevik, G. K. Olsen, and A. Svendsen. Adding Standardized Variability to Domain Specific Languages. In *Software Product Line Conference, 2008. SPLC '08. 12th International*, pages 139–148, September 2008.

[66] George T. Heineman and William T. Councill, editors. *Component-Based Software Engineering: Putting the Pieces Together.* Addison-Wesley Longman Publishing Co., Inc., Boston, MA, USA, 2001.

[67] Markus Herrmannsdoerfer, Sebastian Benz, and Elmar Juergens. Automatability of Coupled Evolution of Metamodels and Models in Practice. In *Proceedings of the 11th international conference on Model Driven Engineering Languages and Systems*, MoDELS '08, pages 645–659, Berlin, Heidelberg, 2008. Springer-Verlag.

[68] Michael G. Hinchey and Roy Sterritt. Self-Managing Software. *Computer*, 39:107–109, 2006.

[69] Mike Hinchey, Sooyong Park, and Klaus Schmid. Building Dynamic Software Product Lines. *Computer*, 45(10):22–26, October 2012.

[70] Edzard Höfig. *Interpretation of Behaviour Models at Runtime - Performance Benchmark and Case Studies*. PhD thesis, Technical University of Berlin, 2011. http://opus.kobv.de/tuberlin/volltexte/2011/3065/pdf/hoefig_edzard.pdf (accessed July 6th, 2014).

[71] Paul Horn. Autonomic computing: IBM's Perspective on the State of Information Technology, 2001.

[72] Tassilo Horn. Model Querying with FunnyQT. In Keith Duddy and Gerti Kappel, editors, *Theory and Practice of Model Transformations*, volume 7909 of *Lecture Notes in Computer Science*, pages 56–57. Springer Berlin Heidelberg, 2013.

[73] Tim Howes. A String Representation of LDAP Search Filters, 1996. http://www.ietf.org/rfc/rfc1960.txt (accessed July 6th, 2014).

[74] Wei-Chih Huang and William J. Knottenbelt. Self-adaptive Containers: Building Resource-efficient Applications with Low Programmer Overhead. In *Proceedings of the 8th International Symposium on Software Engineering for Adaptive and Self-Managing Systems*, SEAMS '13, pages 123–132, Piscataway, NJ, USA, 2013. IEEE Press.

[75] Arnaud Hubaux, Dietmar Jannach, Conrad Drescher, Leonardo Murta, Tomi Mannisto, Krzysztof Czarnecki, Patrick Heymans, Tien Nguyen, and Markus Zanker. Unifying Software and Product Configuration: A Research Roadmap. In *Proceedings of the ECAI 2012 Workshop on Configuration*, 2012.

[76] Markus C Huebscher and Julie A. McCann. A Survey of Autonomic Computing – Degrees, Models, and Applications. *ACM Comput. Surv.*, 40(3):7:1–7:28, August 2008.

[77] IBM. An architectural blueprint for autonomic computing. *IBM White Paper*, (June), 2005. http://www-03.ibm.com/autonomic/pdfs/AC%20Blueprint%20White%20Paper%20V7.pdf (accessed July 6th, 2014).

[78] IEEE Recommended Practice for Architectural Description of Software-Intensive Systems. *IEEE Std 1471-2000*, pages i–23, 2000.

[79] Silvia Ingolfo and Vítor E. Silva Souza. Law and Adaptivity in Requirements Engineering. In *Proceedings of the 8th International Symposium on Software Engineering for Adaptive and Self-Managing Systems*, SEAMS '13, pages 163–168, Piscataway, NJ, USA, 2013. IEEE Press.

[80] James Ivers, Paul C. Clements, David Garlan, Robert Nord, Bradley Schmerl, and Oviedo Silva. Documenting Component and Connector Views with UML 2.0 (CMU/SEI-2004-TR-008), 2004. http://resources.sei.cmu.edu/library/asset-view.cfm?AssetID=7095 (accessed July 6th, 2014).

[81] Andy Ju An Wang and Kai Qian. *Component-Oriented Programming*. John Wiley & Sons, Inc., 2005. http://eu.wiley.com/WileyCDA/WileyTitle/productCd-0471644463.html (accessed July 6th, 2014).

[82] Kyo C. Kang, Sholom G. Cohen, James A. Hess, William E. Novak, and A. Spencer Peterson. Feature-Oriented Domain

Analysis (FODA) Feasibility Study. Technical Report November, Software Engineering Institute, Carnegie Mellon University, 1990. `http://www.sei.cmu.edu/reports/90tr021.pdf` (accessed July 6th, 2014).

[83] Kyo C. Kang, Sajoong Kim, Jaejoon Lee, Kijoon Kim, Gerard Joughyun Kim, and Euiseob Shin. FORM: A Feature-Oriented Reuse Method with Domain-Specific Reference Architectures. *Annals of Software*, pages 1–28, 1998. `http://www.springerlink.com/index/V6901T52316R1350.pdf` (accessed July 6th, 2014).

[84] Christian Kästner, Klaus Ostermann, and Sebastian Erdweg. A Variability-Aware Module System. In *Proceedings of the 27th Annual ACM SIGPLAN Conference on Object-Oriented Programming, Systems, Languages, and Applications (OOPSLA)*, pages 773–792, New York, NY, 2012.

[85] Alexander Keller and Heiko Ludwig. The WSLA Framework: Specifying and Monitoring Service Level Agreements for Web Services. *Journal of Network and Systems Management*, 11(1):57–81, 2003.

[86] Jeffrey O. Kephart and David M. Chess. The Vision of Autonomic Computing. *Computer*, 36(1):41–50, 2003.

[87] Anneke Kleppe. *Software Language Engineering: Creating Domain-Specific Languages Using Metamodels*. Addison-Wesley Professional, December 2008.

[88] Anneke Kleppe, Wim Bast, and Jos B. Warmer. *MDA Explained: The Model Driven Architecture: Practice and Promise*. Addison-Wesley, 2003.

[89] Paul Klint, Ralf Lämmel, and Chris Verhoef. Toward an Engineering Discipline for Grammarware. *ACM Transactions on Software Engineering Methodology*, 14(3):331–380, 2005.

[90] Mieczyslaw M. Kokar, Kenneth Baclawski, and Yonet A. Eracar. Control Theory-Based Foundations of Self-Controlling Software. *IEEE Intelligent Systems*, 14:37–45, 1999.

[91] Bastian Koller, Giuseppe Laria, Paul Karaenke, András Micsik, Henar Muñoz Frutos, and Angelo Gaeta. *Computational and Data Grids*. IGI Global, September 2011. http://www.igi-global.com/chapter/computational-data-grids/58752/ (accessed July 6th, 2014).

[92] Sacha Krakowiak. Component Control. In *Middleware Architecture with Patterns and Frameworks (Distributed under a Creative Commons license)*, chapter 7.4.5. 2009. http://proton.inrialpes.fr/~krakowia/MW-Book/Chapters/Compo/compo.html (accessed July 6th, 2014).

[93] Jeff Kramer and Jeff Magee. The Evolving Philosophers Problem: Dynamic Change Management. *IEEE Transactions on Software Engineering*, 16(11):1293–1306, 1990.

[94] Philippe Kruchten. Architectural Blueprints - The âĂIJ4+ 1âĂİ View Model of Software Architecture. *IEEE Software*, 12(November):42–50, 1995. http://www.cs.ubc.ca/~gregor/teaching/papers/4+1view-architecture.pdf (accessed July 6th, 2014).

[95] Ivan Kurtev, Jean Bézivin, and Mehmet Aksit. Technological spaces: An initial appraisal. In *CoopIS, DOA'2002 Federated Conferences, Industrial track*, 2002.

[96] Robert Laddaga. Self Adaptive Software SOL BAA 98-12. Technical report, DARPA, 1997. http://people.csail.mit.edu/rladdaga/BAA98-12excerpt.html (accessed July 6th, 2014).

[97] Robert Laddaga. Active Software. In Paul Robertson, Howard E Shrobe, and Robert Laddaga, editors, *IWSAS*, volume 1936 of *Lecture Notes in Computer Science*, pages 11–26. Springer, 2000.

[98] Robert Laddaga. Self Adaptive Software - Problems and Projects. In *Proceedings of the Second International IEEE Workshop on Software Evolvability*, pages 3–10, Washington, DC, USA, 2006. IEEE Computer Society.

[99] Kung-Kiu Lau and Zheng Wang. Software Component Models. *Software Engineering, IEEE Transactions on*, 33(10):709–724, 2007.

[100] Linda M. Northrop and Paul C. Clements. A Framework for Software Product Line Practice, Version 5.0. http://www.sei.cmu.edu/productlines/frame_report/index.html (accessed July 6th, 2014).

[101] James Martin. *Managing the Data-Base Environment*. Prentice Hall PTR, 1983.

[102] Tanja Mayerhofer and Philip Langer. Moliz: a model execution framework for UML models. In *Proceedings of the 2nd International Master Class on Model-Driven Engineering: Modeling Wizards*, MW '12, pages 3:1–3:2, New York, NY, USA, 2012. ACM.

[103] Tanja Mayerhofer, Philip Langer, and Gerti Kappel. A Runtime Model for fUML. In *Proceedings of the 7th Workshop on Models@run.time*, MRT '12, pages 53–58, New York, NY, USA, 2012. ACM.

[104] Malcolm Douglas McIlroy. Mass Produced Software Components. In Peter Naur and Brian Randell, editors, *Software Engineering*, pages 79–87. Garmisch, Germany, 1969.

[105] Stephen J. Mellor and Marc Balcer. *Executable UML: A Foundation for Model-Driven Architectures*. Addison-Wesley Longman Publishing Co., Inc., Boston, MA, USA, 2002.

[106] Daniel Mies. Modeling of Dynamic Software Product Lines. Diploma thesis, Universität Koblenz-Landau, Koblenz, Germany, 2012.

[107] Joaquin Miller and Jishnu Mukerji. MDA Guide Version 1.0.1, 2003. http://www.omg.org/mda/mda_files/MDA_Guide_Version1-0.pdf (accessed July 6th, 2014).

[108] Marco Müller, Moritz Balz, and Michael Goedicke. Representing Formal Component Models in OSGi. In Gregor Engels, Markus Luckey, and Wilhelm Schäfer, editors, *Software Engineering*, volume 159 of *LNI*, pages 45–56. GI, 2010.

[109] Linda M. Northrop. Software Product Line Adoption Roadmap. Technical Report September, Software Engineering Institute, Carnegie Mellon University, 2004. http://www.sei.cmu.edu/library/abstracts/reports/04tr022.cfm (accessed July 6th, 2014).

[110] Object Management Group Omg. OCL : Object Constraint Language. *Language*, 36(January):1–11, 2012.

[111] Peyman Oreizy, Michael M. Gorlick, Richard N. Taylor, D. Heimhigner, Gregory Johnson, Nenad Medvidovic, Alex Quilici, David S. Rosenblum, Alexander L. Wolf, and Dennis Heimbigner. An Architecture-Based Approach to Self-Adaptive Software. *Intelligent Systems and their Applications, IEEE*, 14(3):54–62, 1999.

[112] Rolf P. Würtz, editor. *Organic Computing*. Springer; Auflage: 2008, 2008.

[113] Manish Parashar and Salim Hariri. Autonomic Computing: An Overview. In Jean-Pierre Banatre, Pascal Fradet, Jean-Louis Giavitto, and Olivier Michel, editors, *Unconventional Programming Paradigms*, volume 3566 of *Lecture Notes in Computer Science*, pages 257–269. Springer Berlin / Heidelberg, 2005.

[114] Liliana Pasquale, Mazeiar Salehie, Raian Ali, Inah Omoronyia, and Bashar Nuseibeh. On the Role of Primary and Secondary Assets in Adaptive Security: An Application in Smart Grids. In *Software Engineering for Adaptive and Self-Managing Systems (SEAMS), 2012 ICSE Workshop on*, pages 165–170, 2012.

[115] T. Patikirikorala, A. Colman, J. Han, and Liuping Wang. A systematic survey on the design of self-adaptive software systems using control engineering approaches. In *Software Engineering for Adaptive and Self-Managing Systems (SEAMS), 2012 ICSE Workshop on*, pages 33–42, 2012.

[116] Klaus Pohl, Günter Böckle, and Frank J. van der Linden. *Software Product Line Engineering: Foundations, Principles and Techniques*. Springer, 2005.

[117] Yourdon; Press and Larry L. Constantine. *Structured Design: Fundamentals of a Discipline of Computer Program and Systems Design*. Prentice Hall, 1 edition edition, 1979.

[118] Mario Pukall, Christian Kästner, Walter Cazzola, Sebastian Götz, Alexander Grebhahn, Reimar Schröter, and Gunter Saake. JavAdaptor - Flexible Runtime Updates of Java Applications. *Softw., Pract. Exper.*, 43(2):153–185, 2013.

[119] M Salehie, L Pasquale, I Omoronyia, R Ali, and B Nuseibeh. Requirements-Driven Adaptive Security: Protecting Variable Assets at Runtime. In *Requirements Engineering Conference (RE), 2012 20th IEEE International*, pages 111–120, September 2012.

[120] Mazeiar Salehie and Ladan Tahvildari. Self-Adaptive Software: Landscape and Research Challenges. *ACM Trans. Auton. Adapt. Syst.*, 4(2):14:1–14:42, 2009.

[121] Marco Sinnema, Sybren Deelstra, Jos Nijhuis, and Jan Bosch. COVAMOF: A Framework for Modeling Variability in Software

Product Families. In *In Proceedings of the Third International Software Product Line Conference (SPLC)*, 2004.

[122] SLE Conference Homepage, 2012. http://www.sleconf.org/2012/ (accessed July 6th, 2014).

[123] Ian Sommerville. *Software Engineering*. Pearson Addison-Wesley, 8 edition, 2007.

[124] Vítor Estêvão Silva Souza. *Requirements-based Software System Adaptation*. PhD thesis, University of Trento, Italy, 2012.

[125] Thomas Stahl and Markus Völter. *Model-Driven Software Development*. Wiley, 2006.

[126] Sascha Strauß. Application-specific extensions for TGraph schemas in JGraLab. Master's thesis, University of Koblenz-Landau, 2012.

[127] Rick Sturm. *Foundations of Service Level Management*. Sams Publishing, first edition, 2000.

[128] Nary Subramanian and Lawrence Chung. Software Architecture Adaptability: an NFR Approach. In *Proceedings of International Workshop on Principles of Software Evolution*, pages 52–61, 2001.

[129] Clemens Szyperski, Dominik Gruntz, and Stephan Murer. *Component Software - Beyond Object-Oriented Programming*. Addison-Wesley, second edi edition, 2002.

[130] The Object Management Group. OMG Unified Modeling Language Infrastructure. August 2011. http://www.omg.org/spec/UML/2.4.1/ (accessed July 6th, 2014).

[131] The Object Management Group. OMG Unified Modeling Language Superstructure. Technical Report August, The Object Management Group, 2011. http://www.omg.org/spec/UML/2.4.1/ (accessed July 6th, 2014).

[132] The Object Management Group. Semantics of a Foundational Subset for Executable UML Models (fUML), 2012. `http://www.omg.org/spec/FUML/` (accessed July 6th, 2014).

[133] The OSGi Alliance. OSGi Service Platform Release 4. Technical Report April, The OSGi Alliance, 2010. `http://www.osgi.org/download/osgi-core-4.3-early-draft1.pdf` (accessed July 6th, 2014).

[134] The OSGi Alliance. OSGi Core Release 5. Technical Report March, The OSGi Alliance, 2012. `http://www.osgi.org/Download/File?url=/download/r5/osgi.core-5.0.0.pdf`(accessed July 6th, 2014).

[135] The OSGi Alliance. OSGi Enterprise Release 5. Technical Report March, The OSGi Alliance, 2012. `http://www.osgi.org/Download/File?url=/download/r5/osgi.enterprise-5.0.0.pdf`(accessed July 6th, 2014).

[136] The OSGi Alliance. OSGi Alliance "About" Homepage, 2013. `http://www.osgi.org/About/HomePage` (accessed July 6th, 2014).

[137] Dave Thomas. Programming with Models — Modeling with Code The Role of Models in Software Development. *Journal of Object Technology*, 5(8):15–19, November 2006. `http://www.jot.fm/contents/issue_2006_11/column2.html` (accessed July 6th, 2014).

[138] Alfred V. Aho, Monica S. Lam, Ravi Sethi, and Jeffrey D. Ullman. *Compilers: Principles, Techniques, and Tools.* Addison Wesley;, second edition, 2006.

[139] Marina Vatkina. JSR 345: Enterprise JavaBeans,Version 3.2 - Core Contracts and Requirements. Technical report, Oracle America, Inc., Redwood City, California, 2013. `http://download.oracle.com/otndocs/jcp/ejb-3_2-fr-eval-spec/index.html`(accessed July 6th, 2014).

[140] Thomas Vogel and Holger Giese. A Language for Feedback Loops in Self-Adaptive Systems: Executable Runtime Megamodels. *2012 7th International Symposium on Software Engineering for Adaptive and Self-Managing Systems (SEAMS)*, (3):129–138, June 2012.

[141] Thomas Vogel and Holger Giese. Model-Driven Engineering of Self-Adaptive Software with EUREMA. *TAAS*, 8(4):18, 2014.

[142] Thomas Vogel, Andreas Seibel, and Holger Giese. The Role of Models and Megamodels at Runtime. In Juergen Dingel and Arnor Solberg, editors, *Models in Software Engineering*, volume 6627 of *Lecture Notes in Computer Science*, pages 224–238. Springer Berlin Heidelberg, 2011.

[143] Markus Völter. *DSL Engineering: Designing, Implementing and Using Domain-Specific Languages*. CreateSpace Independent Publishing Platform, 2013.

[144] Christoph von der Malsburg. The Challenge of Organic Computing, 1999. `http://graphics.usc.edu/~suyay/class/Slides/CS597-09-18-06-Strategy.pdf` (accessed July 6th, 2014).

[145] Tobias Walter. *Bridging Technological Spaces: Towards the Combination of Model-Driven Engineering and Ontology Technologies*. Logos Verlag Berlin GmbH, Berlin, 2011.

[146] Danny Weyns, M. Usman Iftikhar, Sam Malek, and Jesper Andersson. Claims and Supporting Evidence for Self-Adaptive Systems: A Literature Study. In *Software Engineering for Adaptive and Self-Managing Systems (SEAMS), 2012 ICSE Workshop on*, pages 89–98, 2012.

[147] Danny Weyns, M Usman Iftikhar, and Joakim Söderlund. Do External Feedback Loops Improve the Design of Self-adaptive Systems? A Controlled Experiment. In *Proceedings of the 8th International Symposium on Software Engineering for Adaptive*

and Self-Managing Systems, SEAMS '13, pages 3–12, Piscataway, NJ, USA, 2013. IEEE Press.

[148] Andreas Winter. *Referenz-Meta-Schema für visuelle Modellierungssprachen.* Deutscher Universitäts-Verlag GmbH, Wiesbaden, 2000.

[149] Eric Yuan and Sam Malek. A Taxonomy and Survey of Self-Protecting Software Systems. In *Software Engineering for Adaptive and Self-Managing Systems (SEAMS), 2012 ICSE Workshop on*, pages 109–118, 2012.

[150] Carmen Zannier, Grigori Melnik, and Frank Maurer. On the Success of Empirical Studies in the International Conference on Software Engineering. In *Proceedings of the 28th International Conference on Software Engineering*, ICSE '06, pages 341–350, New York, NY, USA, 2006. ACM.

Printed in the United States
By Bookmasters